D0027530

Get Savvy

Letters to a Teenage Girl
About Sex and Love

Kathleen Buckstaff

Two Dolphin Productions
SAN FRANCISCO

Events described by Kathleen Buckstaff are based on her memory
of real-world situations. Many of the names of her classmates and teachers
have been changed. Any resemblance to persons living or dead resulting
from changes to names or identifying details is entirely coincidental and
unintentional. The views expressed by Kathleen Buckstaff are hers alone
and are not necessarily held by the people she interviewed.

TWO DOLPHIN PRODUCTIONS
San Francisco

Copyright © 2017 by Kathleen Buckstaff
All rights reserved. No part of this book may be used or reproduced in
any form or by any electronic or mechanical means, including information
storage and retrieval systems, without the written permission of the Publisher,
except by a reviewer who may quote brief passages in a review.

Printed in the United States of America. For more information
please visit the author's website at www.kathleenbuckstaff.com.

Original journal handmade by Melissa Oesch, artist and owner of
ReImagined by Luna: reimaginedonline.com,
www.etsy.com/shop/ReImaginedByLuna

Photo credits: front and back cover—by Kathleen Buckstaff.
Back cover photo of Kathleen by Chiara Headrick.

Publisher's Cataloging-In-Publication Data
(Prepared by The Donohue Group, Inc.)
Names: Buckstaff, Kathleen, 1966-
Title: Get savvy : letters to a teenage girl about sex and love / by Kathleen
    Buckstaff.
Description: First edition. | [Tiburon, California] : [Two Dolphin
    Productions], [2017] | Written in the form of letters. | Interest age level:
    13 and up. | Includes bibliographical references and index.
Identifiers: ISBN 978-0-9887642-9-3 | ISBN 978-0-9887642-6-2 (ebook)
Subjects: LCSH: Youth--Conduct of life. | Youth--Sexual behavior. | Rape
    victims--Psychology. | Post-traumatic stress disorder. | Self-esteem in
    adolescence. | Buckstaff, Kathleen, 1966- | Self-help techniques.
Classification: LCC HQ798 .B83 2017 (print) | LCC HQ798 (ebook) | DDC
    305.235--dc23

Book design by Shannon Bodie, Lightbourne, Inc.

FIRST EDITION
10 9 8 7 6 5 4 3 2 1

Neither the publisher nor the author is engaged in rendering professional advice or services to the
individual reader. The ideas and suggestions contained in this book are not intended as a substitute
for consulting with your physician or therapist. All matters regarding your health require personal
attention and care. Neither the author nor the publisher shall be liable or responsible for
any loss or damage allegedly arising from any information or suggestion in this book.

If you are a teenage girl—or you still have a teenage girl inside who needs someone to talk with you about hard subjects—this book is dedicated to you.

With love,
Kathleen

Also by Kathleen Buckstaff

The Tiffany Box, a memoir

USA Best Book Awards Finalist,
International Best Book Awards Finalist

Mother Advice To Take With You To College:
Humor, Inspiration and Wisdom To Go

Savvy ~

Adjective: Shrewd and knowledgeable
in the realities of life; well-informed, streetwise.

(Google Dictionary)

Contents

Discernment ~ 223

Boundaries ~ 269

Dear Reader,

I began working on this book by interviewing current college students and recent graduates. Whether we were a thousand miles apart or sitting face to face over a cup of tea, I asked each person the same question: "Imagine you are sitting with a teenage girl you care for deeply—a younger sister, a cousin, a neighbor, or a girl you babysat. Recall what you've gone through since you left home. What do you wish someone had told you before you left? Try not to think before sharing your answer, and instead, if you can, speak from your heart."

I was twice their age, and what followed were stories full of wisdom and love. Their ability to articulate what they'd gone through took my breath away, and I wished I had known the things they shared before I left home. I am from a silent generation—we didn't talk about hard subjects. This meant that if something horrible happened, we didn't have words to name what had occurred. As a result, I was unable to describe difficult feelings and painful experiences.

One of my interviewees said, "Maybe we're not broken, but one of the first generations that's telling the truth." I found this to be true with every person I interviewed.

I spoke with young people from all over the country who attended public and private universities, state schools, and community colleges. They represented a variety of ethnicities and sexual identities. They had married parents, divorced parents, a deceased parent, and moms and dads who worked part-time, full-time, in the home, and out of the home. Their majors covered a broad spectrum. Some names I changed, and some are real. Each person entrusted me with hard-earned lessons as an offering to you.

I also interviewed professionals who work with teens and twenty-somethings—counselors, health advisors, lawyers, self-defense teachers, professors, and college dorm heads. I attended workshops for college students and read books, academic studies, and news articles, hoping to find pieces in a puzzle.

It wasn't until much later that I realized the puzzle I was trying to put together was myself.

In her book *The Story of My Life*, Helen Keller describes losing her ability to speak, see, and hear when she was 19 months old, following a viral infection. When Helen was six years old, Annie Sullivan arrived at Helen's home, determined to teach the deaf-blind girl words to free her from her isolation and suffering.

Annie began by using finger spelling to make words in Helen's hand. But Helen could not connect the shapes in her hand with objects in her world. Annie spent 10 weeks spelling words in Helen's hand. D-o-l-l was doll. H-a-t was hat. M-u-g was mug. One day, Annie took Helen outside and put one of Helen's hands under a water pump. While Helen felt the flow of water with one hand, Annie spelled w-a-t-e-r in her other hand. Suddenly, Helen understood that w-a-t-e-r meant water.

Helen said that day she was "born into language" and wrote: "Water! That word startled my soul, and it awoke, full of the spirit of the morning... Until that day my mind had been like a darkened chamber, waiting for words to enter and light the lamp, which is thought. I learned a great many words that day."[1]

Each person I interviewed shed light on a hard time in my own life—my three years at a New England prep school and my first year in college. Following those years, I spent decades in the dark—isolated and suffering—unable to name things that had happened. My mind was like a darkened chamber.

When I first started working on this book, I had no intention of sharing my own story. Then I met my daughter for lunch. She was 22 at the time. I asked her opinion; I wanted to know if she thought sharing my story would give my book more meaning for the people who read it.

"Definitely," she said. "A lot of people are offering advice, but it's different coming from someone who's gone through as much as you have. If you tell your story, I think people will be more willing to listen to what you have to say. Your story makes it personal."

After I had lunch with my daughter, I reviewed my diaries, letters, class assignments, and photographs from high school and college, and I consulted with classmates to check details. I also reread my notes from the interviews I had conducted. Each person I spoke with gave me words where I had none. As I wrote my letters to you, I wove in my interviewees' insights and experiences to help me tell my story, and finally, after decades of silence, I was able to describe what happened to me.

I want to add that my interviewees also changed how I think about gender and the role language plays in defining it. Within this book, instead of using "she/he," "her/him," and "her/his," I broke from traditional grammar rules and substituted "they, them, or their" instead. When I shared excerpts, I removed only those few words that detracted from the interviewee's intention, honoring the verbal nature of the interview. I made two other changes: When someone mentioned a college or university by name, I substituted the word "school," and when someone shared memories about a traumatic sexual encounter, I altered identifying details. Their words otherwise remain the same.

Denise, age 25 ~ It has been a long journey. For a long time, it was my Pandora's box. I'm recently on the other side of it, with a lot more perspective and a willingness to talk about it. What I've come to see is if we don't talk about it, then who will?

If you've already been through something sexually traumatic, I am sorry, and it's important to me that you are kind to yourself as you read this book. I was kind to myself as I worked on it and took breaks to talk with close friends and walk in beautiful places.

The young people I interviewed were my teachers. They lit the lamp for me. With their help, I hope to do the same for you.

With love, Kathleen

Grace Miller, Sexual Health Educator, age 22 ~

I graduated from a public high school as salutatorian—I bring that up to show how much I stuck to the rules. I learned everything I was supposed to learn. I got to college and realized how little I knew about sex, and what was even more shocking was how little I knew about my body.

When I graduated from high school, I could tell you how to find the area under a curve using calculus, but I couldn't tell you anything about the area between my own legs. That's just not okay, and I felt betrayed. No one thought it was important for me to know about essential functions in my own body.

I had done everything I'd ever been told to do in terms of being the perfect student. I didn't go to parties, I didn't do drugs, and I didn't think about sex at all. When I got to college and people were honest on the subject, I realized that the environment I'd grown up in had kept me from realizing important truths about who I am. It was terrible.

The reason I got involved in this work is that I want to ensure that what happened to me doesn't happen to anyone else—that moment of realizing how ignorant I was.

A huge part of college for me was coming to terms with what I wanted, who I wanted to do this with, and how I could feel safe doing it.

The bottom line: When entering this new space, there is so much that can seem scary, but you have the right to do only what you feel comfortable with, and there are resources to help you figure out what that is.

Helen Keller, The World I Live In ~

In any case, it is pleasant to have something to talk about that no one else has monopolized; it is like making a new path in the trackless woods, blazing the trail where no foot has pressed before. I am glad to take you by the hand and lead you along an untrodden way.

Part One:
My Story

High School

My Sophomore Year

Helen Keller, The Story of My Life ~

Many incidents of those early years are fixed in my memory, isolated, but clear and distinct, making the sense of that silent, aimless, dayless life all the more intense.

Dear Reader,

As you approach the end of high school, that moment when you put on a cap and gown and receive your diploma, I want to write to you about leaving home.

Zoe, age 22 ~ When you are a senior in high school, all people talk about is how great college is and that it's going to be the best four years of your life. They say you're going to have these amazing friends and life experiences, and I wish I had known how hard the transition was going to be. Basically, I think that first year is really hard. You're leaving home. You have a fresh, new group of friends. You are in a totally unfamiliar place. I wish someone had told me to expect that it would have a lot of challenges along with a lot of ups.

I have discomfort calling up past memories. Already my heart starts to race. But perhaps this time, unlike all the times before, it's not only fear, even terror, that is recalled, but a glimmer of hope—hope that if you see what I've been through, you will take away a self-love that is strong and resilient.

When I was 15, I lived in Phoenix, Arizona. I was the oldest of four children and attended an all-girls Catholic high school. My dream was to become a writer. I started keeping a diary in first grade and hid the key in the top drawer of my bedside table. At the end of my freshman year in high school, I saw that I wasn't getting the writing instruction I wanted. I'd heard New England prep schools offered the best education available. I talked with my parents, and we decided to look at schools in the East. I applied and got in.

Liz, age 23 ~ You're thinking, "Oh yeah, I'm ready to get out of here—get out of my mom's house." I'm so close to my mom, and I still thought that. Even for the most well adjusted person, it's the first time for a lot of people that you have to deal with change by yourself.

I was 15 years old when I left home. The Prep School was surrounded by a pristine forest and situated on a hill overlooking a lake. Most of the students came from nearby towns and cities, and they dressed in styles I'd never seen before.

Mia, age 23 ~ All the girls look the same. They wear silk blouses tucked in with a Hermes belt, skinny jeans, and Tory Burch wedges. The hair is curled to the tens with so much hairspray, heavy make-up, lots of blush, top and bottom eyeliner, eye shadow, and bright lipstick. And it seemed like everyone had a Louis Vuitton purse. Can you imagine? It was brutal. I was shopping at Urban Outfitters in high school. I wore tons of bracelets on my wrists. My friends in college called me the artsy one. My sister goes to art school. She has underarm hair. They don't know what artsy is. It was the hardest adjustment.

Before school began, new students were required to participate in Rise, Run & Dip. Over one hundred of us woke early and ran to the lake. At the water's edge, we stripped down to our swimsuits. As I stood there delaying the cold plunge, I noticed that all the girls were wearing whole-piece swimsuits except for me. I was wearing a bikini. I'd been on a swim team since I was four years old, and one-piece suits were reserved for practice and competitions. Most teenage girls in Phoenix wore bikinis to social swim events. But that misty fall morning, I received disapproving looks. Before classes had even begun, I was labeled by many of my classmates as a slut.

Dear Reader,

I didn't finish my last letter to you. My stomach started to feel nauseated as I recalled that time in my life, and I needed to take a break. When I was at The Prep School, many awful things happened to me and to some of my girlfriends. Because of what happened when I was at boarding school, I had open conversations with my own daughter about guy stuff and sex stuff. There were things I wanted her to know before she left home.

The summer before my daughter went to college, she shared some of the topics that she and I had discussed with her closest girlfriends. They, in turn, asked if I would give them some of my lectures. Each young woman told me, "My mom doesn't talk to me about these things."

My response was one of kindness. My mom hadn't talked to me about these things either. I love my mother dearly, and I know that if she had known how, she would have.

The young women came to my home. I explained that it's awkward to talk about sex and that I often stumble along, but that I'd rather stumble and talk than leave conversations about sex and guys to silence. I knew personally that silence had left me unprepared for things that happened.

Mary, age 23 ~ My ability to be thoughtful and cautious was because my mom was so honest with me about traumatic things that had happened to her when she was in high school and college.

I explained that sometimes sexual things are really difficult to talk about, and, because they feel private, embarrassing, or confusing, we don't talk. This kind of silence can be isolating. This kind of silence needs to be broken.

Together we acted out challenging situations I thought they would encounter in college, and we practiced different responses. I wanted them to know what they were up against and to be prepared. At first, each young woman laughed at my imitations of guys and doubted whether any of it would happen. I assured them that, unfortunately, it would.

When their first winter break arrived and the girls returned from college, they came to our home. They sat around the kitchen table and exchanged stories from their freshman fall. They told me they had encountered every situation I had described and more.

Lauren, age 22 ~ In the fall of my freshman year, I was at a party with a friend who was really drunk and she wanted to stay at the party. My friend was insisting that she was fine and okay to leave with a guy. "No, you're not," I told my friend. I was physically grabbing her, and then I was yelled at by a group of guys for "cock-blocking." They were all yelling, "Cock-blocker! Cock-blocker!" A junior guy was literally pulling my friend's arm, and I was pulling the other trying to keep her from leaving drunk with a guy.

Lela, age 22 ~ When I entered college, I saw rape as something where someone was dragged behind the bushes by a stranger and pinned down and raped. I also thought date rape could exist only when roofies were involved. The older I got, I became more and more aware of everything that was actually happening on campus.

Regardless of your background, your race, your sexual orientation, the color of your hair, where you study at night, or whom you sit with at lunch—the brutal truth is that sexual assault can happen to anyone. Helping to prepare you is what this book is about.

I'll write more tomorrow.

Dear Reader,

My dorm looked like pictures you see of a New England school. It was a three-story, red-brick building with white-trimmed windows, surrounded by old trees, grassy lawns in the summer, and colorful leaves in the fall. On each floor lived thirty freshmen and sophomore girls, who were over-seen by three senior proctors and a faculty corridor master who lived at the end of the hall.

My roommate was from New York City, and her name was Lisel. She had a great sense of humor, and we laughed often. Every night we had two hours of study hall, during which we were required to be in our room. Lisel and I talked during study hall. This meant we often had homework to complete past the lights-out curfew. On most nights our dorm head, Ms. Spike, patrolled the exterior perimeter of our dormitory looking for violations.

Lisel and I had the corner room at the end of a long hallway. I can still close my eyes and hear the sound of Ms. Spike's boots as she walked down the corridor. It's hard to imagine someone's footsteps could sound like anger as they met the tile floor, but hers did. Eventually, Ms. Spike sepa-rated Lisel and me during study hall. A desk was set up in the common room, and I was required to study there.

I was struggling in first-year French. We were graded on making nasal sounds in front of the class. A Frenchman would make a noise like a struggling pig or a stuck donkey, and I was supposed to imitate him. Though I was a girl who prided herself on receiving A's, I'd been awarded a series of failing grades. Being alone in the common room gave me the space to practice making nasal sounds.

My favorite subject was English. Before I met my English teacher, other students had told me that Mr. Jessup was a god at the school and the best writing instructor. On the first day of school, Mr. Jessup asked me to stay after class. He said he wanted to be my advisor and gave me a note authorizing the change. I was thrilled.

In class, we were reading *Romeo and Juliet*. For the balcony scene, Mr. Jessup climbed on his desk and was Juliet, then hopped down on the floor, knelt, and was Romeo. Mr. Jessup delighted us with his charm and impersonations. He could play different characters with ease.

My first birthday away from home was in February. I turned 16. Mr. Jessup made me a lopsided chocolate cake, and the class sang "Happy Birthday".

Helen Keller, The Story of My Life *~ It was my teacher's genius, her quick sympathy, her loving tact which made the first years of my education so beautiful. It was because she seized the right moment to impart knowledge that made it so pleasant and acceptable to me.*

During winter term, Mr. Jessup asked us to write a personal essay every day. At night I reviewed his comments and worked to incorporate his suggestions into my next assignment. I loved the challenge.

Stephanie Seibel, Counselor, age 25 ~ It's especially important to connect with mentors. I did this a lot. For the classes I was interested in, I connected with all of my professors. They have office hours, and I went to them. If you find a subject that interests you, learn more. The teachers are there, and they want to help.

Because I was from Phoenix, I'd never experienced winter. Lisel was teaching me the importance of putting on socks and a coat before venturing outside, and I was learning to navigate icy sidewalks. I wiped out several times on my way to the science building.

Walking to the dining hall had its own challenges. An all-boys dormitory stood between my residence and the main building. A group of boys often gathered on their balcony to rate girls as they walked by. They would whisper to each other, and then one boy would hold up a number from one to 10 written on a large sign. Girls tried to walk in pairs and not look their way, but some boy always shouted out a number, and the group on the balcony always laughed.

Lauren, age 22 ~ I lived with 11 girls in a house, and I'd go to an all-guys house to escape. The way they talked about girls around me was disgusting. It was fully based on looks. They talked about girls as if they were objects and cared only whether or not they had sex with a girl. They cheered each other on, saying things like, "Oh, way to go, nice." They were competitive about getting females. It was a way to one-up each other, who hooked up with whom. They were loyal to each other, but not to the girls they were with.

That winter I competed on the swim team. At boarding school, swimming was a winter sport, and we swam in an indoor pool. Once a week, the girls' team had practice after dinner. One winter night, I walked back to my dorm holding my wet ponytail in the air above my head. My hair froze straight up as I was arriving back to my room, and Lisel laughed at my hairdo.

I always loved to hear Lisel laugh. She could light up a room with her eyes. Lisel and I had a bedtime ritual. We put on our flannel nightgowns and walked down the hall together to the bathroom, where we washed our faces and brushed our teeth. Both of us were unhappy that zits were part of our everyday life. We tried all sorts of products to reduce the red bumps, and we decorated our faces in zit cream for laughs. As we fell asleep, we'd discuss boys—who was cute, who wasn't, who might be cute someday, and who had no prayer. We decided that some of the boys in our grade might eventually mature into good-looking young men, but we preferred the upperclassmen.

Lela, age 22 ~ Everyone talks about a scale of desirability for heterosexual couples. Senior women are often described as least desirable because they're jaded—they're not willing to put up with crap—and the freshmen women are seen as most desirable. Freshmen boys are seen as least desirable because they're zany, with zits on their faces, and haven't filled out yet. Freshmen girls with senior boys are a known thing on campus. And freshmen girls are seen as "freshmen meat." No one tells you this. Instead the freshman girl thinks, "Oh, that senior guy likes me..." Girls think the guys are more into it than the guys really are. Go into it knowing that older guys see freshmen girls as meat, and be a little more wary.

Ice hockey was a new sport to me. I'd never seen a game before. Groups of sophomore girls would go to the rink to watch the boys' varsity hockey team compete. The fast pace of the skates on ice, the cold air, the sound of bodies slamming against the Plexiglas, hockey sticks clacking, voices yelling—it was all exciting to me. After the game, the girls would go to the snack bar, drink hot chocolate, and talk about the players.

It was rumored that several Ivy League colleges were recruiting one of the seniors. His name was Dylan. In the dining hall, the seniors all sat together. Sometimes I would watch Dylan laughing with friends. They talked louder than anyone else and took up more tables, spreading out with their arms, legs, and deep voices—an implicit statement of owning the place.

Liz, age 22 ~ At my school, there are a lot of guys who think, because their family has money, that they can do what they want and get what they want.

There was a dress code that we had to follow. The girls were not allowed to wear jeans, and the boys had to wear a shirt with a collar, khakis or cords, a blazer, and a tie. This gave the seniors a look that was rumpled and sophisticated. Unlike the boys in our grade, they had outgrown zits and knew it.

Once a week, I used the pay phone in the stairwell in my dorm to call home. I'd tell my mom about my friends and things that were going on, but it wasn't the same as talking in her kitchen. Our conversations were never private. I could hear my words echoing up the stairwell. My most frequent communications from my mom were letters that she wrote to me with news from home.

I am going to stop and take a break from telling this story. I will return tomorrow, sit at my desk, and continue. The closer I get to the awful night, the harder it is to write.

Mia, age 22 ~ Freshman year, I had to get out of my dorm and run and listen to music because it's so claustrophobic. Find your alone time.

Mikayla, age 22 ~

My mom and I are really close, and I talk to her a number of times per week on the phone. I can't count the number of small details that we share about our lives with each other, not important things. She likes to call me on her drive home. I call her when I'm walking to class. She doesn't like to give long maternal speeches, but she does love to chat. It makes me feel really connected to her to know these kinds of things, to know what her plans are. And she knows what my plans are.

If I did well on a paper, or was stressed about a paper and something was going badly, I'd bring it up. But she never was calling to tell me what to do. My mom liked me to check in with her a lot, especially freshman year. She liked to know generally what I was up to that night. On Friday night, I'd talk to her for a couple of minutes and say, "Hey, I'm doing this." She'd ask what my plans were and maybe with whom. She would often make comments: "You're doing this and this—okay, make sure to stay safe and be smart." That's how she would bring it up. Be smart. It implies that if something happens, then you're dumb, which I don't think is exactly right. But to me it meant don't get out of control. Stay somewhat reasonable in the amount you're drinking, and don't be overly reckless.

I think I responded, "Yeah, sure," but hearing it that many times—a little comment like "I love you, be safe, have fun"— does affect the way you think about your decisions over time. It's pretty rare not to have at least one story of drinking to crazy excess in college. But I actually never had an experience where I woke up and had no idea what I did the night before. I think my mom's a pretty big part of it. The next day, she'd expect to hear from me. If I didn't check in, she'd call or try to get a hold of me.

Dear Reader,

On the night of my 16th birthday, when study hall was over, some girls in my dorm gathered in the common room to eat ice cream. Halfway through the party, a group of senior hockey players stopped by. This was a rare visit and led to much excitement.

During the celebration, someone slipped a condom on a doorknob. When it was discovered, girls blushed and the seniors laughed. It was the first time I'd ever seen a condom.

Dylan, the varsity hockey player I admired, was there and wished me happy birthday. When he was leaving, he called out to me, "Thanks for the valentine," and I turned bright red. Our school sold valentines that were delivered to students during class. I'd sent one to Dylan anonymously. When the seniors left, I screamed from embarrassment and was comforted by my friends.

After my birthday, Dylan came by my window during study hall a few times, and we talked through the screen. Seniors were not required to be in their rooms during study hall. Dylan said that Mr. Jessup had told him I'd sent the valentine. I had confided my secret action in one of my English essays, and Mr. Jessup was Dylan's coach. Dylan also told me that Mr. Jessup was the one who had suggested he visit me on my birthday.

Two weeks later, Lisel and I went through our bedtime ritual. We were wearing our flannel, floral-print nightgowns with lace around the neckline. We brushed our teeth, washed our faces, and then we fell asleep. Hours later, we awoke to senior guys setting up a party in our room. They were laughing and drunk.

Alcohol abuse is a strong behavioral predictor of both physical and sexual aggression. More alcohol abuse problems have been found among men who perpetrate sexual and physical intimate partner violence than among those who do not.[2] Alcohol acts as a disinhibitor for the man, as an excuse for the rape after it has occurred, and as a means of reducing the victim's resistance.[3] The Campus Sexual Assault Study (2007) reported that, of the men who admitted to attempted or completed sexual assault, 81% reported that they had been drinking before the incident. Of these men who had been drinking, 94% of them reported being drunk before the assault occurred.[4]

Lisel and I would not have called these students friends. We knew who they were—they were the seniors everyone knew, the ones who strutted and talked loudly in the halls. Dylan was there.

Jonathan, age 22 ~ Having girls around makes a party better. You don't want to have a party and there's just 40 dudes and 15 girls. Then it's just kind of weird. Generally, the rule is the more girls the better. Obviously, all of the guys are trying to score with the girls. That's the most basic part of why we want the girls to come to the party. Of course, the alcohol is the lubricant of the whole party. It makes everybody loose. Alcohol is a pretty vital thing. When you don't have alcohol, people are like, "Who are these random people? I don't know what to say or do." And then you add the alcohol, and everybody gets a little drunk, and people are talking, and dancing, and yadda yadda.

On Lisel's desk, they set up Dixie Cups, grain alcohol, and Welch's grape soda. Someone poured grain alcohol into the cups. Someone else added grape soda. "Purple passions!" they yelled. Then they bumped their cups together and drank the shots.

Mary, age 22 ~ So much of being a freshman in college is make-believe. You're pretending you've had these experiences before. You pretend it's casual. You pretend school isn't too hard. You pretend you're not lonely. You pretend you're not struggling. It gets dangerous when you're a freshman at a party and you don't want to turn to your girlfriend and say, "I'm a little uncomfortable. Is what's happening okay?" The nature of freshman year is that you're far from your family and your friends from home. What you don't realize when you're alone at a party is that all the girls you just made friends with feel the same way.

Dylan sat on my bed, and a friend of his sat on Lisel's bed. Several others continued making drinks. Dylan lay on top of me and started kissing me.

Professor Renee McDonald ~ I want every girl to know that most sexual assaults start with a kiss. If a person is going to progress to a sexual assault, they start with a kiss.

Dylan's tongue was in my mouth and tasted like alcohol and cigarettes. I turned my head away and tried to push him off.

Marybeth Bond, Author and World Traveler ~ In the middle of the night, this guy broke into my room. I was staying in a very inexpensive place in India on the beach. It was so hot. I was sleeping under a sheet with nothing on. He broke into my room, and I just jumped up and pulled the sheet off the bed and put it around me, and I started jumping on my bed. "What are you doing in here?" I was shouting. I became the mother tigress. He was so taken aback that he moved around the room away from me, and I was able to run out of the room and scream, and scream, and scream.

Angela Exson, Director of University Sexual Assault Education and Response ~ Oftentimes a survivor will make a check list in her mind of all the things that she could have done differently, but the bottom line is that the perpetrator still could have made a different decision and could have chosen not to hurt you.

Dylan moved off my comforter, lifted it, and then got under the covers with me. Again he was on top of me, kissing me—my neck, my lips. He whispered in my ear, "It won't hurt." He fumbled with my nightgown and tried to lift it up while I used both hands to keep it down.

Allie, age 21 ~ Guys are getting more and more cocky. They think, "I can do whatever I want." They're cocky in what they think they can do to girls. They treat us as if we're their property and as if they can do whatever they want. I say, "We're not your property. Chill out and talk to me like I'm a real person instead of just coming on to me like a sexual object."

Dylan was rubbing his erection on my underwear. I tried to get him off of me. He was touching me all over my body. I shifted my face from side to side to avoid his kisses while he bruised my pelvic bone.

Zoe, age 22 ~ He sexually harassed me when I was home from college. It was the summer after freshman year. There were a lot of people there. We were camping. The biggest thing was that it was the first time in my life where I was physically trapped, and I couldn't get away. I couldn't remove myself from the situation. That was the scariest thing. I'd never been in a situation before where I felt like I couldn't leave. There was forwardness and touching that I wasn't comfortable with. He wasn't letting go. That's the biggest thing. I was pulling away. I was trying to get out, but I couldn't. I was trying to get out of his arms and get outside, and he wasn't letting go.

And then one of the seniors making drinks said it was time to go for a swim at the pool. He was bragging about having the keys to the school. The guys taking shots at the desk began packing up the alcohol and grape sodas.

Other factors that often indicate a history of sexual and physical aggressiveness include delinquent behavior,[5] dominance motives for sex, and consorting with peers who condone and encourage sexual conquest.[6]

I was relieved when I heard the suggestion to go to the pool. It felt like a fast way out of an awful situation. Eventually Dylan got off of me, and the senior on top of Lisel got off of her. She and I put on jeans, sweatshirts, and shoes. As we were leaving the dorm, we ran into more upperclassmen guys and lowerclassmen girls in the stairwell, coming down from the second and third floors. The guys carried bottles of hard alcohol. Together we walked across the snow-covered field to the gym.

Laura, age 22 ~ Alcohol is the biggest date-rape drug—more than getting roofied.

We entered the gym through a back door and walked up a dark set of stairs to the girls' locker room. Once inside, I knew my way around because I was on the girls' swim team. One senior suggested that we all shower before swimming. In an open, rectangular room, a row of showerheads extended from the wall. Although it was almost completely dark, I could see the silhouettes of couples standing together under the water.

Dylan and I stood under one nozzle. We were wearing our clothes, and water covered us. He started kissing me again and running his hands over my body. He was touching me everywhere—my breasts, my belly, my hips. His touch was aggressive. My heart was racing. I used my hands to block him from putting his hands down my pants. He was getting more forceful in his efforts and held me tighter and harder, and then he pinned me against the wall. I felt afraid, deeply afraid.

I could hear girls gasping and gulping around me. There was no laughter. There was no talking or joking. It sounded as if some of the girls were struggling to breathe. The excited voices that had accompanied the sounds of sneaking out, shoes walking across hard snow in the moonlight, a key successfully opening a heavy gym door, and cheers of celebration accompanying the break-in—all faded, and what was left was the spray from the showerheads and the sound of girls drowning.

I told Dylan I had to use the bathroom. I said it several times, and he released me. I walked in the dark to a bathroom stall, locked the door, and stood there for a long time.

I knew how to make my way to the pool in the darkness. I walked through a narrow hallway and down a few steps. When I arrived, I saw Dylan sitting on the side of the pool near the diving boards, toward the far end of the room. He was smoking a cigarette. He blew smoke circles that bounced off the surface of the pool. It was the first time I'd ever seen someone make rings with cigarette smoke. I dove into the water with my clothes on and felt safer there.

I watched couples emerge from the locker-room shower. Some people swam. Some girls sat by themselves. The guys were loud. The girls were quiet. Eventually Lisel came out of the shower. She looked as if she was about to cry. I tried to catch her eye, but she wouldn't look at me.

Catherine Criswell Spear, Title IX Coordinator and Attorney ~ The reality is that a perpetrator of rape is likely to be someone you know.

Seventeen years after the shower incident, I was at The Prep School for a reunion, and a classmate of mine told me that she had been raped that night at the pool party. She said she hurt so badly the next morning between her legs that she couldn't sit on the chair in her Biology class. Since then, two other women told me that they were raped in the shower that night.

93% of juvenile sexual assault victims know their attacker; 58.7% were acquaintances, 34.2% of attackers were family members, and 7% of the perpetrators were strangers to the victim.[7]

Helen Keller, The Story of My Life ~ *Once a gentleman, whose name I have forgotten, sent me a collection of fossils—tiny mollusk shells beautifully marked, and bits of sandstone with the print of birds' claws, and a lovely fern in bas-relief. These were the keys which unlocked the treasures of the antediluvian world for me. With trembling fingers I listened to Miss Sullivan's descriptions of the terrible beasts, with uncouth, unpronounceable names, which once went tramping through the primeval forests, tearing down the branches of gigantic trees for food, and died in the dismal swamps of an unknown age. For a long time these strange creatures haunted my dreams.*

Dear Reader,

News about "the pool party" spread throughout the school. The upperclassmen involved walked with swagger and bragged about their conquests.

Elisa Pinto de Magalhaes, Studied Bro Culture, age 22 ~ *Bro Culture is a small group, but on campus it's the most visible and powerful group. They're very close-knit. So much power is given to so few. They get to choose what girls they want. They can be picky, and they don't really care. Women are not important to them. They value being part of a strong culture, and their identity is built on this group of men. How many girls a guy has been with is seen as badges on a belt—not to show to other girls, but to show to other men. Women are used as bragging rights.*

Classmates and teachers celebrated the guys who had been involved in the pool incident, and the girls were taunted and shamed. In my dorm, female peers snickered and said, "I heard you were at the pool party. I bet you enjoyed it."

Jessica Chapman-Segal, Reproductive Health Educator, age 25 ~ *I know sexual assault happened at my school. I'd hear about it in the halls. A lot of times girls blame other girls and say things like "She's such a slut. She's such a whore. She had it coming. No wonder. Okay, obviously she would get raped." That's a really, really nasty thing to say. It wasn't until I was older that I began to understand the complexities behind rape. If someone blames a girl and says, "Well, she did this and she did that," it belittles the person's experience. Her past behavior, if it* exists, doesn't matter. If she was raped, she was raped. That's the end of the story.

That spring, my math teacher was drawing an illustration on the chalkboard to prove a theorem. Halfway through, I realized that he had drawn my dorm. With chalk, he put an "X" on the corner room —Lisel's and my room. Above it he wrote, "The Den of Promiscuity." And then he laughed, and the students laughed with him.

Many teachers seemed to be enjoying the sex lives of the seniors, and sex with an underclass girl was seen as "scoring." It was a cruel game, in which select students asserted their dominance at the expense of others, and the people in positions of authority smiled in approval. No one called foul.

In the dining hall, an English teacher made tsk-tsk sounds at me about what he called "the night of infamy." And then he smirked and said, "Boys will be boys."

Grace Miller, Sexual Health Educator, age 22 ~ Men are not mindless sex-craved beasts. That's a dehumanizing way to view them. It's important to recognize when a behavior is wrong and is not an innate way of how someone can act. The conversation on a societal level tends to focus just on women changing their behavior; however, I think it can be extraordinarily helpful to recognize that rape isn't a given. There is no reason why rape should ever occur. You don't ever ask to be raped. Recognizing that the situation is changeable is the only way I can have any modicum of hope.

Dear Reader,

At the graduation ceremony that spring, the senior hockey players held trophies above their heads and were given Varsity letters to sew on their jackets. These young men were the pride of the school. Many would be enrolling in Ivy League colleges in the fall, and teachers posed to have their pictures taken with them. After the ceremony, the seniors left to attend parties, while underclassmen stayed on campus to study and take final exams.

The day after graduation, Ms. Spike called Lisel, me, and another friend of ours into her apartment. We were 16. We didn't know why we were being summoned. Then Ms. Spike began questioning us about "the midnight pool party."

"Did you leave the dorm after hours? Was there alcohol involved? And how much did you have to drink?"

Debra, age 22 ~ When people ask, "How much did she have to drink?" they blame the woman and neglect to hold accountable the perpetrator of the crime.

Three months had passed since the seniors had used a master key to enter our room. I didn't understand why Ms. Spike had waited until after the seniors graduated to begin her interrogation. Junior hockey players who were in the shower room that night were still on campus, and they were never questioned.

Jessica Chapman-Segal, Reproductive Health Educator, age 25 ~ Whoever is making the school a lot of money—like star athletes—the school will turn a blind eye to the allegations and do their best to push it under the rug.

After several hours of questioning, Ms. Spike decided that the three of us needed to be severely punished. One week later, she presented her case to the faculty at the year-end meeting. I was later told that the faculty considered expelling us and decided instead to place us on General Probation. This meant that if we broke one rule during our remaining time, we would be kicked out of school.

Sofie Karasek, Co-founder End Rape on Campus, age 22 ~ People in authority handled everything horribly. What the school did to me was worse than what happened.

There is so much more I have to tell you, but the daylight is waning. Do I keep writing? You see, you are the future to me. All these events are in the past, and it's over—well, not completely over, because the horror and the violation are still in my mind and in my body.

Catharine MacKinnon, Professor of Law ~ This past isn't over. It is all still here…and there will be no end to it until it is changed. Until there is truth, there can be no reconciliation. All of this denial of responsibility by perpetrators and institutions… is what keeps this past alive.[8]

The story lives on in me, as much as I wish that weren't so—but if I share it with you, maybe you can use it to make yourself more savvy. Know you are beautiful, and if and when they blame you or shame you, don't listen. Don't listen.

Sofie Karasek, Co-founder End Rape on Campus, age 22
~ At our core, we tend to blame ourselves because society has
told us that it's our fault. I push back against self-blame every
chance I get because it's at the root of so many problems.

I still don't know who gave the seniors the keys to the school. A nod of approval from an adult in charge to one student can change another student's life.

Thomas, age 19 ~

Guys will talk about girls behind their backs. It's common dialogue. The guys are educated to act that way—by the media and adults. They're taught that it's okay when really it isn't. I learned that my fall-back wasn't standing up for someone. When others were saying bad things, I'd go along and be quiet. And then I realized how many parts of my identity I had changed to get myself accepted. There was a group of guys laughing about a nude picture they had of a girl. They were laughing and talking bad about girls. It made me uncomfortable, and so I said something and made them delete the picture. It's really hard to advocate for someone, especially someone of the opposite gender. I ended up not alienating my friends like I thought I would.

Grace Miller, Sexual Health Educator, age 22 ~

I believe in the ripple effect. These days I'm making more of an effort to talk with my male friends as issues come up. I'm actively challenging problematic assumptions. It's powerful. If I can shape how a male friend views these incidents, then that can have a huge effect.

If you hear someone say, "She's such a slut," ask, "Why is she such a slut?" If you hear a guy say, "Oh, she's so drunk, I should go for it," say, "No, she's too drunk, you should not go for it." If you hear a guy say, "Oh, she asked for it," ask, "Why?"

This is really hard to do, but it can be helpful. I've been in situations where I'm the only woman with guys, and they start talking about women's bodies. When I say something, they say to me, "Oh, you're such a buzz-kill." I still say something.

Dear Reader,

I was sitting on my mom's bed, telling her good night. It was the summer following my sophomore year. Her room was dark. I wanted desperately to talk, but I didn't know how. My heart was racing, and I was quiet.

Annie Clark, Co-founder End Rape on Campus, age 25 ~ How are we supposed to talk about rape when we can't talk about sex?

Catherine, age 22 ~ My mom did such a good job with us, keeping us on our feet, but there were some times when we were in pain and she couldn't see it, or vice versa—she was in pain and we couldn't see it. It might be because we didn't talk too much about feelings.

Eventually I brought up the subject of the night at the pool. I paused, and then my mom said, "You broke the rules. The school must have known what they were doing when they put you on General Probation. It was a consequence for breaking the rules."

I was silent. It was as if a dungeon door had dropped shut, leaving monsters inside where they were free to roam.

Elizabeth, age 17 ~ Not knowing how to talk about something really traps you.

How many times have I thought back on that conversation and imagined it differently? I imagine my mother saying, "You don't seem like yourself, you're not smiling or laughing. What happened?"

I see myself having the words to begin talking—but how could I? I didn't know you could be raped or sexually assaulted by someone you knew.

Maybe she asks, "Did something happen that you don't know how to describe? Did something terrible happen?"

And I say, "Yes."

And then she says, "There were upperclassmen in your dorm room and alcohol—seniors with sophomore girls. That's a dangerous combination. Did you get hurt?"

And I say, "Yes, I got hurt. And other girls got hurt too."

And then my mom says, "I'm really sorry this happened, and I love you. I really, really love you." She takes me in her arms, and she holds me in the dark.

The dungeon door lifts, and I say, "He rubbed so hard on me that when I peed it burned for days. I never knew that people do things like that to other people. Guys I know hurt girls I know. Badly. It was really scary. No one is talking about what really happened. Some people think it was fun, or funny, or cool. They're bragging about it, but it wasn't funny, and it wasn't cool. It was terrifying and violent and cruel."

Emma, age 22 ~ I came home for a family vacation, and my mom said, "You're miserable. You're not yourself." I said, "I'm fine. I'm just adjusting." She said, "You're not fine," and she took me to a therapist. My mom said, "We need to get you out of there." And she was right.

I imagine my mom saying, "No supposedly top-notch education is worth your health and happiness, ever. We trusted that the school would do everything they could to protect you, and they didn't. We'll take care of you. We'll get you help." And then she asks, "Was anyone kind to you? Anyone?"

And I say, "No."

Madison, age 21 ~ I honestly don't know if I've come to terms with it. It happened two years ago. I never got counseling. I never went to the doctor.

A prayer-poem I wrote in my journal ~

I wish you healing and health.
I wish you people who are kind, patient, and loving.
I wish you friends who laugh and cry and
    get angry on your behalf.
I wish for you a justice system that works.
I wish you peace within when it doesn't.
I wish for you the sanity that accompanies truth.
I wish for you the healing that comes
    with tears and kindness.
I wish for you a peaceful night of sleep.
I wish for you a gentle reclaiming of your body and spirit.
I wish for you laughter again like rain after a drought.
I wish for you joy.
I wish for you love.
I wish for you peace.
I wish for you hope.
I wish for you a deep knowing that you are sacred,
    most dear, a beloved.
Always worthy. Always worth protecting. Always.
May you be wrapped in rose petals and gold light.
May birds sing to you.
May warm, gentle breezes comfort you.
May you hear whispering words in the wind that say again
    and again, "You are loved, you are cherished, you are
    honored, you are believed, you are beautiful."
May you be comforted by faith.
May you be energized by hope.
May you rediscover joy.
May you be healed by love.

High School

My Junior Year

May 29, 1898

Dear Mrs. Hutton,

Each day is filled to the brim with hard study... You will be pleased to hear that I did three problems in Geometry yesterday without assistance... I felt somewhat elated myself. Now I feel as if I should succeed in doing something in mathematics, although I cannot see why it is so very important to know that the lines drawn from the extremities of the base of an isosceles triangle to the middle points of the opposite sides are equal! The knowledge doesn't make life any sweeter or happier, does it? On the other hand, when we learn a new word, it is the key to untold treasures.

Helen Keller

Dear Reader,

When I was 16, I wanted to be a virgin when I got married. My mother had presented this as a virtuous and desirable path for me to follow. "It's good to be a virgin when you get married," she had said. It was a one-sentence discussion where my mother spoke and I felt uncomfortable and waited for the "conversation" to be over.

When I imagined having a boyfriend, I wanted someone who would hold my hand, be my friend, kiss me under the stars, and talk with me about interesting subjects. I was eager to love someone and to have someone love me.

In sixth grade, I played "Truth or Dare" in a friend's backyard behind a wooden fence and was kissed on the cheek when a boy I liked chose "Dare." In eighth grade, I struggled with braces and kissing and trying to keep a boy's hands away from my bra buckle. I didn't want my body to be someone else's anatomy book.

I spent years holding back boys' hands that wanted to venture up my shirt or down my pants. When I was a freshman in high school, I had a boyfriend break up with me because I was only willing to kiss him and then I was shunned by his friends for being a prude.

My prep-school reputation as a wild and sleazy girl was foreign to me. Both definitions—the prude and the slut—defined me as a sex object. One criticized me for being too sexual and the other for not being sexual enough, as if who touched or didn't touch certain parts of my body defined who I was as a person. As if.

When I returned to The Prep School for my junior year, I was determined to stay out of the gossip firing line and to focus on academics. One fall weekend, a young-alumni reunion took place. Recent graduates came back to the school to party.

In the dining room I saw Dylan from afar, and my stomach felt sick. He had returned to campus with a group of friends. They strutted around as if they still owned the place, which, on many levels, they did. That night, Dylan woke me up in the middle of the night. He was drunk and stood beside my bed. I lived in a different dorm that year, and my room was on the third floor.

Dylan was telling me how much he missed me, and then he started to touch me.

"Leave. Leave now," I said. "Get out. Get out of my room. I really mean it." And he did.

Grace Kaimila-Kanjo, Girls' Empowerment Educator, Africa ~ Violence against girls is a major problem. Not just sexual violence. Physical violence. Emotional violence. Girls are harassed. They are sexually assaulted, and the community does not really take this seriously. In a number of communities in rural Africa, it's like, "Oh, it's okay for girls to go through those kind of experiences." The boys are trained that after you try your luck with a girl, then you are man enough. It is socially sanctioned that you harass girls. You touch their boobs. You touch their behinds. You touch them in inappropriate ways to prove that you are maturing as a boy. This really brings a lot of mental problems among the girls. If they don't feel safe in any environment, it affects their participation. It affects their education rights.[9]

High School

My Senior Year

Helen Keller, Optimism ~

I know what evil is. Once or twice I have wrestled with it, and for a time felt its chilling touch on my life.

Dear Reader,

I started my senior year wanting to focus on improving my writing and doing well in school. I was the captain of the swim team and a proctor in an underclass dorm.

Gabby, age 22 ~ I'm ambitious. I have big dreams. I wanted to do what I love, and I knew what I had to do to be successful: Do well in school and take the right classes. Each year I check in with myself and ask, "Do I still want to be a writer?" Giving up on a dream is really easy. It takes work to stay focused. I imagine and dream in my mind and see myself doing what I love a lot.

That fall, teachers pulled me aside to tell me what a remarkable turnaround I'd made—implying that they were stunned that I had transformed from a slut into a student, an athlete, and a school leader. When they complimented me, I smiled.

No one cared that before I attended The Prep School I had been president of my freshman class. To them, I was the girl who had been at the pool party with varsity hockey players, and the faculty prided themselves on my transformation. One even wrote me a letter praising me for my change.

In the fall of my senior year, I was placed in an Honors English section with an aging teacher who was struggling to speak in complete sentences. I had waited years to take this class. Mr. Jessup taught the other Honors English section, which was considered the best class the school offered.

A few weeks in, I met with Mr. Jessup in an alcove off the dining room and asked to be switched into his section. I said that I wanted to be challenged during my last year and that I planned on majoring in English in college. Mr. Jessup said that if he transferred me into his class, others would see that he favored me. I was devastated. As I imagined a year of studies lost, my eyes filled with tears. And then Mr. Jessup pulled me close to him, pressed his body against mine, and kissed me.

Stephanie Cyr, Lawyer and Self–Defense Instructor ~ There are levels of sexual assault. As soon as I receive unwanted touch—that's an assault.

I felt Mr. Jessup's tongue in my mouth and his hands on my body. I froze. He was decades older than I was. He was my advisor and my friend. I was 17. Mr. Jessup ran his hands over my shoulders and down my waist as he pressed his hips against mine. When I pushed away, he said, "Kat, sometimes a teacher is attracted to a student, and things like this just happen. I couldn't help myself."

Mr. Jessup was one of the most respected teachers at the school. He told me it was my fault that he had kissed me, and I believed him.

Sofie Karasek, Co-founder End Rape on Campus, age 22 ~ If it does happen, the blame rests solely on the perpetrator.

After the kiss, Mr. Jessup switched me out of Honors English into a lower English class. I felt guilty that I had caused a great man to stumble, and I accepted his punishment. I dove into a world of schoolwork and shame. Mr. Jessup was married. I respected and knew his wife. With his kiss, all of the hateful snickers and knowing smiles sank in. In my mind, I was definitely a slut.

David Wolowitz, Lawyer and Consultant on Student Safety ~ One way for a teacher to be popular with the students is to act as a peer. It is normal for adolescents to seek peer approval. There is no more special peer than an adult peer who is acting like a child. The teacher wants to be the pied piper and have kids adore them. When the teacher becomes special to the student and the student becomes special to the teacher, the relationship has become a power-dependent relationship. The power-dependent relationship can lead to abuse and an unhealthy relationship in many different ways. It isn't always sexual abuse. It can also be social, financial, or emotional, and it can deeply hurt the student.

Helen Keller, The Story of My Life ~ I got used to the silence and darkness that surrounded me and forgot that it had ever been different.

Dear Reader,

My senior year, there was another English teacher whom many girls admired. His name was Mr. Lyon. At the start of winter term, I was heading into the library to study after dinner, and Mr. Lyon pulled me aside. He'd never spoken to me before, and I was surprised that he knew who I was.

"Kat," Mr. Lyon said, "can I talk to you for a minute?" He called me by the same nickname that Mr. Jessup used for me. Mr. Lyon told me about a study-abroad program that he was chaperoning in the summer and invited me to his apartment to see the brochure.

Gavin de Becker, Author and International Expert on Predicting Violence ~ There are two kinds of predators. There is a power predator. That's someone who charges like a bear and knocks somebody down, and that's a very rare predator because it's a much riskier thing. The persuasion predator actually persuades the victim to participate, persuades the victim to be in an environment that is without advantages, only has advantages for the attacker.[10]

The next night, I went to see Mr. Lyon. He was a faculty dorm head and lived at the end of the hall of an all-boys dorm. Mr. Lyon sat beside me on his couch and showed me pictures of Europe. When he finished, he told me that Mr. Jessup had suggested he get to know me better.

Mr. Lyon had a book on his coffee table called *The Curtis Creek Manifesto: A Fully Illustrated Guide to the Strategy, Finesse, Tactics, and Paraphernalia of Fly Fishing.* Mr. Lyon told me he loved fishing—the game and the hunt. He said he experimented with bait to determine which worked best to catch a fish. He said he was patient while he stalked a fish, and that sometimes a fish would pull hard on the line and he'd have to let it run or else the fish would get away. He said he'd let the fish tire itself out, and then he'd reel it in. Other times, he said, he'd feel a quick tug, and that he knew how to set the hook.

After that night, Mr. Lyon invited me back to his apartment often and asked me to help him grade papers. When I reviewed his students' essays, he said he was impressed by my insights into literature and writing. He played the guitar for me, ordered pizza, and taught me card games. He enjoyed winning. At the time of our first meeting, I was 17. One night he asked me when my birthday was. I said it was at the end of February.

"That's so long for me to wait," Mr. Lyon said. "In the meantime, I want you to call me Ben."

Mr. Lyon's words filled the air with excitement, and I wondered what he meant. The invitation to call him by his first name surprised me. He was handsome. Some of the girls thought he looked like Michelangelo's statue of David.

Anne, age 25 ~ When he was saying really, really flattering things involving me—it's embarrassing to say, but he said he fantasized about me, and that he thought I was really gorgeous, and I was very aware of the difference between how it was affecting my body and what I needed to do. If I had been in a more vulnerable place, I could have given in and fallen for the flattery—and given the flattery back to him. Instead I kept my boundary clear, and I didn't give him the flattery back. That was huge for me because I think as women we don't want to hurt their feelings, we feel we owe them something, and I was very clear that I didn't owe him anything. That was big for me, realizing not to give him the flattery back.

In the dining room and in the school hallways, I would often look up and see Mr. Lyon following me with his eyes. He'd nod his head and smile. I liked the secret attention.

David Wolowitz, Lawyer and Consultant on Student Safety ~ The one who has the responsibility to make the relationship healthy is the adult. Kids will worship and follow teachers. This is developmentally part of being an adolescent. It's the teacher's responsibility to set boundaries and set limits.

Decades later, I was in a therapist's office taking apart what had happened when I was at The Prep School. I realized that Mr. Lyon had waited for me to turn 18 before beginning a sexual relationship to avoid being charged with statutory rape. The courtship preceding my 18th birthday could be described as grooming by a pedophile.

Statutory Rape: Sexual activity in which one of the individuals is below the age required to legally consent to the behavior. (Wikipedia)[11]

Grooming: When a sexual predator gives toys and other things to a child to gain trust and sexually harm the child. (Urban Dictionary)[12]

Pedophile: An adult who is sexually attracted to children... It's a sick f#@%ing fetish, acted out by vile human beings who cannot tell right from wrong. (Urban Dictionary)[13]

Sometimes Mr. Lyon left me gifts in my mailbox, and then he'd stop by my dorm room to visit me. His attention made me feel special. He thought I was pretty and told me often. In his apartment, his hand would touch mine when he was reaching for a book or a deck of cards. He offered me wine and beer. And after I turned 18, he kissed me.

Professor Renee McDonald ~ I want every girl to know that most sexual assaults start with a kiss. If a person is going to progress to a sexual assault, they start with a kiss.

Laura, age 22 ~ Alcohol is the biggest date rape drug—more than getting roofied.

I was one of three proctors on my floor, and we rotated who was overseeing study hall for the freshmen and sophomore girls. On my nights off, I went to Mr. Lyon's apartment. I felt grown up and sophisticated, drinking wine and talking about literature. Out of all the girls, he could have had his pick, and he had chosen me. I enjoyed the charge that he and I got from maintaining a secret relationship, but, at the same time, it also made me worry—something about it didn't feel right.

Gwyn, age 22 ~ It's easy to look back and see all the glaring red flags. I knew my opinion didn't hold the same weight as his. I felt he had more social status than I did. There was an imbalance there.

Mr. Lyon wrote letters to me several times a week and left them in my school mailbox. I hid the letters in a textbook and took them into a bathroom stall to read between classes. In his letters, Mr. Lyon gave me instructions on when and where to meet him and told me he'd never had this powerful an attraction to someone before. He always told me how beautiful he thought I was, and he said that he'd tried to resist entering into a relationship with me but couldn't.

Hersh and Gray-Little, (1998) ~ Men who report increased levels of sexual aggression also report higher levels of manipulativeness.[14]

Mr. Lyon said it had been over seven years since he'd been in love and that the last woman had hurt him badly. He said that when he was with me, he was finally happy.

David Wolowitz, Lawyer and Consultant on Student Safety ~ A healthy relationship between a teacher and a student focuses on the child's development and their social, emotional, and academic needs, not on meeting the teacher's needs.

When Mr. Lyon and I were in his bedroom, he would take out a condom and explain how desperately he wanted to make love to me. Again and again, I told Mr. Lyon that I only wanted to make love with someone when I was certain I was in love.

"I'm sorry," I apologized. "I'm not ready."

www.futureswithoutviolence.org ~ When you tell someone NO or that you're feeling uncomfortable, he or she should stop the situation and respect your decision.

Mr. Lyon would pout and look dejected. He'd tell me how much I was hurting him, and then he'd tell me other ways he liked to experience sexual pleasure. And then Mr. Lyon would give me specific instructions, and I would do what he asked.

Grace Miller, Sexual Health Educator, age 22 ～ It's not consent if you're feeling pressured to say yes.

Denise, age 25 ~

I never felt like I fit in in high school. I wasn't blond-haired. I wasn't blue-eyed. And then, my freshman year, I met a guy who was a year older than me. He was tall, dark, and handsome, so handsome and quiet in a mysterious way. He was the "it" guy. I gave him a lot of power without realizing it. Many guys don't start out abusive. It's a development.

We were pretty serious. We had fun together. We were the cool, hot couple that first year. There were little glimpses of him saying to me, "Don't do this, don't do that," but it was very minimal.

The second year of our dating, I was a sophomore and he was a junior. It really picked up fast, and he started to be very controlling, possessive, and jealous. "Don't go out without me. I don't trust you. If I'm studying, you're staying here." That's when I didn't fight back, and I started to do what he told me. Early on, I did everything he asked because I was a people-pleaser. I didn't want to disappoint him.

This is about the time that I was learning that when I did disobey him, he would unleash on me. He was very verbally abusive at this point. I was so scared of the verbal abuse that I did whatever it took to avoid it happening. If it was a Friday night and he said he needed to study and that he wanted me to stay in, I did it. I didn't want to deal with the consequences.

I was terrified of the verbal abuse. This was my Pandora's Box. He called me a dipshit and a whore all the time. It was continuous. I wasn't talking to anyone about it, and it got continually worse his junior year and his senior year.

That verbal abuse destroyed my sense of self, and I started depending on him more and more. It was a vicious cycle because

I wasn't telling anyone this was going on. I was very quiet about it. Subconsciously, I knew this was bad, but I was like, "I need him. I need a stabilizing force."

The harder his life got, the worse he was to me verbally and the more controlling he became. That's when the physical abuse started. It was the same issue: I wasn't talking about it. He had this ridiculous standard. My entire being annoyed him—anything I did, anything I said, I was too social, too extroverted, too flirty, too absentminded.

If I did something that annoyed him in public, he would pinch me really hard under the table. I mean, the guy was 6'4". His pinches were bruise-worthy, and I did have bruises from them. Sometimes he would grab my skin and pull it in two directions and burn the skin. It was excruciating. But those aren't slaps in the face or punches in the face, right? So I never considered it physical abuse. I was thinking, "He's just letting me know how he feels, but he can't verbalize it in public." Once that started, it just got worse and didn't stop.

Warning Signs of Abuse

- Checking your cell phone or email without permission.
- Constantly putting you down or telling you what to do.
- Extreme jealousy or insecurity. Possessiveness.
- Isolating you from family or friends.
- Explosive temper or mood swings.
- Making false accusations.
- Physically hurting you in any way.
- Pressuring or forcing you to have sex.[15]

Dear Reader,

The first time Mr. Lyon and I went out to together, we met at a restaurant close to campus. As a boarding-school student, I thought going out to dinner was a treat and riding in a car was a special occasion—both were privileges other students would envy. Mr. Lyon and I were having a candlelight dinner when another faculty member was seated at the table next to ours. She looked at Mr. Lyon and then scowled at me.

The next time he and I went out to dinner, Mr. Lyon decided it would be best if we went farther from the school. Late one afternoon, I walked to a nearby town and Mr. Lyon picked me up at a gas station. We drove to a bordering state, where we had dinner at a small inn. We sat at a table for two in a corner. It was the first time I was served wine at a restaurant.

Allie, age 21 ~ My mom would say, "If a guy comes up offering to show you puppies in his van, do not go with him to see the puppies."

The third time we had dinner together was in New York City. Some classmates and I took a train to Manhattan for the weekend. Mr. Lyon pre-arranged that he and I would meet at The Lone Star Café. I left my friends and took a cab to the restaurant.

Mr. Lyon bought me dinner. In the bar afterward, we drank beer and danced to a country western band. I knew many of the songs. The music reminded me of my home in Arizona. It was after midnight when we got into a cab together. Mr. Lyon asked the driver to take us to his hotel. In the car I told him I wasn't going up to his room, and he got angry. Mr. Lyon said he'd come all the way to the city and couldn't believe I wouldn't go back with him to his hotel.

We had not discussed my spending the night with him as part of our plan.

Professor Renee McDonald ~ The first stage is just chit-chat. The second stage is mild flirtation and an expression of interest. The third stage is beginning pressure to kiss or do something. The fourth stage is the male increasing pressure with anger that the girl is not relenting, and the male is arguing back and combatting her defenses.

For the first time since I had begun my interactions with Mr. Lyon, I felt afraid. At a stoplight, I got out of the cab in the middle of a street in New York City. I'd had a few beers. I didn't know where I was or what time it was—if it was two or three in the morning. It was the night in early spring when the clocks change. I passed groups of men huddled around fires burning inside garbage cans, and I asked strangers for directions. Hours later, I found my friends.

Madison, age 21 ~ My roommate was raped in high school. A guy took her to a motel. They were friends. He was older than she was. He kept her there for 24 hours. It was a nightmare. Eventually, she told her dad about the guy at the motel. She and her parents are really close. She made her dad promise that he wouldn't tell her mom. She thought it would hurt her mom too much.

After the weekend, Mr. Lyon wrote several letters to me apologizing for his outburst and asking me to come see him. He told me how much he loved me and how sorry he was. He seemed incredibly sad.

Zoe, age 22 ~ I've very much always been a golden retriever. I want to please everybody. I'm really bad at conflict and confrontational situations. I really like everything to be all good, and I'd do anything to make the other person happy.

I'd been taught to be forgiving and to give someone a second chance, and I did. But when Mr. Lyon continued to pressure me to have sex with him, I tried to end things with him.

Gwyn, age 22 ~ There was an emotionally abusive component, and there was sexual violence. He was telling me that I was crazy and that everything he was doing was fine and normal. He didn't own up to anything. After I ended it, he started apologizing, and he showed up in front of my dorm and wouldn't leave. He literally followed me and stood outside my dorm. He was writing me poetry and sending me flowers. What he did still wasn't right. My advice to you is to really, really trust your own sense of right and wrong.

I tried to ignore Mr. Lyon—all I wanted was to go to school. But he kept writing me letters and then, one day, he came by my room.

Laura, age 22 ~ I had to punch a guy in the chest because he was trying to push me into my room. I said, "Get the hell out of here," and he left. You have to have the courage to trust your instincts and not be afraid to act. Be willing to say, "Hey, you're not going to push me around." I didn't know what his intentions were, but I felt if he got in my room, it wouldn't have been a good situation.

Once inside my dorm room, Mr. Lyon told me how much he'd missed me, and then he asked me to come by his place to discuss my feelings. He said he wanted to hear what I had to say. In his apartment, he put on music and poured me a glass of wine, and I talked and talked. The night ended in his bedroom.

Mr. Lyon told me he loved fishing—the game and the hunt. He said he experimented with bait to determine which worked best to catch a fish. He said he was patient while he stalked a fish, and that sometimes a fish would pull hard on the line and he'd have to let it run or else the fish would get away. He said he'd let the fish tire itself out, and then he'd reel it in.

After my high school graduation, Mr. Lyon met me secretly at one of the graduation parties. He told me how deeply I was hurting him by going to college and begged me to have sex with him in the back of his car.

"If you knew how much I love you, you would," he said.

I said no and felt proud of myself for saying no—despite how much pain he said I was causing him.

After I returned home to Arizona, Mr. Lyon called me often. He said he had purchased a round-trip plane ticket to Phoenix. He asked me to lie to my parents, tell them I was spending the weekend with a friend, and stay with him in a hotel instead.

When I told him to cancel his trip, Mr. Lyon was furious, and I said that things were over. A week later, I received a letter from Mr. Lyon telling me what a terrible person I was and how cruelly I had treated him.

Chloe, age 20 ~

When I told her I wanted it to end, she exploded. She kept trying to make it work, and she wanted me to give her another chance.

Throughout the whole relationship, it was clear from the start. There were a lot of red flags. I didn't see them. She would use a lot of "you" statements. We would fight or talk about things that weren't working, and she would say, "You're selfish," or "You don't like to do this," or "You think this way."

Because she was the person I most cared about, she was the person I most wanted to please and make happy, and she would tear me apart. She would get into all the reasons why I wasn't enough, even if it wasn't true, and then later she'd say, "I didn't mean it." I'd get in this mindset that was awful—I didn't feel appreciated, and I didn't feel good enough.

This is a broader issue with social anxiety and needing people's judgments of me to define myself. I suffer from—no, not suffer, I deal with, cope with, work with—high levels of social anxiety, which manifests in my taking these projected judgments, what others say about me, and defining myself based on them.

My main mantra now is "My social interactions do not define me."

There was a manipulative dynamic, her trying to control me and not wanting me to be happy without her. It was so messed up. She'd either be super loving, charismatic, and everyone loves her, or within a night, she'd turn into the complete opposite and rip into me because she saw me as all bad.

It was narcissism because she saw me as a tool.

People like me see other people as windows and see inside them: They're their own people, they have stories to tell, and there are things to learn about them, and they're super fascinating. Each person has a story and intricate details that make up who they are.

Narcissists look at other people as mirrors and don't acknowledge their individuality because they see everybody as elementary for their own goals as a person. They see other people, and there's no registering of that person's individual existence or entity.

With Heather, she didn't respect my complexity or respect that we are different people in a relationship, that we are joined by the relationship but we are not the same people. She wanted me to want the same things that she wanted. Narcissists want you to want the same things they do. Heather didn't want to break up, and because I didn't want the same thing she wanted, she ripped into me. That's the all good or all bad. If you do want what they want, it's great. They're super nice to you. If you exercise your free will, then it's all bad.

As long as you are going along with what they want, they're happy, but then it gets scary because you're afraid to do what they don't want. Over the summer, I was worried every time I had to go to a family dinner because I had to tell her and sign off and still be on high alert in case she texted me.

I didn't really have a voice. Her narcissistic mindset created a power dynamic—which is super unhealthy in relationships—where she was the type A, had all these ideas, and always wanted to be the leader and expected me to follow.

It is interesting because it was a same-sex relationship, and you normally hear about the power dynamic with the guy being controlling, but with this it was the same thing. It was totally unexpected, but it was the same thing.

It's been a long process of untangling myself and my head.

Anne, age 25 ~

Once I said, "This is over," I had to make it over in my mind as well. I told myself, "I don't need to invest any more energy in this." I did tell a very trusted mentor, an older woman, and she said, "Now that you've said this was your last meeting, you have no obligation to return his calls." That felt really good too—to get that affirmation that I don't owe him anything and I don't need to feel bad about it. Years ago, I would have thought, "Oh, I don't want to hurt his feelings. Oh, I feel bad." Instead I said to myself, "No! The guy is sick. You need to cut him off. I don't need to follow up and see how he's doing. We're done." It's helpful for me to see the pitfalls that I would fall into normally as a woman and that I didn't go there, and so I'm really proud of myself.

Dear Reader,

I need to tell you about Claire. She was one of my best friends my senior year at The Prep School. We were proctors together in an underclass dorm. She was a beautiful poet and would leave me poems she'd written on my desk before she left for class.

An English teacher named Mr. Wickham picked Claire to be his lover. He was considered to be one of the best teachers at the school, and Claire felt delighted that Mr. Wickham had special feelings for her.

Every day, Claire and I would meet and discuss what letters or presents we had received. We both felt lucky that we had been chosen. Claire confided in me details about her sexual interactions with Mr. Wickham. I confided in her that I wasn't ready to have sex with Mr. Lyon, and she supported my decision. Claire told me that after she and Mr. Wickham made love, he'd serve her pancakes in bed. As Claire's birthday was later than mine, she was 17 when she was having sex with Mr. Wickham.

I don't know if I should keep writing now that I'm in the middle of telling this story. I need to start making dinner, cut up celery, and peel carrots to make a soup. Do I keep going? Do I take a break?

After I moved with my husband and children to California, I was sorting through boxes and came across items I'd saved from my senior year. There was a piece of folded notebook paper. I opened it. It was a poem Claire had written and left on my desk. It was in her handwriting—crisp letters made with a blue fine-point pen. When I reread it, I could hear her voice—laughing, joyful, alive.

Claire, age 17 ~

Good morning! Good morning!
Isn't it a beautiful day?
Last night you sent me to bed with dreams smiling.
I'd do anything to make you smile.
I'd stand on my head or sing a song or give you a hug.
I just wanted to write you to say that
Wildflowers bloom all over in unexpected places.
You're always a wildflower for me, Kathleen.

When I found Claire's poem, I cried.

I don't know how to tell you what I'm going to say next. Years after we graduated from The Prep School, I got a phone call and was told that Claire had killed herself.

Helen Keller, The Story of My Life ~

That night, after I had hung my stocking, I lay awake a long time, pretending to be asleep and keeping alert to see what Santa Claus would do when he came... Next morning it was I who waked the whole family with my first "Merry Christmas!" I found surprises, not in the stocking only, but on the table, on all the chairs, at the door, on the very windowsill; indeed, I could hardly walk without stumbling on a bit of Christmas wrapped up in tissue paper. But when my teacher presented me with a canary, my cup of happiness overflowed.

Little Tim was so tame that he would hop on my finger and eat candied cherries out of my hand. Miss Sullivan taught me to take all the care of my new pet. Every morning after breakfast I prepared his bath, made his cage clean and sweet, filled his cups with fresh seed and water from the well-house, and hung a spray of chickweed in his swing.

One morning I left the cage on the window-seat while I went to fetch water for his bath. When I returned I felt a big cat brush past me as I opened the door. At first I did not realize what had happened; but when I put my hand in the cage and Tim's pretty wings did not meet my touch or his small pointed claws take hold of my finger, I knew that I should never see my sweet little singer again.

Dear Reader,

My senior year in high school, there was a friend of Claire's and mine—he was a classmate of ours. Decades later, this friend told me that during our senior spring, Claire had confided in him that she was having sex with Mr. Wickham. My friend said he was deeply disturbed by what Claire had shared with him, and that he went to his advisor and told him that Claire and Mr. Wickham were having sex. This friend said that he and his advisor had met with the Assistant Headmaster that spring and told him that Claire and Mr. Wickham were having sex.

Professor Luci Herman, Resident Fellow and Student Advisor ~ We have a responsibility to report if there are implications of sexual assault or relationship abuse—not necessarily physical, it can be emotional too. If names are named, we legally cannot keep it confidential. We have to report.

This means that, more than 30 years ago, two adults in administrative roles, an advisor and the Assistant Headmaster, were informed that a teacher was having sex with a student. Adults in positions of authority had the opportunity to intervene.

Rape can have long-term emotional consequences that can lead to suicide, and research studies show that intervention can save a life. Fifty percent of youth who have been victims of rape attempt suicide, compared to 12.5% of non-abused girls.[16] It is quite common for rape victims to suffer from depression, and untreated depression is the number one cause for suicide. For survivors of sexual assault, suicide attempts may occur years after the rape.[17] If a victim of sexual assault receives care early, however, then the long-term negative effects are significantly diminished.[18] Many negative effects often follow sexual assault: shame, self-loathing, anorexia, bulimia, depression, anxiety, addiction, alcoholism, PTSD, and suicide. It's a horrible, horrible list. No one talks about sexual assault being a gateway to unhappiness. But it is. For someone who has been sexually assaulted, getting help matters. It matters a lot.

Denise, age 25 ~ I went back to my dean after I was a year sober. He teared up and said, "As a doctor, I need you to know that with the amount of pills you were taking and drinking, you should be dead. You 100% should be dead. And you have no heart damage." He had me go to a cardiologist to check out my heart. I tear up when I talk about him. He saved my life.

If people in administrative roles had followed the law and reported the abuse, it is possible that the intervention could have saved Claire.

I can't write any more tonight. The tears in my eyes return. The soup is almost ready. My son is home. My husband is home. And I need to return to them—to dinner and feeding the dog and dishes. But there is always a lingering thought for me, a memory of a girl who loved to write poems and leave them on my desk before she went to class.

I will leave you with her words.

Claire, age 17 ~ Wildflowers bloom all over in unexpected places.

Zoe, age 22 ~

I texted a friend at school and I told him, "I don't think I can do this any more. It feels like a me-problem. These people are attacking me, and I can't do this any more."

I was really down on myself for everything that had gone on since we'd gone camping. I was really close with the guy who'd sexually assaulted me. And then he sent me a text and said really hurtful things. I was attacked again and again.

My friend from school texted me back and said, "Put your time into what makes you happy. The people who share that happiness will be drawn to you, and that's where your genuine relationships are going to come from. You have to find your happiness. It can't come from others, and you can't let people bring you down."

Now I know I'm the only one who can say if I'm a bad friend, and I know I'm not a bad friend. I know I went above and beyond trying to be a friend to that guy. I know he had other things going on in his life that probably caused him to attack me. Finding that ability to have me be the strongest source of self instead of others is my focus.

This is the first year I ever saw a therapist. It was through the health center. I stopped seeing her after four times because I thought I was doing a lot better. It was really helpful.

I also have two not-official therapists—one of my roommates and one of my RAs. I talk to them about everything. They know everything about my life and are constantly there to listen. My RA will read my poems and talk about thoughts with me. They've been awesome, and I am very grateful for them.

I feel like they hear me and see me. They are both incredible listeners. They both know "Don't offer advice, offer support."

A lot of times there are situations where there's no advice that can make it better, but to feel supported is huge. They definitely taught me that existence is a genuine form of support for others. A lot of times you don't need advice because there's nothing you can really do. You just need someone to talk to or snuggle with. Both of them have held me as I cried myself to sleep. Those are the best kinds of people.

I was on a run with my RA, and we were talking about feelings about college and purpose, and my RA was talking about wanting to make a difference in the world. And I said, "To you, I might just be one person, but to me, you essentially saved my life. This is my entire world, and you've made an incredible difference. This is the biggest difference you can imagine. You don't even know what you've already done."

My RA smiled and said, "Oh, I didn't think about it like that."

Now, when I get to that place and I feel really down, I know I can get through it, which is huge. It's everything.

Your life is extremely valuable, and people care about you. Please reach out for help. Never act on your thoughts of suicide. Never. (www.suicide.org)

Dear Reader,

My son is home sick today. That's why I was making soup last night. I boiled a chicken and cut vegetables, taking breaks as I wrote to you. This morning I put our dog in his room, and she curled up beside him.

He's a junior in high school, and I watch the stress he carries with friends, girls, school, athletics, and considering colleges. I hope he sleeps deeply. There is a cloud cover today, and the house is quiet.

I was the same age that my son is now when Mr. Jessup kissed me. I can't imagine my son's advisors pulling him aside, hugging him tightly, and kissing him. The sickness of it is easy to see now, but it wasn't easy to see then.

I didn't tell you what Mr. Jessup kissing me did to my confidence. He was powerful—his praise filled me with hope, and a disparaging comment from him wrecked my day.

December 20, 1900

My Dear Mr. Copeland,

When I have written something that seems to be fresh and spontaneous and worthy of your criticism, I will bring it to you, if I may, and if you think it good, I shall be happy; but if your verdict is unfavorable, I shall try again and yet again until I have succeeded in pleasing you.

Helen Keller

After Mr. Jessup kissed me, I believed that all the compliments he'd ever given me were false flattery to gain my attention, and I questioned my worth as a writer and as a person.

Luke, age 24 ~ When a young person starts to question their self-worth, we are all deprived of their full potential.

In my garden at home, I've noticed that where I water, the plants grow. This is true of people as well, and I began to see myself in the ways that I was being seen—as a sexually powerful young woman.

Jessica Chapman-Segal, Reproductive Health Educator, age 25 ~ Young women are given the message that they are sexual, and you use your sexuality as a power, and you use your body. You are told that you get power and attain power through your body. You should not have to use your body to get attention, or to have power. You should be appreciated for your contributions as a human.

Too often our culture blames women's sexuality for the transgressions of men, and I accepted that blame. I was 15. I was 16. I was 17. I was 18. I was a girl becoming a woman. The teachers—Mr. Jessup, Mr. Lyon, and Mr. Wickham—were false gods full of false praise, who quoted Shakespeare to woo female students. To have a young student's adoration, laughter, and start-struck gaze made them giddy and high.

David Wolowitz, Lawyer and Consultant on Student Safety ~ The people with the most serious problems usually have the least amount of insight, and they need to be identified by a colleague. My mission is to help teachers identify high-risk behavior in their colleagues and report it before children are harmed.

I look back on who could have intervened. There was the female teacher who sat next to Mr. Lyon and me at the restaurant, who saw that he and I were more than friends. Other female faculty scowled at me in the halls. Why was I blamed, and why did no one contact the police?

Mr. Jessup had supreme status at the school, and he encouraged both Mr. Lyon and Dylan to "get to know me better." Was Mr. Jessup vicariously enjoying the sexual conquests of his followers while creating a culture that celebrated rape?

Professor Phil Zimbardo, The Lucifer Effect: Understanding How Good People Turn Evil *(2007) ~ Evil consists in intentionally behaving in ways that harm, abuse, demean, dehumanize, or destroy innocent others—or using one's authority and systemic power to encourage or permit others to do so on your behalf.*

In the yearbook, my senior year, my classmates gave me the award of "Self-Appointed Faculty." A lot of people knew about what was going on. Instead of condemning the sexual predators, they blamed the victims.

Professor Phil Zimbardo, The Lucifer Effect *~ Our usual take on evil focuses on the violent, destructive actions of perpetrators,* *but the failure to act can also be a form of evil, when helping, dissent, disobedience, or whistle-blowing are required. One of the most critical, least acknowledged contributors to evil goes beyond the protagonists of harm to the silent chorus who look but do not see, who hear but do not listen.*

A lion makes a kill, and when he's finished with his prey, vultures tear meat from the carcass. "She deserved it. She had it coming. She asked for it." It makes me wonder if the sound of nails going into the coffin of a dead girl is the sound of snickers in the hall.

My first night at boarding school, when I was 15 years old, Ms. Spike went to each room to check in students. Lisel and I stood in our doorway, listening to the echo of Ms. Spike's boots as she walked down the corridor. When Ms. Spike met Lisel and me for the first time, she pointed her long fingers at our eyes, glared down at us, and said, "You two are going to be trouble." If she had spit on us, it would have felt the same.

Young, female sexuality is powerful. Often, we as a society turn that power against girls: Boys hate girls, girls hate girls, teachers hate girls, and parents hate girls. This needs to stop now. We need to value and protect our girls, and it starts by valuing and protecting the feminine within all of us—the part inside us that is mysterious, powerful, unique, and beautiful.

Many adults—teachers, administrators, coaches, dorm heads, and advisors—failed to protect children who were in their care, and terrible things happened to children as a result. Resist the urge to be quiet when you see someone putting someone else down. Resist the urge to be silent when someone puts you down. Resist the urge to make yourself feel better by stepping on someone else, and reach out a hand instead. If you see that someone is hurting someone else, say something.

The only way out is to be kind and brave—even when no one else is. When you practice kindness to others, you will perhaps be able to do what is even more difficult, and that is to practice kindness to yourself. This ability could save your life.

Irene Tsai, Watcher and Alcohol Educator, age 21 ~ We recommend that people take the initiative and intervene because they shouldn't be scared of negative consequences or the backlash that comes with being accused of being a cock-blocker. We're trying to emphasize that it doesn't matter if you are called a cock-blocker, because ultimately we're trying to watch out for the other person's wellbeing.

College

My Freshman Year

Hannah Gribetz, Sexual Assault Peer Educator, age 22 ~

High school, they were preparing you for academic challenges, not social challenges. Fortunately, one person told me that socially it can be a hard transition. He told me he felt sad a lot. When things were really difficult for me and I was feeling sad or lost—normal things freshmen feel—I would think back on that person I admire: He was good at everything, and I knew that he'd also had a hard time. It's not unusual. This let me know that there wasn't something wrong with me.

Sophie, age 22 ~

Within two weeks of leaving home, you're starting classes, and you're asked to answer all these questions: Tell us three things about yourself. You could say anything, and no one would know the difference. In high school, everyone knows you—if you say something about yourself that doesn't ring true, someone will challenge it. In college, you're in charge of making your identity. You have the power to determine it. People ask you casually, and they want an answer quickly—as if who I am is an easy answer. It's like asking someone what a tattoo means. That's such an ordinary question. You could ask that question to someone you don't even know, and, the answer is probably a long, personal story. Nine times out of 10, the answer isn't casual.

Dear Reader,

I started my freshman year in college eager to take as many English classes as I could. I was ready for a fresh start.

Lindsey, age 24 ~ The first few weeks of college were really rough because you meet so many people you never see again. I was trying to make friends. I'd sit down next to someone at the dining hall and introduce myself, but it never went anywhere. It was a dead end. It wasn't that I wasn't meeting great people, I was, but I quickly realized that if you don't have a structure like a club or a team to build a relationship around, it's hard.

I lived in a co-ed dorm. The girls across the hall built a hang-out area in their room with throw pillows, pipes, and tapestries. Sometimes I'd sit with them and laugh and talk, but smoking pot didn't appeal to me.

Hannah Gribetz, Sexual Assault Peer Educator, age 22 ~ If I was hanging out with friends and someone offered me a joint, even if everyone else was smoking, I was perfectly happy to say no thanks, pass it along, and sit back and sip on my beer or water, or nothing. This is corny, but saying no to drugs actually makes me feel cool, in a weird way, though I'm not sure I can explain it... I guess confidence is cool.

Other students regularly offered me mushrooms, cocaine, and acid, and I passed. My mother was a nutritionist and frequently sent me articles on the negative long-term effects of drugs. I was afraid of being out of control and didn't want to harm my body or my mind.

Catherine, age 22 ~

In the spirit of making friends and thinking my freshman room-mate might become one of my really great friends, I told her that my dad was an addict and is now a recovering addict. This came up because she was asking me how I felt about the drug and alcohol culture. I told her that I feel comfortable drinking, but I would never do any of these addictive drugs because it's in my genes and I saw that unravel.

I told her all about this, and a week later she was like, "Let's meet up with some friends." It was freshman year, in the fall right before Thanksgiving break. I walked in and saw all these people sitting in a circle around lines of coke, which I'd never seen before. A bunch of the people in the room were upperclassmen, and they were seriously trying to get me to do it. They were like, "Do it. Do it. Do it." I said, "No, I'm fine. I have a drink." They were all saying, "Are you going to be a party pooper?"

It was a small group setting, so it was even more uncom-fortable, and I was new to college, and here I was thinking my roommate was kind of cool and maybe I wanted to be friends with her. I had to continuously say "No," and it was so uncom-fortable, and so awkward. Eventually I just walked out of the room because I didn't know what else to do.

Looking back on it, I am so glad that that's what I did, and I started to distance myself from her immediately. I'd never been peer-pressured before. I am proud to this day of how I handled myself. I said, "No, I'm fine. I have a drink," and I walked out. Nobody brought it up again. In the moment it was hard because they were pressuring me, but I knew I didn't want to do it, and the moment passed, and I'm glad I dealt with it the way I did.

Dear Reader,

Sometimes I'd go to fraternity parties with a few of my dorm-mates. I liked to dance, and many of the houses had good music. As freshmen girls, we were always welcomed when we arrived at a party.

James, age 22 ~ The freshmen girls ditch their freshmen guy friends to hang out with older guys and party with them. The houses are really cool. They have big budgets, lots of booze, and fun activities: ice luge, dancing on tables, drinking games, beer pong, slap cup, flip cup. The girls complain about it, but they always go back.

Gwyn, age 22 ~ I fell into the deep end a lot in college. I still studied and got good grades, which is the scary part because I was able to look fine on the surface. But being fine in college and being mentally healthy isn't just about being able to check off good grades, friends, in clubs, and going out. I was a mess.

My first semester in college, I felt profoundly alone and suffered from migraines. The highlight of my week was the volunteer work I did at a local after-school program, where I helped children learn how to read. The kids were always happy to see me when I arrived at the trailer that had been set up for them. In the corner, I sat on a beanbag with children on my lap, and we sounded out words together from picture books.

D-o-l-l was doll. H-a-t was hat. M-u-g was mug. W-a-t-e-r was water.

Jack, Watcher,[19] age 19 ~

Every fall and every spring there's a giant festival at our indoor track, and you can check out clubs. I signed up to be a Watcher at the first club fest and went to their training and started working parties.

As Watchers, we track different types of partygoers, and we attempt to intervene with them in a certain way. We allocate them as the tipsy partygoer, the person who's wavering a bit; the rowdy partygoer, the person who drinks a lot and starts jumping on tables; the sick partygoer, the person who drinks a lot and starts throwing up; and the creepy partygoer, the guy who drinks a lot and starts eyeing women.

When we see signs that people are getting into any of these areas, there are different intermediate actions that we take to stop that situation from progressing from iffy to worse. For example, if we encounter a rowdy partygoer, the recommendation for the intervening action is to literally be rowdy with that guy or girl because they'll tire out more quickly because someone is joining in.

I've done that once or twice, and it does work. Once there was a guy who was bobbing around and yelling really loudly. It was a party that had taken place after a hockey game. He was yelling out, "Yeah, hockey!" And I started yelling, "Yeah, hockey!" Once someone acknowledged him, he relaxed and started talking in a more normal voice. That's a lower-risk situation.

I probably go to one event every two weeks. Watchers is based on teamwork. You never watch a party alone. Usually teams are between three and eight people, and we try to keep the group of Watchers as diverse as possible so we can tackle different situations.

We meet up at the party about 15 minutes before, and the host of the party will show us around the place. If it's a frat or a home, someone will give us a general tour and point out all the entrances, all the exits, places outside, all the nooks and crannies, places we'd want to know about so we can understand the entire grounds beforehand.

When we are at the party, we're required to be sober, and we're wearing normal party clothes. I'm trained to notice everything. We roam around with our partner and mingle. We have a rotation, and we do a small loop around that area. Then we go to the second floor. We check bathrooms every half hour.

Some of our interventions are more secret agent. For the tipsy partygoer, you would be trying to get him to drink a little less. Say he's drinking a rum and coke. You say, "Oh, I'll get you another one." You take his glass and put it somewhere. You go up to the bar, pour a coke and dip your hand in the rum and rim the glass with rum so he thinks it's really strong even though he's drinking coke.

For the creepy partygoer, if you see him edging up on a girl, the girl might be pressed against a wall. You can tell by the physical and facial gestures of the guy and especially of the girl if it's heading in the wrong direction. With the guy, it's mischievous intoxication. The guy is inebriated. His eyes are glazed over a bit, but he's still sort of thinking straight, and you can see in his face that there's a slight energy to it, even though that energy shouldn't be there because he's inebriated. The energy has intent. It doesn't look specifically evil or bad out of context. It looks purposeful, like he's trying to concentrate on something and enjoying the fact that he's concentrating on something. He looks as if he's trying to get an enjoyable task done—I think would be the best way to describe what it looks like to me.

In my experience, there aren't many guys who look mean. The fact that the guy is drunk may be threatening in and of itself, but I don't think the menace comes through in the facial expression. Think of an enjoyable task, like a guy who's playing a video game or a physical sport—the enjoyment is subtle, but it's there. More evident is the purpose that I'm seeing in his face. He knows he is the instigator in an offensive way, and he's enjoying it. That would be the subconscious thought that I think is projected in his mindset.

The girl is easier to read by her facial expressions. It depends on how intoxicated she is. With a medium intoxication level, the main emotion I see is less dread at first and more uncomfortableness. She's not really feeling it's a dangerous situation, but she's feeling that she doesn't really want to be there. You can tell from her subtle foot movements that she's maybe trying to inch away from the area really slowly so that she might get separated from the guy in the crowd, to slowly tip-toe back so that maybe a couple of people might cut them off and she could head out. You can also see it in her eyes. The guy's eyes are more consistently focused. They never really move. They're pretty much focused on the girl, who is their objective. With the girl, her eyes are constantly very fluttery, and they're looking in different ways, and very rarely are they consistently looking at the guy. Those are the main tells. The girls are a lot easier to read.

For me, this is one of the trickier things to handle because it's harder for a guy to do this and have it not be blatantly obvious and effective. Usually, if I can, I have someone of the same gender help get the girl away. Since we're on teams, we'll have one of the girls run over to that girl, even if she doesn't know her, and shout out, "Hey, I haven't seen you in a while, let's get a drink." And they roll off together. Because it's sudden and rather unexpected, the guy doesn't track it as well, and the girl's going to go with it because she's trying to get out of there, and she's noticing what's going on around her, and seeing that it's dangerous. By the time she's away, the guy's lost her. That is the best tactic. And then we keep an eye on that guy to make sure he doesn't go after someone else.

Dear Reader,

I am uncomfortable writing about what happened next.

Angela Exson, Director of University Sexual Assault Education and Response ~ Oftentimes a survivor will make a check list in her mind of all the things that she could have done differently, but the bottom line is that the perpetrator still could have made a different decision and could have chosen not to hurt you.

Emma, age 22 ~ When I was a freshman I felt a lot of pressure to go out. People always would say to me, "The college years are the best years of your life. Go out and party. Be crazy." That put a lot of pressure on me. I felt like I was wasting my youth when I wasn't going out. Then I would go out, and I would be miserable. I'd be with people I didn't love, and I'd be doing something I hated.

It was a Saturday night. I was at a party with girlfriends, and we were playing drinking games with a group of guys. A guy was flirting with me by challenging me to drink.

Lela, age 22 ~ When you're a freshman in college, it's exciting when guys like you, but, with hindsight, you realize that drunk guys in a basement like all girls.

Laura, age 22 ~ Alcohol is the biggest date-rape drug—more than getting roofied.

Tally, age 22 ~ It can be really dangerous if you're taking shots at each station. It can also be really fun if you know your limits, what's okay and what's not okay for you, and you know how to turn down a drink. Sometimes I'd say, "I want to play, but I've had enough to drink," and people were okay with that. If these are your friends or people you're getting to know as potential friends, it's a good indicator if they're accepting that you don't want to drink.

Jack, Watcher, age 19 ~ If girls are with a group that has guys, and the girls are trying to drink as much as the guys, the alcohol will impact them significantly more than it will the guys. There are differences between gender and weight that are dividing factors. If a girl tries to keep pace with a guy who drinks, she is going to get drunker much faster than that guy.

And then he started kissing me.

Professor Renee McDonald ~ I want every girl to know that most sexual assaults start with a kiss. If a person is going to progress to a sexual assault they start with a kiss.

He suggested we go into another room. We were making out on a bed. I was wearing a skirt. When he lifted it, I told him I didn't want to have sex. And then he started rubbing his erection on my underwear.

Professor Charlene Senn ~ Break things off immediately if a guy is pushing drinks, ignoring your "no," or trying to get you alone.[20]

Zoe, age 22 ~ I was physically trapped, and I couldn't get away. I couldn't remove myself from the situation. That was the scariest thing. I'd never been in a situation before where I felt like I couldn't leave.

I had been in a similar situation before. It was in my dorm room the night of the pool party.

Zoe, age 22 ~ He wasn't letting go. That's the biggest thing. I was pulling away. I was trying to get out, but I couldn't. I was trying to get out of his arms and get outside, and he wasn't letting go.

I told him again that I didn't want to have sex. But then he pinned my arms, and I froze.

Cora, age 24 ~ It was sort of like a rape. It's one of those gray areas. I'm not 100% clear that it was rape. A lot of women have experiences like it. I was at a party. I'd been drinking. I drank a bit too much. I was with a couple of girlfriends. One decided to stay the night. I decided to stay with her because I didn't want her to be alone. Somehow I'd had too much to drink. I knew I didn't want to have sex with a guy that night. I would have been comfortable kissing him, but not going all the way. He was cute, and we were dancing. We were flirting, and we went into a room and ended up making out. I was so drunk. I don't remember all of it. I don't know how much I stood up for myself. It's definitely a gray area. It's debatable. I was probably blacked out. I was saying, "I'm not sure I want to do this." I remember saying no. And it happened.

Afterward, I felt separated from who I wanted and hoped I would be.

Hannah Gribetz, Sexual Assault Peer Educator, age 22 ~ It's hard for someone who has been sexually assaulted to come out and say they've been sexually assaulted by someone in their peer group.

Sofie Karasek, Co-founder End Rape on Campus, age 22 ~ So often people blame themselves, and this self-blame becomes the core for so many other problems that perpetuate sexual assault. For example, if you're blaming yourself and you don't feel you can tell a friend, then you are depriving yourself of essential support during a time when support could be really helpful. If you're blaming yourself, you're less likely to get counseling and you're less likely to report the incident. Overall, self-blame contributes to the silence around sexual assault and allows people to pretend it does not exist.

I didn't tell anyone, not even my closest friends. I pretended it didn't exist.

85–90% of sexual assaults reported by college women are perpetrated by someone known to the victim; about half occur on a date. The most common locations are the man's or woman's home in the context of a party or a date. The perpetrators may range from classmates to neighbors.[21]

Cora, age 24 ~

I definitely felt really bad about it immediately after, but I think I numbed myself to it and tried to move on. I rationalized it. I didn't realize it had affected me until a couple of years later.

In work I was having boundary issues. I wasn't standing up for myself. It impacts you. It was sabotaging me and keeping me from doing my creative work in the world. I did see a therapist, and that was really helpful.

It can keep showing up in other areas if you don't untangle them. It brought up things for me—understanding my boundaries, learning how to say "No" and how to take care of myself. There was an inner disappointment. I didn't process it fully until later.

It's tricky because I feel one of the gifts of youth is that we're so trusting and naïve. It's challenging because we want to hold on to a trust in life and feeling open-hearted, and we still have to protect ourselves.

The sad truth is that as women we really need to protect ourselves and have awareness. We need to be aware of the situations we're putting ourselves in and have limits and boundaries. When we're young, we're thinking, "I'll just stay and drink the night away with all these strangers and sleep on the couch."

I haven't put myself in a situation like that since. While it was painful after, the healing process broke my heart open. Ironically, I was able to experience more compassion in life. It's through hardship that we learn there is suffering in the world, and that everyone is suffering in their own way, and that life is hard.

Annie Clark,
Co-founder End Rape on Campus, age 25 ~

If I go on CNN and talk publicly, I can seem okay, but sometimes it's hard. Sometimes, not every time, I need to cry, or go on a run, or do something to take care of myself.

Survivors go on TV shows and tell their stories, and they're strong, and then they go home and need to process it. That's okay. Sometimes you tell your story and you're fine afterward. Sometimes you cry. Healing, recovery—it's all different for everyone, and it's all valid.

Suzanne, age 23 ~

Survival is possible, but you've got to do the work and trudge through it. You're going to cry.

Stephanie Seibel, Counselor, age 25 ~

I think it's probably a real wounding in the men that's causing this problem. I think it's how the male culture is raised and our ideas of masculinity. We put a lot of pressure on the men—they have to be the provider and meet the image of the strong man and never be weak or sensitive. I think a lot of men cut themselves off from their empathy to deal with that pressure. It starts when they're kids: "No crying. Suck it up."

We wind up with this real shadow side of masculinity, and a lot of men feel inadequate and overcompensate with aggression.

It's tricky. I think society perpetuates it. Pornography perpetuates the image of man conquering woman as an object. It devalues women and sets standards that men feel they can't meet: "You're not man enough." I think a lot of men feel that way. It's hard to be a man today—all that pressure. They find unhealthy ways to deal with it.

Aggression is like a virus. It spreads. Everyone is acting out the pain that was inflicted on them. A boy has a feminine side, and he's told it's bad. Him doing that act—raping someone—is not going to heal the pain. It's only going to make it worse. And he has to live with what he did and the person he's become.

Professor David Lisak, Predators:
Uncomfortable Truths about Campus Rapists (2004) ~

Here is what we know about them: They come from all racial and ethnic groups; they are sophisticated sexual predators who plan their attacks exhaustively and with astonishing cunning... Their violence and predatory behavior mirrors precisely that of the sexual predators who have been incarcerated and studied, except that by targeting non-strangers and by refraining from gratuitous violence, they have escaped prosecution.[22]

Jack, Watcher, age 19 ~

We put a watch on the creepy partygoer. We communicate this to the other group members, and we say, "Watch the guy in a white t-shirt with a Led Zeppelin logo on it and jeans." You want to know who it is, and, in your mind, you add the person to a list you have and observe them longer than anyone else.

I have a poster on my dorm-room wall of the Green Arrow. It's one of the few TV shows that I actively follow. The most popular superhero is Batman and has been for two decades. Green Arrow is grittier. He fights crime and eventually gets a small team of people who work with him. Even if they don't get any credit, they see the effect, and that's all they really need.

In the middle of season three, the Green Arrow delivers a couple of bad guys he caught to a police officer he works with. The police detective yells after him, "Hey, I never told you thank you." And the Arrow says, "That's not why I do this." His point isn't to get any fame or admiration; it's more that he wants to do good in the world regardless of how much credit he gets.

We're trying to step in before a situation causes harm.

Lauren, age 22 ~

Bystander training is stepping up in a situation and saying, "Wait a second, this doesn't look good. I'm going to do something about it." Stepping Up has five aspects:
1) *Notice; be more aware of your surroundings.*
2) *Investigate and ask questions.*
3) *Take personal responsibility to help, and don't assume that someone else will.*
4) *Learn what to do and how to help.*
5) *Take action and be a leader; decide to make a positive difference in someone else's life. Be there for your friends.*[23]

Mark, age 21 ~

The bad guys are the ones who rape girls. They're predatory. They say, "Let's pump some vodka shots with these chicks so they'll hook up with us." A man-slut will hook up with anyone. They brag about it, and they're looking for admiration. These guys are in it for the game, the hunt, or the conquest. But there's no glory in that. Glory comes from real-life accomplishments.

I have good close friends who are girls. We hang out. We don't hook up. At a party, I tell them, "I won't let you within 20 feet of that guy."

Guys look out for girls by peer-pressuring creeps to not be creepy.

Then there are the polite scoundrels, the smitten Romeos. They're respectful. They hook up with girls. They honor boundaries. They really like girls.

A drunk guy in a corner is not going to attract girls. Guys, do something cool with your life, and girls will come talk to you. Be you. And don't show off. Showing off leads to trouble. If you're showing off, it means you're compensating for something—people would rather know you.

I've also had drunk girls throw themselves at me. I can't even push them off. I have to find a girlfriend of hers and say, "Help get her off of me," or else I could be charged with assault. Guys on this topic are scared. One girl saying, "I don't remember, I was too drunk," could ruin your life.

On this topic, there's a big gray zone. There's "I'm shy, and I drank a few beers to get up the courage to say yes to you." Girls do this. Guys do this.

Or there's "I'm really drunk, and because I'm really drunk I said yes, and that yes wasn't really a sober-like decision." Then that's 20 years in prison versus consensual sex. And that tiny difference can change someone's life.

It's important to develop life skills—practice talking to people in class so you're comfortable talking to people at a party, and don't drink too much because you're feeling uncomfortable. When you drink because you're uncomfortable, that falls into the category of drinking to solve other problems. Other problems are harder to solve and important to identify.

If there's a guy who is getting girls drunk, or using drugs to get a girl drugged up to have sex with her, he knows what he is doing, and that is very clearly rape.

But for the innocent guy who has no ill intent, who can't differentiate between "Yes, I also want this," and a girl who is just saying yes because she's drunk, that guy is not a rapist. He might be making a poor decision and should stop, and they should revisit the decision when they're both sober, but this is not realistic. If a girl is really drunk or a guy is really drunk, you don't do it. It's obvious. It's bad. The gray zone is gray.

What if she doesn't verbally say yes, but she was taking your clothes off and then you had sex? Was that technically sexual assault? By law it was.[24]

What if you didn't say yes? If neither person said yes, it's technically sexual assault on both parties, but it falls on the guy. Technically, every movie sex scene is sexual assault.

If you ask her out loud verbally, and she says yes, you can progress. I should write a book, How to Hook Up with Girls Safely for Guys, to Make Sure You Don't Go to Jail for the Rest of Your Life. Guys need to know this.

What if the guy is going with a girl, and she's going along physically, and she hasn't verbally said no, and the guy thinks she's saying yes. Six month later, the girl speaks up and says she didn't consent, and it was sexual assault.

If the girl says, "Yes, yeah, I'm not sure," not sure is not good. Hopefully the girl is clear. A girl giving a guy a condom is not consent. She has to verbally say yes. It's geared toward the girl's safety, and a guy does have to say yes too.

Why doesn't the girl ask, "Hey, do you want to do this?" or say, "Hey, I'm just getting to know you, I don't want to"?

If she says no early in the night, it's a no for the entire night.

When people are drunk, they're not thinking. You have to be super careful. You have to look out for your friends. You have to bring up the conversation, even though it's awkward: "Do you want to do this?" You can't say, "Hey, do you want to go to my room and hook up?" Hooking up is vague. You need to ask, "Do you want to have sex with me?" Every time you want to get creative, you need to get out a new consent form.

There are a whole lot of problems that come with drunk sex:

- *You don't remember, and then why is that fun?*
- *Whisky dick: You can't get it started, or you can't finish it.*
- *You decide certain places are okay, and they really aren't; they're too public—like the 50-yard line of the football field, or on the washing machine, or on the subwoofers, and you end up being called "Subwoofer" for a year. Everyone knows—the entire campus knows—and it's really awkward. It sucks for the guy and the girl. If it was something you did secretly and it gets out, the girl can be embarrassed, and she'll never speak to you again, and her friends will never speak to you.*

At parties, sometimes I go around and toss condoms on couples who are making out. I want them to snap to it. Sometimes they say, "Thanks, we'll need this later." Sometimes it's a way of saying, "Hey, this is where your night is heading, do you both want to do this?"

That's why we created the policy: No Drunk Sex. It's to protect the girls and the guys.

Talk about it, guys. Talk about it, girls. I'm all for guys being safe and girls being safe. I'm all about equality and making sure that everyone has the best opportunity to succeed as a human being.

Olivia, age 22 ~

The awkwardness of going to get yourself birth control is far better than unintentionally getting pregnant. Lots of girls carry condoms. They'd rather have it, than not. It's better not to assume.

Plan B is a morning after pill and can be taken within 72 hours after having unplanned sex. Plan B doesn't require a prescription or parental approval to buy it. It's best to use it within three days of having unprotected sex. It costs between 35 and 60 dollars and many pharmacies sell it. It does not end an existing pregnancy, but prevents sperm from impregnating an egg.

The day after pill, Plan B, should not be used as your first line of defense. First should be a male condom, a female condom, the pill and a condom, the NuvaRing and a condom, or an IUD and a condom if it is a new, unknown partner. Save the day after pill for unplanned sex.

Grace Miller, Sexual Health Educator, age 22 ~

Part of the reason why it is important to get that verbal consent is that people are afraid to talk during an interaction. They're afraid they'll wreck the mood if they stop to take a break or emotionally step back to reconsider.

This is true about birth control too. People think that by talking about it they're ruining the moment, if they stop to get a condom or talk about STIs. People glorify the mood. They see it as the ideal sexual interaction.

Forget the mood and the idea of there being a sexy mood that you're destroying. Sex can be so much more than that one narrative. It can be fun, or funny, and people can laugh, and you can define it how you want.

Know your right to say "No" at any point during a sexual interaction, and know that you have a right to be having a good time. You can't force someone to do something they don't want to do, and you have the right to make your wants known.

Your body is your own, even when you are in an intimate interaction with someone else. It doesn't mean you've given up the right to your own body. Even if you're naked in bed, you have the right to say "No" to absolutely anything.

There is a difference between being aggressive and being assertive. For a woman, being assertive is important in terms of what your wants and needs and boundaries are. For both men and women, being assertive about what you want sexually is fine. Being aggressive is where it crosses the line.

Women, in the traditional narrative, are not supposed to start anything. They're not supposed to make any moves. They aren't supposed to be sexually experienced, and, therefore, they aren't supposed to ask for anything in bed. This whole thing is messed up.

If you want to be the one who asks someone to be sexually intimate with you, that's fine. You aren't a slut or a skank for doing that—those are words used to punish women for being sexual beings. You have just as much right as anyone else to be sexually engaged or a sexual being.

On the flip side, a woman can be called a prude for not wanting to do things. Know that you have just as much of a right not wanting to be sexual or to do things.

I've been involved in sex education. Everyone will tell you that everyone's body is different. What feels amazing for one person may be uncomfortable for someone else or do nothing for them. Partially because sex is a taboo subject and there's very little comprehensive positive sex education, people don't learn what a positive sex interaction looks like. The best way to have the best time in bed is to communicate with your partner.

If you know that you will only be comfortable being in a sexual relationship with someone wearing a condom, you have the right to ask for that every single time. You don't have to compromise. They are a guest in your home, and you have a right to feel safe.

Even if you aren't having sex in a way that may get you pregnant, there's still the chance to spread STIs. STIs can be undetectable to the naked eye. You may not know if you have an STI, or your partner may not know if they have an STI, which is why its important to be checked regularly. Health centers at universities can generally do this. Planned Parenthood can do this. Use protection when being sexually intimate with someone. It's a myth that oral sex can't give you an STI.

Something to keep in mind is that no one is having as much sex as you think they are. The hook-up culture can seem overwhelming. This has been shown in study after study, that the hook-up culture isn't as pervasive as it often seems, and there isn't as much social pressure to act in certain ways as it might seem.

The second piece of advice I'd offer is to know your body and know yourself. It can be really hard, especially at first, to know what you want and what you feel safe and comfortable with, but something that really helps is taking time to be with yourself. That can mean, if you're comfortable, being intimate with yourself, physically exploring your own body, which is a great way of exploring what you would want from someone else, and it can be a good time for yourself as well.

It can also mean sitting down with yourself and thinking through what kind of interaction you personally feel ready for.

Dear Reader,

A few days ago, I drove to a local university to attend a workshop. I parked my car and followed hot-pink flyers with arrows drawn on them. They were taped to the sidewalk and were covered with the words "I Love Female Orgasm."

I tried to walk as if I were completely comfortable heading to a presentation on female orgasms, but internally I was having trouble breathing. When I couldn't find the next flyer with an arrow, I worried that I was lost. I usually ask for directions, but I didn't have the nerve to stop a student and say, "Can you tell me how to find the workshop on female orgasms?" A group of students were walking with purpose, and I decided to follow them.

We crossed a bridge and entered an engineering building. An engineering building? I could see holding a lecture on the female orgasm in a biology lab or even a poetry classroom, but engineering? The hot-pink signs reappeared with arrows that led us upstairs and down a long corridor. I could hear music blasting and people laughing—a bit too loudly. They were uncomfortable too. At the door, students waited in line to purchase the book, t-shirts, buttons, and posters that read, "I Love Female Orgasm."

When I entered the lecture hall, I saw an image of a Georgia O'Keeffe flower projected onto a large screen at the front of the room. The painting looked like a giant, colorful vagina. I took an open seat in the second row and hoped I would blend in with the crowd.

I thought of all the conferences, panels, and workshops I'd attended on sexual assault. I had never felt uncomfortable walking into those auditoriums. What a crazy world, that a subject as delightful as a female orgasm would make me want to hide, even turn around and head for my car. Clearly, I had discovered another silent topic: female pleasure.

I put on my glasses and wrote the date and time in my notebook. The lecture hall continued to fill with students. I looked around—it was packed, and I was the only one taking notes. The presenters stood at the front of the room. The two open seats left in the auditorium were on either side of me. As it turns out, college students don't want to sit next to a woman who looks like a mom during a talk on the female orgasm. Feeling defensive, I wondered, "How do they think they arrived on earth?"

Dorian Solot and Marshall Miller co-authored the book *I Love Female Orgasm*, and Marshall was one of the presenters. When he began talking, the rowdy room quieted. Marshall was trying to help those standing in the back find seats.

"There's some benefit to coming early," he said, and the students laughed.

Marshall asked people to raise a hand if they had an open seat next to them, and I broke out in a sweat. Fortunately, the students in the back assured him that they were happy to stand.

Marshall said their goal was to increase our knowledge of and comfort with our own bodies, and to help us discern what is healthy, responsible, and right for us and our partners. And then Kate Weinberg, the other presenter, showed a film clip from the movie "When Harry Met Sally." In the scene, Meg Ryan is sitting in a coffee shop and pretends to have an orgasm to prove that men don't know when women are faking it.

Miller and Solot ~ 44% of men say their female partners always have orgasms when they have sex. 22% of women say they always have orgasms when they have sex.

Kate explained that she used to do things sexually because she thought she should. She said she thought it was her job to make her boyfriend happy while she pretended things were good for her, when in reality they were "kind of blah." Eventually, she began figuring out what she liked and what she didn't like. She said, "I had to get curious about exploring what I liked and not be drunk every time we hooked up." She said she wanted to put a sign over her bed that said, "Orgasm: I would like one of those too."

"Why?" Kate asked the crowd, and then answered her own question: "Because orgasms feel good."

Kate said, "It's a myth that a person you just met can do this. All bodies are completely different, and it's essential to communicate to promote the process of orgasm." She then shared a few facts: 70% of women need stimulation of the clitoris to have an orgasm. The average length of time it takes a woman to have an orgasm is 20 minutes of direct stimulation of the clitoris (ranging between 15 seconds and 30 minutes). The average length of time it takes a man to have an orgasm is two to five minutes. Marshall added, "The guys in porn movies who keep at it for a long time—that's not accurate."

On the large screen, they projected an image of the female reproductive organs. Kate said that a lot of female anatomy classes cover the female sex organs—the uterus, the ovaries, the fallopian tubes—but leave out the clitoris. It's part of the external genitalia, the vulva. It's a small bump, also known as the "eye of the storm." It's right above the urethra, where your pee comes out. It's important to learn where the clitoris is—the thing that will result in an orgasm when stimulated. 30% of women can reach an orgasm from penetration alone, but 70% of women, in order to have an orgasm, need to have stimulation of the clitoris.

During the talk, I learned that the clitoris has more nerve endings than any other organ in the entire body, male or female. And to experience physical pleasure with another person often requires a profound sense of vulnerability on the woman's part. She reveals herself as worthy of time, attention, affection, and communication.

As I listened to the presenters, I thought, "This is where our work is. Maybe not for all, but certainly for many girls and women—to be able to say physically what we like, what we don't like, what we want, what we never want, and what we'd like to try sometime, but not now. Our needs matter, our wants matter, and our words matter."

Hannah Gribetz, Sexual Assault Peer Educator, age 22 ~ Get to know what you're comfortable with, and get to know what you like. And learn how to say "No" to things that don't fall in those categories.

Toward the end of the presentation, Kate offered encouragement: "Learn, explore, be curious. If you're with a partner, learn to ask questions. 'Is this okay with you?' Talk to the person. It's okay to pursue joy. It's okay to desire to slow down and take time and attention. It's okay to know, 'I'm worth this.' You are worthy of time and experiencing pleasure. You can be the receiver. You can be center stage. You can let it all be about you."

As I walked back to my car, I thought about my personal beliefs. I believe that intimate love is one of the best experiences on earth. This includes being vulnerable, being playful, taking turns, communicating, and setting boundaries. It may start with holding hands, or kissing, or taking a long walk and talking.

Humans long for connection and to be loved. To experience another person's uniqueness requires conversation, care, and the development of trust. To be experienced as unique requires conversation, care, and the development of trust.

Is the interaction one-sided? Is there mutual respect? Are both people being kind? Are both respecting boundaries? How can we balance giving pleasure and receiving pleasure, loving another and allowing ourselves to be loved?

Know that you are worthy of love.

Olivia, age 22 ~

Obviously it's flawed, but there are some things about hooking up that I enjoyed. I'm glad I got to focus on making good girlfriends, and I'm also glad I got to experiment with guys and see what I liked and what I didn't.

It's fine as long as you're clear about what you want and don't want—by that I mean clear to yourself beforehand—and then clear with them when it's happening. I'd go out, and I'd think, "Yeah, it would be fun to meet up with this person. I know I don't want to have sex with him, but I'm okay going back to his room." I know what I'm okay with, and I know that before I start drinking.

I'm very clear with them. I say, "I'm happy to go back to your room, but I'm not having sex or whatever." Or in the moment, they ask, "Should I get a condom?" and you say, "I don't want to do that," or whatever feels comfortable to you. As long as you're clear about what you want beforehand, and as long as you're clear with them, then I think it can be a great time for you to discover what you want and what you don't want—because there are a lot of different types of people out there, and you're not going to know if you don't experience it.

But you want to do it in a way that is safe and in a way that feels right for you, and that might not be the way that your friends are doing it. I had a lot of friends who would go out and sleep with a different guy every weekend, and I knew that wasn't what I wanted. And as long as I knew that and I was clear with myself and the people I was with, it was fine. Keep in mind, what you want and what you're comfortable with might be different from what your friends want and what they're comfortable with. And that's okay.

As soon as a guy isn't treating you the way you want to be treated, get out of there. It's college—it's the best time to be meeting people. There are tons of guys. Don't waste your time on someone who isn't treating you well, because you'll be able to find someone else who will.

Charlotte, age 22 ~

There's so much pressure now for everyone to be "chill" about sex and dating and the hook-up culture. And yet there's still a very strong double standard. If a girl genuinely wants to sleep around, she gets labeled as a slut. If she wants to be in a relationship, she's seen as clinging, or over-emotional, or needy.

People say, "Oh, all things are equal now." It's not true. I don't want to fall into the category of saying all women would rather have closed relationships with emotionally attached sex— that's not true. But if women want traditionally feminine things, it's still valued less than if they want traditionally masculine things. Romantically attached sex is still seen as a feminine ideal, and it is valued less. No-strings-attached sex is viewed as more masculine.

If a man wants to become emotionally involved, he's seen as sweet: "Oh, wow, he's so sweet." If a girl is doing the same things, she's seen as a stalker or as creepy.

There's a lot of talk about hook-up culture equalizing sex. I don't think it did. A lot about the hook-up culture feels like there's a double standard. We're given all these handouts and flyers saying, "Consent is sexy," but the administration and the culture don't hold to what they're paying lip service to.

This is a generalization about heterosexuals, but even at my very progressive liberal arts college, a guy is seen positively if he is sexually active or if he is sexually attached. A girl who is sexually active is seen as a slut, and a girl who is sexually attached is seen as clingy and "not a chill girl."

There's a lot of pressure to be laid back, to not have strong feelings, and to conform to the stereotypes of what men want out of love and sex. Girls stuff their emotions to get male affection. You listen to people tell you how free you are and how liberated you are, and then at the same time you have to have sex freely, not care, drink a lot, and be really chill. Can you imagine a culture where boys are liking Pride and Prejudice and white-wine spritzers?

I had a deep desire for intimacy, and it was minimized. I was told to be chill and that I wasn't liberated if I withheld sex. As a culture, we've gone so far toward making intimacy taboo that's it's not healthy for anyone.

Garcia, et al., (2010) ~ 63% of college-aged men and 83% of college-aged women would prefer a traditional romantic relationship as opposed to an uncommitted sexual relationship.[25]

Jonathan, age 22 ~

I wish things could be more like when my grandmother and grandfather were dating. The old dynamic of how relationships worked was so different from what it is now. I was ticked off about it, and I talked to my grandmother. She was describing to me her dating situation when she was 16. She would go on three dates a week, and she wouldn't necessarily become girlfriend-and-boyfriend with any of the people, but she got to interact with all these people. The dating situation was a million times different, which would be kind of cool.

As a high school kid, I was always intimidated to ask girls on dates. Nobody had girlfriends. The percentage was tiny. Compare that to back in the old days, when everyone had boyfriends and girlfriends all the time, and it was a casual thing to ask a girl on a date. It seems to me that it's changed so much since then. I don't know why. It's obviously super different. I think to myself, it would be easier for someone like me if things were more like they were back in the day; it would be easier for me, for fringe people, to get through and be reasonably successful.

There were several cases with girls in high school where I totally should have asked them for a date, and I never really did it, and I know my buddies should have done the same thing, and they never did it either.

Tally, age 22 ~

I think that a lot, lot, lot more people, both guys and girls, would like more dating and more daytime activities. I've seen some people do that really successfully. From my perspective, it's more the sporty, outdoors people—the people who would rather go surfing on a Saturday, or go hiking on a Saturday, or go climbing on a Saturday—it's a lot easier for those types of people to say, "Hey, we would both rather go on this cool hike than go to this party and get really drunk on Friday. Let's not do that, and let's plan to go on a hike on Saturday." It's easier to have connections develop over a shared activity in the daytime—when you're on a hike with someone, or doing an activity that you both like—than while drinking.

I've been encouraging my friends who are very jaded with the bar scene—they're like, "Its sucks," or "We never meet good guys." The guys I hang out with say, "The good guys aren't at the bars. They want to go surfing on Saturday. They're skiing on the weekend. They're doing much more interesting things. They're not at the bar." These guys think it's funny that girls want to find great guys at bars.

One girlfriend of mine just bought a mountain bike, and she's been doing a lot of biking. I told her, "That's awesome. You're going to meet much more interesting guys doing that." The first few weeks that she had her mountain bike, she had several guys say to her, "Oh, wow, you mountain bike? We should go sometime." They probably thought she was cute, but they also probably thought, "Wow, it's a girl who shares something I like to do, that's awesome." She definitely did not get the mountain bike because she wanted to meet guys. She got the bike because she wanted to do something on the weekends other than go to bars. By doing that, I'm sure she will meet guys who also want to be doing something other than going to bars. I think pursuing your own interests and finding people who are also interested in those things is a really great way to find quality people.

Dear Reader,

Most students I spoke with want something other than getting drunk and hooking up with someone they don't know.

Lauren, age 22 ~ You can think, "Oh, I'm fine. I haven't had that much to drink—I'm making this decision to hook up with this person consciously." But you also need to assess how drunk the guy is. The next day, they don't remember, and your feelings are hurt.

What I'm hearing is that there's a huge desire for something different—something combining friendship and intimacy. Part of the solution is being willing to go through the awkwardness of asking someone to spend time with you, and learning how to talk about easy topics first.

When I was researching this book, I read about a philosophy professor named Kerry Cronin. For extra credit, she gives her students an assignment—to ask a legitimate romantic interest on a date. Her class has become quite popular. I watched a video of Professor Cronin giving her students this assignment. After she explained the homework, uncomfortable laughter filled the lecture hall. And then she smiled and said, "I know this is why you're all in my class."

Professor Cronin's Guidelines:

- You ask the person in person, no texting.
- The person asking has to know what they want to do, and they have to pay.
- You go somewhere within the next three days, to reduce anxiety about the event.

- The date has to last for at least 45 minutes and occur during daylight. No group dating or third wheels allowed.
- No kissing, touching, alcohol, or checking cell phones during the interaction. An A-frame hug at the end is allowed.
- Afterward, write a two-page reflection on how it went: What it felt like to ask someone out, how you planned the date, and how the conversation went.[26]

I've been interviewing girls and guys, and everyone wants to try dating. A lot of it comes down to saying, "I'm going to be brave and ask."

Donnovan Somera Yisrael,
Sexual and Emotional Health Educator ~

This is an opportunity to practice courage. Go up to someone and say, "Hi." You have to be willing to experience discomfort. We're afraid of feeling awkward. We do everything to avoid feeling awkward. Movies are made about one awkward scene after the next. No one likes feeling awkward, and yet you have to risk awkward in anything you're going to do.

God forbid that you have something awesome happen in your life and there's no one you can celebrate with. Or, if something awful happens, you want someone who will cry with you. Companionship is essential, and to get it requires risk and feeling awkward. The next great love of your life could be around the corner. Smile. Work on learning how to flirt. Get your face out of your phone, and make eye contact with people.

College

My Sophomore Year

Alyssa, age 23 ~

*I call it "friend searching." Freshman year, you're trying out dif-
ferent friend groups. You're looking for the group where you feel
genuinely happy. This is a big struggle for girls in all stages of
life. You find that you're with a group of girls and you don't feel
at ease—maybe it's the things they talk about, or the things they
don't do or don't say. Maybe it's your intuition. And then you
have to deal with your fear of leaving that friend. What are they
going to say about me if I do leave? I'll have to start from scratch.
Where am I going to go?*

*I've done this before, and it all works out, and you're going
to be so much better for it. You're going to be in a better place. It
might not happen overnight, but you'll get there, and it's worth it.*

*You want to find that group that will make you happy and
appreciate things. I get goose bumps because I found the greatest
group of friends. It's great when you do and it just clicks.*

Dear Reader,

During my freshman year, I realized that I wanted new friends and sunshine. My solution was to transfer schools and start fresh as a sophomore.

Hannah Gribetz, Sexual Assault Peer Educator, age 22 ~ One reason I stopped being sad after freshman year is that I stopped hanging out with a certain group of friends I didn't actually like. I didn't realize at first that I didn't like them, because they were "my friends." When I stopped being friends with them, my life got a lot better.

Physical distance was the grace I needed to establish a new way of being in the world. I put everything that had happened when I was 15 to 18 in a sealed vault in my mind, and I resolved that I would make my life in California better.

Donnovan Somera Yisrael, Sexual and Emotional Health Educator ~ All of a sudden you're new to the scene, and it's scary and awkward. It's important to be willing to meet new people and see new things. Be cognizant of how much time you are texting. A lot of people take out a cell phone and hide behind it. Put in an effort and get to know people.

Emma, age 22 ~ A lot of my transfer friends stayed within the transfer-class circle, and they felt like they never fully integrated. I saw that happening, and I didn't want that to happen to me, so I did everything. I went to the club fair, and I put my name on every list. You go to the first meeting, and if you don't like it, you don't ever have to go back. I even went to a knitting club, if you can believe it, and I made one of the best friends of my life there. We found out that we both didn't want to go out at night, and we'd stay in and hang out, watch TV, and bake. She's from London, and she taught me how to make English muffins. I learned that all those nights I had forced myself to go out, if I'd just gone to the knitting club I'd have been so much happier.

Laura, age 22 ～ When you're making new friends, you have to be brave.

At each meal, I made myself sit with different people in the dining hall. I'd introduce myself and start conversations. I volunteered as a Girl Scout leader and sold cookies out of my dorm room, which turned out to be a great way to meet new people. I also joined a sorority.

Liz, age 23 ～ After I got into my sorority, I had a very good friend who was older and really grounded. I was able to let down my guard with her, and she helped me learn how to say to myself, "Whatever, I don't have to do that perfectly."

Abigail, age 22 ～ Being part of a group makes everything a lot safer for a girl. A sorority might be too big. They don't have the same accountability structure. A pledge class could work. My team has my back.

Mary, age 23 ～ It's exactly the people who support you in that moment when you decide to leave a party early who will be friends with you for the rest of your life. That's what college is about—finding those kind of friends.

When I did go to parties, I went with a group of friends, and I'd hold a cup to avoid being pressured to drink.

Lindsey, age 24 ~ There were so many things we did as girls to look out for each other.

- *We'd go to the bathroom together.*

- *We kept track of our drinks and made sure no one put anything in them.*

- *I always told my friends if I was leaving the main vicinity of a party, where I was going, and they'd check on me.*

- *We had a code we'd use when you wanted to stop dancing with someone. You'd look at your girlfriends, and they'd pull you away from that person.*

- *I stayed on guard at Greek events. In those circumstances, I was careful, never going past lightly tipsy. This meant I had a few drinks max the whole night, two or three at the most. For some other girls, it meant they had less.*

- *We only left a party when we knew where everyone was.*

I don't know if this is very common, but I never let myself feel out of control with alcohol unless I was in a really safe place with people I felt safe with. That tended to be at an apartment with 15 close friends, and we weren't leaving.

I prioritized school, which had great consequences for me. I did an Honors Thesis senior year. But it also had trade-offs. There were important college-life things I may have missed because I was stressing about some school thing.

As a transfer student, I focused on my schoolwork and enjoyed the sunshine, reading 19th-century novels, and writing poetry.

Dear Reader,

Dan's college dorm room was across a grassy courtyard from mine. He and I had been in the same graduating class at The Prep School. After I was accepted as a transfer student, I reached out to Dan and asked him about classes.

When I arrived on campus, Dan checked in on me. It was nice to see a familiar face. A few nights a week, he would stop by my room after he'd finished studying at the library.

Sometimes, during the afternoon, Dan and I would take walks together. California oaks surrounded the campus lake, and we would talk under the trees. I liked hearing about his engineering projects and telling him about the books I was reading.

Tally, age 22 ~ The best way to get to know someone is in the daylight.

Cora, age 24 ~ It affects your next relationship for sure. Learning how to feel safe with the next person is really a beautiful journey, especially if we can be conscious in choosing our next partner and find someone we feel safe with. What I went through taught me how to recognize a good man. There are bad men and good men, and I have a new appreciation for good men. Even though it was so painful, it taught me how to connect and love because I developed empathy. I brought more depth to love, which winds up being more beautiful in the long run. There's a quote that I love by Kahlil Gibran. It goes like this: "The deeper sorrow carves into your being, the more joy you can contain."

Dan was kind to me. He was also really cute and had a smile that lit up my day. During winter term of my sophomore year, Dan and I started dating.

Catherine, age 22 ~ I knew something was different right away because we could spend hours hanging out and laughing, and I was truly just enjoying being there with him. He makes me laugh. He helps me through all sorts of insecurities and problems and makes me a better person in the process. He knows me so well and supports me when I need it. Even in the bad times, when we're having arguments and we're crying or upset, it's a brief argument, and then it very quickly transitions to both of us trying to understand what the other person is feeling and working it out together.

At first, boys are kind of stupid. At the beginning of the relationship, I would tell him, "I would really have appreciated it if you had done this," and he would say similar things to me, and then we'd both work at it.

I enjoy life more with him. I can say without question that I am a better person than I would have been if I had never met him. We fit together really well. I'm really lucky.

Dan and I went dancing in San Francisco. We drove to the mountains and skied. At an outdoor concert, Dan put me on his shoulders so I could see the band, and I knew what it felt like to have my spirit lifted.

Helen Keller, The Story of My Life *~ I also enjoy canoeing, and I suppose you will smile when I say that I especially like it on moonlight nights. I cannot, it is true, see the moon climb up the sky behind the pines and steal softly across the heavens, making* a shining path for us to follow; but I know she is there, and as I lie back among the pillows and put my hand in the water, I fancy that I feel the shimmer of her garments as she passes. Sometimes a daring little fish slips between my fingers, and often a pond-lily presses shyly against my hand. Frequently, as we emerge from the shelter of a cove or inlet, I am suddenly conscious of the spaciousness of the air about me. A luminous warmth seems to enfold me. Whether it comes from the trees which have been heated by the sun, or from the water, I can never discover. I have had the same strange sensation even in the heart of the city. I have felt it on cold, stormy days and at night. It is like the kiss of warm lips on my face.

Catherine, age 22 ~ In college, I experienced so many things, what they truly can be, for the first time, like being in love and having really good friends. I saw breathtaking landscapes. I learned to do things that were physically and mentally challenging and saw where they could take me. I had this realization that going to college for me was like seeing things in color for the first time. Now I understand fully that life can be amazing. It can be wonderful in all kinds of ways. I am so lucky to have ended up where I am. I can't imagine it any other way.

The Underworld

My Daughter Is a
High School Sophomore;
I Get PTSD, and the
Eight Years that Follow

Kayleen Asbo, Cultural Historian ~

In Greek mythology, Persephone is the daughter of Zeus and Demeter. She is a beautiful, young maiden who is raped and dragged off to the underworld by Hades where she gains knowledge of darkness and death and learns more about beauty.

Helen Keller, Optimism ~

I can say with conviction that the struggle which evil necessitates is one of the greatest blessings. It makes us strong, patient, helpful men and women. It lets us into the soul of things, and teaches us that although the world is full of suffering, it is full also of the overcoming of it.

Dear Reader,

Dan drove me to the second psychiatrist's office. I was in tears. I felt terrified of crossing the Golden Gate Bridge from our home in Marin to San Francisco. I was imagining driving into a wall to end my suffering. I had been awake in the night, agitated with night sweats and heart palpitations. I felt as if hundreds of knives were stabbing my stomach, and my nausea was severe. And since I had begun taking the prescription medication, the few hours I did sleep were filled with vivid nightmares and seeing myself in car crashes.

The first psychiatrist I'd seen had a waiting room full of African masks adorned with mammal teeth protruding from their nostrils. He prescribed a highly addictive anti-anxiety medication, which left me feeling as if I were submersed in a Plexiglas fish tank watching the world go by. I thought he was creepy, and I decided to find another doctor.

Emma, age 22 ~ Part of me learning to know myself was learning to recognize when I needed help and then going to get it. Getting therapy can be stigmatized, but it's become less so—which is good. It depends on where you're from and where your family comes from. My friends would come talk to me about relationship problems, and I'd suggest they go talk to someone. "It's no big deal," they'd say. And I'd say, "It doesn't have to be a big deal to get help with it. You don't have to be alone in it. The thing about little deals is that they become big deals if you don't deal with them. You might think you're fine, but don't bottle it up until you're not fine."

The second psychiatrist had an office across the street from a hospital in San Francisco. He had a copy of one of Vincent Van Gogh's self-portraits on his wall. Van Gogh eventually lost his mind, cut off his own ear, and killed himself. The portrait did not offer me hope. The psychiatrist sat 15 feet away from me, crossed his legs, clasped his hands, looked over his glasses, and occasionally jotted down a few notes. I felt like an animal at the zoo being studied from afar.

The Van Gogh doctor determined that I was clinically depressed and in need of medication. Finding an antidepressant that works can be like searching for a needle in a haystack. I knew this, and, after the anti-anxiety prescription, I was reluctant to try any drug. I told the doctor that I was sensitive to medicine and that, if there were side effects to be had, I usually got them.

The Van Gogh psychiatrist told me that with therapy and medication I would get better, but that I would not get better without medication.

I had taken his prescription once a day for three weeks. Since starting the medication, I felt as if I had fallen into a cavernous pit without handholds to climb out. I was descending when I arrived in the Van Gogh doctor's office with Dan at my side.

"If you want your spouse to join you for an appointment, you need to get my permission and schedule it ahead of time," the Van Gogh doctor said, and he showed Dan the waiting room.

During our meeting, I cried and tried to explain to the doctor that I wanted to crash my car to end my life, and that Dan had come home from work to drive me to my appointment. I said that I felt as if I were trying to hold onto the edge of a cliff with my fingernails and that I was slipping. I told him I was significantly worse, and I didn't think I should stay on the medication.

The doctor took a few notes, looked over his glasses, and said, "You want to get better, you take the medicine."

I questioned his opinion, and he told me how many decades he'd been a psychiatrist. He said that I should be hospitalized and that he would arrange it. He took out his phone.

I was stunned. A psychiatrist was proposing that I spend time in a mental institution. Did he think I was crazy? Was I? I was curled up in my chair, shaking and crying.

I had just turned 42. I was married, and the mother of three children. We'd recently moved to Northern California. Within a few months, I had developed severe stomach pain and lost thirty pounds. I was able to eat only crackers and canned peaches. I had heart palpitations and migraines, and I couldn't sleep. After months of testing—an EKG, blood work, an outpatient stomach-lining test, an ultrasound of my uterus and heart—cancer was ruled out, and the doctors determined that I was suffering from extreme anxiety. I'd never had anxiety before. I wanted to crawl out of my skin and out of my mind. My brain was like a screaming woman who wouldn't stop.

The Van Gogh doctor started to punch in numbers on his phone. If I wouldn't take the pills, he'd have me locked up.

Denise, age 25 ~ After about five weeks at this psych clinic, it's lock down: no shoelaces, as demeaning as possible. That's when I started the process of sobering up and learning who I am and who I want to be.

I sat in silence and thought about my children's ages: 15, 13, and 10. I was trying to see the impact that my death would have on them. I was close enough to the edge that I was searching for a reason to step back, and fortunately I found one. I understood that if I killed myself it would hurt my children, and I didn't want to cause them pain. I decided that, as profoundly as I was suffering, I would do everything I could to live through this time for them.

"I don't want to be hospitalized," I said.

What the Van Gogh doctor didn't know was that my husband and children were keeping me alive. Every step I was making in the pursuit of getting better was for them. I was living for their smiles, their hugs, and the details of their days.

I told the Van Gogh doctor that putting me in a hospital away from my family and forcing me to stay on the medication might kill me. Then I left his office and stopped taking the medication.*

The following year, a book was published revealing that the drug company responsible for manufacturing the anti-depressant that the doctor had prescribed for me had altered its trial findings, which had originally showed that the medication increased suicidal thoughts in some patients. In the light of those findings it was determined that, if suicidal thinking occurred, the use of the medicine should be discontinued immediately.[27]

---

* If you are currently taking any medicine, please consult with your doctor before making any changes.

Dear Reader,

This is how I found my way into Ruth's office. I was broken, shaking, still nauseated, weighing less than a hundred pounds, not sleeping, with severe stomach pain, but alive. Someone had told me that with anti-depressants it can take a few months to feel better, but without them it can take two years or longer. I decided that it was my fate to have to climb a higher mountain, and if I could stay alive during the process and be alive at the end, then it was the only way.

Helen Keller, The Story of My Life ~ *Have you ever been at sea in a dense fog, when it seemed as if a tangible white darkness shut you in, and the great ship, tense and anxious, groped her way toward the shore with plummet and sounding-line, and you waited with beating heart for something to happen? I was like that ship before my education began, only I was without compass or sounding-line, and had no way of knowing how near the harbour I was. "Light! Give me light!" was the wordless cry of my soul, and the light of love shone on me in that very hour.*

Ruth was a therapist. In her waiting room was a picture of a winter landscape: leafless trees in a snowy meadow. I thought it was too somber for those of us sitting there agitated and vulnerable, but later I came to appreciate the winter scene as a symbol. That time in a therapist's office can be a season in one's life, not one's entire life—a place to pause and feel the bareness of branches in the cold wind, while the seeds and bulbs beneath the earth rest and prepare for new growth. It can be a time to take stock, to revisit, and to untangle.

I learned that the way in which one processes events as a child or teenager is not always accurate or complete. Children often blame themselves for actions that were not their fault. Carefully, memory by memory, Ruth and I walked through my past.

Denise, age 25 ~ I had a lot of shame, a lot of guilt.

In our sessions, we unearthed the unimaginable. It involved hockey players, teachers, classmates, and a dead friend. It was a slow, week-by-week process. I asked a friend who was a therapist how long I needed to keep seeing Ruth, and he said, "Until you're no longer anxious."

Denise, age 25 ~ When I was in the middle of it, it was just get through the next 10 minutes. Just get through the next hour. It was very slow, very patient. When you're in the middle of it, it's just survival skills—putting one foot in front of the other with care. It's being patient and reminding yourself this is not a punishment, there is true purpose to this. And that's what helped me more than anything.

Dear Reader,

Ruth and I met once a week, on Wednesdays at noon, for four years. Together, we took apart what had happened to me and came to see why I had lost my mind.

During my last appointment with Ruth, we reviewed our time together. I told her that I understood that I suffered from PTSD. I had learned that when someone has experienced severe trauma, old memories and emotions can surface when their own child reaches the age of the original event. I read about one Vietnam veteran who collapsed with PTSD when his 18-year-old son registered for the draft. The bell tolled for me when my own daughter was a sophomore in high school, the same age I had been when the seniors came into our dorm room. I had been fine for years, and then I wasn't.

Helen Keller, The Story of My Life ~ *As my knowledge of things grew, and I learned more and more words, my field of inquiry broadened, and I would return again and again to the same subject, eager for further information. Sometimes a new word revived an image that some earlier experience had engraved on my brain.*

When I began to see a fuller picture of what happened, my heart broke, and that took longer to heal than my mind.

Although my anxiety wasn't gone, the severity had lessoned, and I was ready to stop seeing Ruth. I knew, for the most part, how to identify a PTSD episode—to breathe, pray, and get help. I told Ruth that the most important thing I had learned during our time together was that I wasn't crazy, not even close. What had happened at The Prep School was. My true north was trusting myself.

Gwyn, age 22 ~ I chose myself over the universal need for validation—which is so hard.

A kind, compassionate listener can witness insanity, cruelty, manipulation, and evil. Sharing these experiences with another human does not change the truth of them, but having a witness and being heard changed me.

Helen Keller, The Story of My Life ~ For, after all, every one who wishes to gain true knowledge must climb the Hill Difficulty alone, and since there is no royal road to the summit, I must zigzag it in my own way. I slip back many times, I fall, I stand still, I run against the edge of hidden obstacles, I lose my temper and find it again and keep it better, I trudge on, I gain a little, I feel encouraged, I get more eager and climb higher and begin to see the widening horizon. Every struggle is a victory. One more effort and I reach the luminous cloud, the blue depths of the sky, the uplands of my desire. I am not always alone, however, in these struggles.

Dear Reader,

My youngest son and I use the same printer in our home. When I finish writing a letter to you, I print a copy to read later. A few days ago, my son printed out an essay and grabbed some of my letters to you by accident.

"What happened, Mom?" he asked.

When I had lost my mind, he was in fourth grade. When I finally accepted that I was suffering from anxiety, I had felt private about it, even ashamed.

Around the same time, a woman I'd recently met was diagnosed with breast cancer. People brought her meals, formed prayer circles, and sent her cards. I longed for support, but I felt deeply embarrassed that my disease was in my mind. I wanted desperately to be able to talk myself out of it, to get a grip, to pull myself together. But no amount of resolve or tough love could get my heart rate to calm down, the knives in my stomach to stop slicing my gut, or my brain to stop circling in fear and worry.

I went for a hike with a group of women. My family and I had recently moved to the area, and these were new friends. The woman who had breast cancer was there. She had lost her hair and wore a bandana to cover her head. She led us up the hill, and I admired her strength and courage. I was weak from the weight I had lost. I was anemic and had to take breaks. I trailed behind the group. A woman who was a nurse stopped and waited for me. I didn't know how to tell them that I was suffering from anxiety and didn't know why. Instead, I was quiet.

I'm not sure why I'm remembering this now. Perhaps because my son asked me what happened, and I felt sorry that I hadn't been able to tell him at the time that I was sick. Instead I hid it from my kids the best I could. I have since developed compassion for myself and what I went through, and this has made all the difference.

Slowly, I began to tell my son what happened when I was in high school and how I had lost my mind when his sister turned 15. I told him how kind his dad had been to me during the years it took to get better. I told him that for a while the only thing that had kept me going was wanting to stay alive for him, his brother, and his sister. My eyes were full of tears, and so were his.

And then he thanked me. He thanked me for fighting to get better. "I'm glad you did," he said.

"So am I," I said.

Helen Keller, The Story of My Life ~ *You cannot touch the clouds, you know; but you feel the rain and know how glad the flowers and the thirsty earth are to have it after a hot day. You cannot touch love either; but you feel the sweetness that it pours into everything.*

Reader,

Today is my birthday. My letters to you are my way of bridging the gap between my past and your future. What I want most is for you to experience the sweetness of love—offering it and receiving it.

Part of getting to experience love is being discerning about people and taking time to evaluate how they treat others.

Catherine, age 22 ~ Not everybody is completely trustworthy, and it's better to be safe than sorry.

If I can open your eyes and show you the violence and manipulation that some people are capable of, then perhaps you will be more savvy as you go out into the world.

Laura, age 22 ~ I think it would have helped if I had taken more time to really understand that not everybody has the best intentions. When I meet somebody, I tend to want to trust them immediately and make friends. I really like meeting new people. But you need to understand in the back of your mind and remember that you don't really know what their intentions are or if they're a good person. You can't just blindly trust, even if they were screened by admissions people.

I also want you to know in the depth of your being that you are worth protecting—with words and with actions.

Stephanie Cyr, Lawyer and Self-Defense Instructor ~ Words are effective. Use your voice. "I'm worth defending. My body is my property. I am the most valuable thing I possess." There are levels of sexual assault. Any form of unwanted touch is an assault. If someone touches you and it's unwanted touch, you say, "Stop," and you create a boundary with your hands. If they cross that line again—if they violate—look them in the eye and say, "Stop!" If they still touch you, all bets are off. Do whatever you can to remove them. No wishy-washy "You're making me uncomfortable." You do not plead with someone who is violating you. You put your shoulders back. You put up your boundaries. You draw from your chi, your gut, your core. That's where your power comes from. That STOP is not in your head. It comes from deep down. You have to work at it to find it and practice finding it. Practice at home. Practice in the mirror. If someone is too much in your face, "Stop." Even if it's a friend, you say, "Don't ever touch me again." You're clear. You're strong. You want to get in the habit of standing up and speaking up for yourself. "I'm worth defending. My body is my property. I am the most valuable thing I possess."

Understand these words. Take them in. It is my birthday wish for you.

Tally, age 22~

At first I used this line in a bad situation, and then later I realized how well it had worked. When you just need to leave, say, "Oh my gosh, my friend is way too drunk. I'm really worried about her. I have to go check on her now." Then bail! Keep saying it as you head out the door. "I'm so sorry about so and so. She's way too drunk. I have to go check on her." In reality, you're thinking to yourself, "I'm in a bad situation, and I have to go now." The reason it works is that you are no longer fun, you're worried—and it doesn't hurt their confidence as much because it makes it seem as if it's not about them.

Professor Renee McDonald,
Co-creator Virtual-Reality Training for Girls ~

Virtual environments train people how to react under stress—pilots, fire fighters, policemen, soldiers. They put people in these conditions, and the people learn to respond in the conditions under stress so that their response becomes automatic.

In our training session with the girls, a facilitator models how to use a firm voice, show confident body language, and state limits. And then the girls practice in a virtual reality with a male actor as a male avatar.

The set-up was that the girl was in a car with a stranger she'd just met, an acquaintance, a guy at a party. They chit-chatted, he was nice, it started raining, and he offered her a ride home. He pulls over in the rain and starts coming on to her.

In many instances, when the guy said, "Can I kiss you?" the girl would say, "No, thank you."

No, thank you? No, thank you? When we talked to the girls afterward, they were unaware that what they were communicating was "Thank you for offering to kiss me, but no." Even when they felt concerned that this was a person they didn't know very well, they were so trained to be polite that they said, "No, thank you."

They also never viewed a request for a kiss as the first step. They thought the sexual stuff was later, when the men asked them to take their shirts off. They thought, "A kiss is just a kiss; it's not sexual." That was fascinating.

Afterward, we asked the girls, "Wher *going with this?" And they got it. But ir* *happened, they did not interpret the des* *is trying to get me to do things I don't* *thinking, "He wants to kiss me, and th* *began asking for more that they thought, "This is w.. _* *what I'm comfortable with."*

If *ther* ... (partial text obscured)

What we taught the girls is that when they say yes to a kiss that is unwanted, they are saying yes to the possibility that more could happen in the guy's mind. If they don't want that possibility in his mind, they need to say "No" there. And they need to say it clearly—not "No, thank you."

We taught them to say, "No, I don't want that." "No, I don't want to do that." "No, I'm not interested." "No, this is uncomfortable." "No, I don't want to have sex with you, so stop asking me." Clearly saying "No."

If they're not comfortable only saying "No," they can also say what they do want. For example, "No, I don't want to do that. I want you to take me home." Something that is very clear, not a squeaky, mousy kind of response. They don't have to yell it. We want to them to be very clear. Very assertive. "No, don't ask me again."

In our scenario, they are with an acquaintance, someone they've just met. As he pressures them more, they are not going to want to do anything with this person. Where it becomes complicated or tricky is when they are with someone who they do know and perhaps do like a bit, and they don't want to cut off the possibility for something in the future. Then they can say, "No, I don't know you well enough for that yet," or "No, I'm not ready for that yet," or "No, we're not there yet," or "No, you're moving too quickly." The first word always needs to be "No."

*you do want the kiss, and you don't want to go any far-
then you need to recognize that allowing the kiss opens the
possibility at least in the other party's mind that "Okay, maybe
there's more," and you need to make it clear where the boundary
is and let the person know that you're going to stop there.*

*A lot of times they're afraid of being disapproved of or afraid
that the guy won't like them anymore. One thing we talked with
the girls about is, if he doesn't accept your "No"—that you're not
ready—is he really showing you respect? And if he's not showing
you respect, is this really someone you want to be involved with?
If he's ignoring you, he obviously doesn't care about how you
feel. Why would you want to continue with someone like that?* [28]

Marybeth Bond, Author and World Traveler ~

*My mother and father taught me always to be a nice girl.
Someone asks you a question, you look them in the eye and you
answer them. You're polite to people. You're not rude. It was a
shock to realize that the whole world doesn't treat you properly. I
realized I had to learn how to stand up for myself. I had to learn
how to be just as tough as they were, even though it was against
my upbringing.*

*Men would impose upon my space, my time, my smiles. I
learned that I couldn't just smile at anyone. I couldn't just look
anyone in the eyes because, unlike in my own culture, it was an
invitation in other cultures. And so I had to do away with all
that upbringing and learn to be tough. No more nice girl. You
don't owe them anything.*

*It's part of the safety thing. It's being aware of what's around
you and what's going on. You're walking down the street. You're
alone on a sidewalk. It's a tiny sidewalk because it's Europe, and*

three young guys are coming toward you. Somebody's going to have to get off the sidewalk. You're going to be very close to them. They're coming toward you—so cross the street. Go out in the street. Don't get so close that someone can grab you. It's the same at a bus station or on a bus. Can you stand next to a family? Can you sit next to a woman? Rather than putting yourself in a questionable environment, try to avoid the situation before you get into it.

Even here at home, you get on an elevator where you park your car downtown, and a really creepy guy gets on, and it's just the two of you—Get out, if you can, before the door closes. "Oh, I forgot something in my car!" and get out. But if you can't get out, humanize yourself. What you do is make yourself not an object but a person. Look him in the eye. Rapists know that once they've been identified, you could pick them out of a line-up. Look him in the eye and talk to him. "Oh my gosh, isn't it beautiful weather today." Or "My friend is waiting for me." Or "I'm in such a hurry. I'm late." Something that makes you a person, not an object.

And the other thing is that, when you're scared, you tend to pull in and get small. NO! Chin up. Shoulders back. Don't-F-with-me attitude. You want to walk down the street that way. And you want to have that attitude toward someone you feel a little threatened by. Don't F with me. Stand up straight and make yourself a real person.

The biggest thing is No Nice Girl. Someone sits down at your table. Why did they do that? They're invading your space. You're working on your computer or just enjoying yourself, and somebody imposed upon you. Get up and move before it becomes a problem. If someone is inappropriate, yell and scream at him—maybe you'll stop him from doing it to the next nice girl.

As soon as someone is invading your space or your sense of propriety—they're talking dirty to you, they're following you, they're being suggestive—say to yourself, "Why do I have to put up with this? I don't have to be a nice girl. He's not being nice to me." First of all think, "That person is not respecting me. Now I don't have to be nice back." In fact, you want to be Not A Nice Girl. Not only in body language, but in your speech: "Leave me alone!" You don't owe anyone anything.

Gabby, age 22 ~

I grew up in Manhattan, and we had mugging training every year. Don't trust everyone, and make sure you know what to do in case of a mugging—scream, and throw your bag away from you because they'll go after your bag, and then run. If they have a gun, it's okay to say, "I'll give you my stuff, but will you please put the gun down because it's scaring me." The most important thing is to give them your stuff. Your life is way more important than your wallet.

Also, know the city you're in. Learn the subways and the buses in case your phone dies and you need to get back to campus on your own.

I know what to do instinctively. I keep my eye on whoever is making me nervous, and I go into a building with a doorman or a hotel. Or you can call someone and talk to them on the phone. People debate this strategy: Some say that being on your phone can make you look distracted and more vulnerable; others say that when you're on your phone, you show that you are in contact with someone and can easily report a problem. Read the room. You have to look at the situation and decide what you can do that will most likely make the person go away.

It might be making a phone call or pretending to be on your phone. It might not.

Jessica Chapman-Segal,
Reproductive Health Educator, age 25 ~

Everyone calls me Sassy Mama. I'm really clear with what I want and don't want. If some guy is hitting on me or making me feel uncomfortable and it's not wanted, I don't have any issue saying, "F— off." That was a skill that took me a long time to harness. We're taught at a young age to be kind and respectful to everyone.

When I was 18, I was backpacking in Europe with a friend for six weeks, and I learned really quickly that if I smiled or was trying to be polite or trying to be nice, that would invite advances I didn't want. There were occasions when we got chased down a street or got inappropriately touched.

Unfortunately, we don't live in a world where it's safe for you to be a woman. There are certain advances in the Western world, but if you have boobs and a vagina, it's a different game. If some person, woman or man, approaches you and you don't want to talk to them—whatever it is—if you're not interested in a sexual way, women should feel empowered not to be sweet and to say "No." When the line is crossed, you need to be assertive and clear and say, "That's not cool. Leave me alone. Go away."

I've pulled a lot of my friends away from guys, and I've been called a bitch often, but I don't care. I'm saving my friends from what might be a huge problem. It used to upset me when I got called names. As I've gotten older, I've realized I've probably done my friends a lot of big favors.

Madison, age 21 ~

Let me just say, I think it's really important for girls, when they go out and they get drunk, to always have a friend with them. Always. My friends were drunk, and they left me. I ended up having to take a train home all by myself.

It was about 3 am. We'd gone out at about 11, me and my friends. We were drinking. I was with my best friend. All of my friends were pretty drunk. I was pretty drunk. We were heading home, and I ended up having a problem with my train pass. Everyone ended up going up to the train platform without me. When I finally swiped my train pass, everyone had already gotten on the train, and the train had left. I ended up standing on the platform alone.

They didn't see me having a problem. Sometimes the train pass is quirky, and I went over and talked to transit authority person to try to get myself through. I ended up getting on the next train.

There was a really creepy guy on the train. He was just staring at me. The train was empty except for me and him. When I went to a different train car, he followed me. I just sat there until my stop, right next to my dorm. I saw him come out of the train car when I got off, and so I started walking really fast.

Then he pulled me into an alley, and he tried to rape me. But he did not. I fought back.

One thing I want to say to girls is that you need to fight back. If I hadn't fought back, he would have raped me. He punched me in the face. He tried to choke me so that I couldn't breathe. I have to tell you, I was literally five hundred feet from my dorm.

I told him, "There are security cameras everywhere. People are going to see this."

The struggle was him trying to get me to be still because I was fighting. There was one point where I thought I was going to die because I couldn't breathe. I was scratching him, and kicking my feet, and doing whatever I could do. I don't remember the exact thing I did that got him to stop choking my neck, but I do remember that I was scratching him. I went for his face. That obviously really bothered him because he was trying to put my hands down. Always go for the face.

And I was screaming, "STOP! HELP! STOP! HELP!"

I was a freshman in college. I had just gotten back to school. It was literally my first day back. It was March.

He was on top of me on the ground. I was using my feet. I was kicking. I was using anything I had. I was trying to move my whole body so that he could not pin me down.

My mom put me in a self-defense course before I went to college. I didn't want to go, and I was upset with my mom for making me go. My friend and I went together. It was a one-day class. We got to beat up people. It was actually really fun. We learned how to attack people if they came for us. I learned how to go for the face and poke people in the eyes. It was really helpful. I think every girl should have some training in self-defense, because one in four girls is sexually assaulted.

People think this will never happen to them. I thought that it would never happen to me, and it did.

The ironic thing is that two cops were sitting outside my dorm. They were literally 20 feet away, and they couldn't see me because I was in the alley.

After I'd gotten away, I walked across the street to the cop car. I got in the cop car and started hysterically crying to the cops. I was severely beaten up. I had a black eye. I had scratches all around my neck.

But the police were not that sensitive to the whole thing. I was really drunk, and I kept saying, "This guy tried to rape me in the alley." They didn't really care. They said, "File a police report," and that was it.

I feel lucky because I did get away. I was beaten up, but I wasn't raped. I think you have to go into it with the mindset of "This is not happening." It's really important to not give up. That was the mindset I was in. I thought, "I'm not about to get raped right now. It's not going to happen to me." I literally fought with everything that I had to fight with. You can't give up fighting.

I was screaming—no words, just screaming. Then I got out my phone and tried to call 911. He saw me trying to call 911, and I think he decided to steal my phone, and he got off of me, took my phone out of my hands, and ran out of the alley. He stole it. I think he thought, "This is going to be too hard to do, so I'm going to steal her phone and call it a night."

Eventually, they're going to be like, "This is too much." I'm happy there wasn't a rock nearby and that he didn't hit me in the head with a rock. I'm happy I was conscious the whole time.

I honestly think you have to go into it thinking, "I'm going to get out of this." Obviously I was thinking, "I'm about to get raped right now," but I was also thinking, "This is not going to happen."

I really did fight. You can't give up. It's so important to keep fighting with all you have. It sounds so simple, but it's imperative to have that will to fight back.

Mary, age 23 ~

I was in Greek life. The sexual assault statistics are high there. I tell women to drink less. I take drinks out of their hands. I don't like anything that could happen to you when you're that drunk. I don't like that you could stumble in front of a car. I don't like that you could spike your blood alcohol content so much that you die. I don't like that you could be unconscious and someone could rape you. These women struggle with that for a long time.

My intention is to acknowledge the dangers I believe exist and to equip you the best I can to avoid them. The alcohol situation on college campuses is exorbitant. It feels like we are intentionally drinking in excess to lose control, and that makes it hard to stay safe. This is happening every weekend at big college parties.

Why do we define freedom in college as a loss of control? Do we not know where the line is? Is it because you don't know that you'll black out on four drinks because you've never had four drinks and you don't know your own limit? Is it because you think everyone else is doing it? Or is it really just because you feel insecure, and you're trying to find a way to feel comfortable and fit in? This is dangerous. This could ruin your life. Are you really weighing the costs and benefits of drinking to excess?

In an ideal world, you should be able to drink to excess and be safe, but that's not real. That's an illusion that you want to believe and your parents want to believe. That's not real. The 5% of guys committing these crimes on campus are predators, and they are preying on young women who are drunk and alone. That's the unfortunate reality of the situation.[29]

Lela, age 22 ~

The biggest piece of advice that I have to offer you is to make sure your protect yourself. That's #1. You cannot undo something that's happened.

Protect yourself and surround yourself by friends you trust, because they are going to be the ones who pull you out of a frat basement when they realize that's not where you want to be in the morning.

Some of my advice is controversial. I agree with trying to create new policies, but I still go back to not putting yourself in a dangerous situation—especially when there's alcohol involved. Alcohol and the hook-up culture are worse the younger you are.

The reality is that you can't stop all sexual assaults from happening. Most policies are about dealing with how to handle the situation after the fact, which means basically that you can never undo what happened, even if it's the best policy.

At the end of the day, you are your only true supporter— we only really have ourselves. You owe it to yourself to protect yourself, and that goes for both genders.

I can tell you what I think is okay, but you will probably learn only through your own mistakes and watching a friend's mistakes, or maybe, by chance, if you happen to listen and think my advice is worthy.

Tally, age 22 ~

If you have a friend who is blacked out, do not leave their side. People think it's funny, but it's actually really scary.

Madison, age 21 ~

Never go out alone. Ideally you should have two other people with you, especially if you're a girl. It's so dangerous, even for two girls alone. I can tell you for a fact that the assault happened to me because I was alone.

When you're out on your own and getting drunk, it's fun when you're a freshman and there's that freeing feeling of, "Oh my gosh, I'm into college, I can do whatever I want. I'm away from my parents." But you have to act in a way that will make you happy with yourself the next day. Don't go crazy. You have your whole life to drink. You don't have to go to great lengths to get F—d up every night just because you can. It's important to live with a personal code that you're comfortable with. You really have to take care of yourself and hold yourself as most important.

Mary, age 23 ~

What if three girls didn't give consent to the same guy? Can we create a social stigma against that guy? We need to go to other guys in his frat and say, "Your brother in your frat rapes unconscious women." The other 95% of campus men need to band together against that 5%.

Every girl who has talked to me about an experience like that thought it wasn't going to happen to her. There is no mold for the type of person who ends up in this situation. It's happening to everyone. Maybe 5% of those girls told their parents. Most of them are not telling their parents. Half of that is because their parents said, "You're not that type of girl," or "That's not going to happen to my daughter," or "You're smarter than that."

What does that mean?

That's victim-blaming of its own kind. My school is full of the smartest kids you can find. That doesn't mean girls aren't getting raped. You'd never say, "My daughter is too smart to get mugged."

You tell your 17-year-old daughter that she's too smart to get raped, and you're equipping her in exactly the wrong way.

She's very confident in thinking, "I can have one more drink, I'm smart, I won't end up in a bad situation." Instead you need to have the conversation, "How do you stay in control and surround yourself with good people? You've never had this kind of independence before. You've never been in a situation where you could make a decision that could destroy you."

I also understand that college is a time when you can test boundaries and when you have the ability to try a whole bunch of things that may have been off limits to you when you were in high school and under your parents' roof. I'm not saying, "Don't have any fun." Learn where your boundaries are. But do it in such a way that you can wake up the next morning and look at yourself in the mirror and like the person you see—however that manifests itself for you.

For me, I don't get my pleasure feeling out of control of myself or my life. Any decision I'm making, I want to be comfortable making it at any time of day, around any group of people.

The number one discussion I've had in college is about the definition of rape. If something happens that you're not okay with, talk to someone. I have a lot of conversations where I hear, "I don't know if it was rape. I was really drunk. He wasn't mean to me. He was cute."

I ask, "Can you remember consenting?" And so often the answer is "No."

You can't give consent if you're drunk.

Be with very supportive friends. Control what you're drinking. Don't be alone. The more of an audience you have around you, the less chance you have of being taken advantage of. It's just as much about healing as it is about protecting each other.

Grace Kaimila-Kanjo,
Girls' Empowerment Educator, Africa ~

During personal safety sessions, I talk to the girls and ask, "What situations put you at high risk? What kinds of activities make you very vulnerable?" I talk about these rowdy parties they go to. The girls call them shindigs. I tell them, "The shindig that you do is what puts you at the greatest risk for personal harm, sexual harassment, or gang rape, because you are there stoned or drunk, and you don't really know what is going on. You may not even remember the following day that you were raped. You are there catching diseases or getting pregnant and putting yourself in such a huge problem."

I ask them to think about how to focus on good habit and not bad habits, what you should avoid growing up, and peer pressure. A lot of these things are the result of peer pressure. We talk a lot about the importance of having good role models. Seek out peers who are very well-behaved, who are doing something with their lives. Look for the ones who are getting good grades or who are getting very good opportunities. You can use those ones as role models and also as peer educators. The peer educators become leaders among their peers.

We have sessions on building self-confidence to help them resist peer pressure. It is this whole issue of self-worth. A lot of them get caught in peer pressure because they want to be accepted, they want to be seen as cool. My message is to tell them, "You are worthy the way you are. You are an important person. You are valuable. You don't need anybody else to validate you."

Self-acceptance, self-validation are very important in resisting peer pressure. If you want to be seen as the cool girl in school, it is usually because there is something lacking in you.

Self-acceptance is lacking. You want other people to validate you, rather than you validating yourself and knowing that "Whatever I am, whatever I do, I am worthy, and I am responsible for my own choices and my own actions whether somebody likes what I do or not."

I focus on girls working together, and also individual girls, teaching them how to carry themselves, how they can be confident, how they can surmount their problems. Of course, I keep telling them, "You are a collective." The battle is not launched on an individual girl. It's launched on all girls. All girls are vulnerable, and you can do something about your situation only if you are working together. Teamwork among girls is very important. Working together is very important, but we also really need to raise the bar of every individual girl so that on their own they know, "I am worthy. I know I can persevere. I know I can become whatever I want to become, and I know I am as good as anybody else."

Dear Reader,

When I was still seeing my therapist, I was looking for pieces that might help me put myself back together. Anything—letters, diaries, drawings. I was trying to remember who I was before I lost my mind, before we moved to Northern California. In one old box, I found a shoebox filled with letters that Mr. Jessup had written to me when I attended The Prep School. I reread his letters and was stunned. I didn't recognize the man that his own words and handwriting were revealing him to be.

I took Mr. Jessup's letters to my next appointment with Ruth and read some of them out loud. I felt nauseated and confused. I had to keep taking breaks. I had loved Mr. Jessup dearly for years. This was the teacher who had stood on his desk and recited Shakespeare; the mentor who had taken me for walks in the woods and taught me about trees and flowers; the advisor who had made me milkshakes in his kitchen and visited me in my dorm room when I was sick.

When I was a teenager, I had been delighted to receive Mr. Jessup's letters. I had treasured them. But now, as an adult, I read them again. I went into my mind, took out events, and looked at them. This time I was the mother of a teenage girl, and I saw a truth that was impossible to fathom.

Helen Keller, The World I Live In *~ My fingers cannot, of course, get the impression of a large whole at a glance; but I feel the parts, and my mind puts them together. I move around my house, touching object after object in order, before I can form an idea of the entire house.*

The letters were addressed to "My Sweetheart," "My Dearest," and "My Dearest Sweetheart." They were filled with excessive praise, flirtatious comments, and a longing to be reunited with me. They were love letters written from a married man to a high school girl. It was painful to see my own naiveté and the depth of his betrayal, deception, and sickness.

He had meant so much to me. To Ruth I kept saying the word "but." "But he taught me to love words… But he brought me hot apple cider when I was sick… But he admired the flowers that came through the snow in early spring."

Ruth held out her arms like a giant cross. "For you to get better, you are going to have to stretch," she said. "You will need to embrace the word 'and.' The same man writes creepy letters to his student *and* admires the flowers that come through the snow in early spring."

It was a challenge for me to accept both aspects of Mr. Jessup as true. In my mind, I worked to replace the word "but" with the word "and" when I thought about Mr. Jessup. I discovered that as I expanded my understanding of who he was, my confusion diminished, my self-doubt lessened, and my sanity returned.

One man can love Shakespeare and be a sexual predator. A-n-d. For the first time since Mr. Jessup had pressed his hips against mine in the alcove beside the dining hall, I saw the situation differently. I understood that I hadn't caused him to kiss me. If this had happened to my daughter, I would never, ever have blamed her.

Dear Reader,

That summer I started reading about sexual predators, and I saw that Mr. Jessup's behavior matched textbook descriptions of grooming a young girl: making her feel special with compliments and gifts, isolating her, touching her, excusing himself, blaming her, and making it a secret.

And then I read that sexual predators' behavior is usually serial—that a predator often has many victims, and I froze.

Often... often... often.

Did Mr. Jessup have other students whom he "loved" the way he "loved" me? Were they "special" to him as well? Did he hug them for a long time, rubbing his hands up and down their back the way he did with me? Did he praise their insights and beauty in exchange for kisses and other sexual favors? Did he confess that he couldn't help himself when he crossed the line?

In my research, I saw that Mr. Lyon also fit the textbook description of a sexual predator. He had told me that he was waiting until I was 18 to kiss me, and he spent months prior to my birthday wooing me with love letters and wine.

I learned that sexual predators "are extremely adept at identifying 'likely' victims and testing prospective boundaries."[30] Was I a "likely" victim? Had my loss of self-confidence—stemming from the night at the pool, the General Probation, the kiss from Mr. Jessup, and having my body rated for its sex appeal when I walked back and forth to the dining hall—rendered me wounded and vulnerable? Mr. Lyon had tested me with compliments, pushed alcohol on me, and ignored my "no."

I read that sexual predators "plan and premeditate their attacks, using sophisticated strategies to groom their victims for attack and to isolate them physically"[31] How many times had Mr. Lyon invited me to his apartment alone? Begged me to go to a hotel with him alone? Driven me off-campus and taken me into the back of his station wagon alone?

I read that sexual predators often "coerce their victims into submission" and "use psychological weapons—power, control, manipulation and threats."[32] I can still hear Mr. Lyon telling me how much I was hurting him by refusing to make love to him, and how angry he was when I said I wouldn't, and then how calm he was when he suggested other sexual things I could do that would feel good for him; he said they would make up for the pain I was causing him.

I read that sexual predators "use alcohol deliberately to render victims more vulnerable to attack."[33] There was always wine or beer out on Mr. Lyon's kitchen table, and he'd pour me a drink when I sat down on the couch to help him grade papers—even when I said I didn't want any.

Craig, (1990) ~ Men with higher levels of sexual aggression have reported coercing a victim by giving her alcohol or drugs, directing a victim into a place or situation where she is more vulnerable, and verbally misleading a victim.[34]

Dear Reader,

That fall I started to wonder if there were other female students who had shoeboxes full of "love letters" from teachers at The Prep School. Mr. Lyon used a green felt-tip pen when he wrote to me. Did other students have letters written in green ink as well, telling them they were special and beautiful? Were these "gods of the school" serial child molesters?

Potentially there were decades' worth of students who had attended The Prep School, who had been taught to believe, like me, that they were special, and who had entered into secret, sexual exchanges with these teachers.

Professor Luci Herman, Resident Fellow and Student Advisor ~ The assailant often repeats offenses and continues to oppress and glean energy. Getting away with it can be exhilarating for them.

Were there other students who had suffered from feelings of self-blame, shame, and despair? Were there other mothers who looked at their daughters and thought, "If someone did this to you, it would never, ever be okay"?

Then a new fear possessed me. I felt terrified for current students attending The Prep School. Taking apart my brain was no longer an exercise that involved uncovering what had happened 30 years ago, acknowledging it, bearing it, and hopefully making peace with the past and moving forward. There were moral and ethical issues that involved current high school students.

I went on the internet and searched The Prep School's website. Although Mr. Jessup had retired, the school continued to parade him around at fundraising events in New York City and Boston and posted photographs of him on their website and in their alumni magazine. He was still one of their gods.

Then I searched the list of current faculty. Even though decades had passed, Mr. Lyon and Mr. Wickham, the teacher who had seduced Claire, were still teaching there.

Professor David Lisak ~ Sexual violence remains as much a dirty secret on our campuses as it is in the larger society. It flourishes because, to confront it, an institution must be willing to shine a bright light on aspects of itself that are both ugly and painful.[35]

Dear Reader,

On December 10th, I sat down, wrote one letter, and sent it to seven people at The Prep School: the Headmaster, the Assistant Headmaster, and several teachers, including the three I named as abusers. I informed the Headmaster and the others that two teachers had emotionally and sexually abused me and that a classmate of mine had been emotionally and sexually abused by a third teacher. I named names and gave details. I informed them that my friend had killed herself and that I felt it was important for the school to be notified in order to ensure the safety of their current students.

Within a week, I received a letter back from the Headmaster assuring me that he took my "allegations" seriously and that he would get back in touch with me immediately.

When I wrote my initial letter, I had no idea what would follow.

Helen Keller ~ People don't like to think, if one thinks, one must reach conclusions. Conclusions are not always pleasant.

Dear Reader,

Four months after I had notified the Headmaster that he had sexual predators teaching at his school, he called me and told me that his lawyers wanted to interview me. His voice was cold and formal—he had lawyered up.

This meant I also needed lawyers and supporting documents. I had a better network in Arizona and retained two attorneys there. Prior to my meeting with the school's lawyers, I spent three months going through diary entries, class assignments, notes, letters, and photographs, marking relevant information with post-its. I had boxes of saved material from my time at The Prep School.

In July, I met with four lawyers. Two represented me, and two had been hired by the school. We had agreed to meet at my attorney's office.

It makes my heart race to recall the meeting. I flew to Phoenix and carried a suitcase on the plane with all of my documents. I felt as if my life depended on them.

I wasn't suing the school. I wasn't asking for money. I was asking for something different: I wanted the school to do the right thing. I wanted The Prep School to set the safety of its students as its highest priority and take every step possible to ensure it.

David Wolowitz, Lawyer and Consultant on Student Safety ~ In my line of work, I talk to many victims, and every time it breaks my heart to see the damage done. Kids at boarding schools are vulnerable, and we have a special responsibility to them.

I arrived early at my attorney's office in downtown Phoenix. Before The Prep School lawyers arrived, I arranged my documents in chronological order. The conference table was covered with rows of papers, notebooks, envelopes, and photographs. I reviewed the words I'd written on post-it notes. During the questioning, I wanted to be able to refer to supporting material easily.

When The Prep School lawyers entered the room and saw the documents covering the conference room table, they froze. It took them several minutes to regain their composure.

A friend of mine later said, "Guys don't count on girls keeping diaries."

We introduced ourselves and shook hands.

Helen Keller, The Story of My Life ~ *The touch of some hands is impertinence. I have met people so empty of joy, that when I clasped their frosty fingertips, it seemed as if I were shaking hands with a northeast storm.*

On the wall, there was a painting of the Grand Canyon. I have since come to see it as a symbol of the divide between why I was there and why the school's lawyers were there. I believed that the teachers were a threat to current students, and the school's lawyers, Poulet and Duey, treated me as if I were a threat to the school.

After we made our introductions, Poulet took out an essay I'd written several years earlier and held it toward my face. He suggested that perhaps I was bitter about what had happened my sophomore year and made up a story about esteemed teachers violating students as a way to get back at the school.

I had written the essay for an event commemorating The Prep School's 25th anniversary of being coed. It had been shared with many students and alumnae. In the essay, I had mentioned the pool night and focused on the unjust punishment of a few girls, myself included, that had followed.

I also had a copy of the essay with me. I showed it to Poulet and Duey. I told them it was that essay that had prompted several women to confide in me that they had been raped in the shower that night. I explained that the pool incident was widely discussed on campus and that no teachers or administrators had offered help to any of the girls involved. I told them that this indifference reflected the culture of the school—certain male students and male faculty were protected and revered and were not held responsible for their illegal actions.

I carefully went through a number of letters written to me when I was in high school and the summer after I graduated from friends who referred to my involvement with Mr. Lyon. I read some of the teachers' letters out loud. I shared photographs of Mr. Lyon that were taken off-campus during the spring of my senior year. And I read from my diaries descriptions of sexual interactions between Mr. Lyon and myself.

When Poulet asked for explicit sexual details about what had occurred between Mr. Lyon and me, his tone was accusatory. I was grateful that one of my lawyers was a woman. Her presence helped me as I answered question after question.

During Poulet's interrogation, I had to take a break. I went to the bathroom, and Sandra, my lawyer, followed me. When I started crying, Sandra reached into her purse and gave me a tissue. I tried to regain my composure, but I was shaking and nauseated. Sandra opened her purse again and pulled out an origami crane made from red paper. She said that her teenage daughter had made it and that it symbolized a hope for peace. She gave it to me. I held the red crane in my hand. Sandra reminded me of why I was there. She said that it was hard work but important work. I splashed my face with cold water. I took deep breaths, and then we walked back to the conference room together.

During Poulet's questioning, I stopped many times to be certain that Duey had time to write down verbatim the words I was reading out loud from my diaries and letters. He took pages of notes. The Prep School lawyers had scheduled a golf game for the afternoon. I think they had thought that they could fly from the East coast to Phoenix, discredit me, and then play golf. Poulet and Duey had to interrupt the meeting to cancel their golf game.

The session lasted almost four hours. When we concluded, I was exhausted, but I believed that The Prep School would be a safer place for its students.

To my horror, when The Prep School began again in the fall, both teachers whom I had named were still teaching full-time.

Helen Keller, Light in My Darkness ~ *Science may have found a cure for most evils; but it has found no remedy for the worst of them all—the apathy of human beings.*

Gwyn, age 22 ~

I was in an abusive relationship, and I was deciding if I would report it. I was emotionally raw. I asked a counselor if I should report it, and she said, "No, it will stress you out."

I went to Safety & Security to report to them that my boyfriend had threatened to commit suicide when I told him that I was ending the relationship. The female officer asked if I was okay. I told her that I needed to report other stuff as well.

"Well, don't report anything illegal," she said. "If you do, we'll have to follow up on it."

She told me to go home and think about it and then talk to an Equity Officer or a counselor. I'd already talked to a counselor. I went on a mission trying to get the administration's attention. I went to the Equity Office, and she gave me the "Go home and think about it before you ruin someone's life" talk.

I saw that the administration didn't have my back, but what hurt the most was that my friends didn't have my back. I had to accept and know that I needed to trust my own sense of right and wrong rather than what other people were telling me.

People didn't feel comfortable saying that anyone was wrong. They'd tell me I was holding to a rigid moral code. I felt conflicted. I'd ask myself, "Am I standing my ground too much? Do I harp too much on these impossible morals that I've set up?"

I had to come to the point where I knew I loved my friends and valued their opinion, and, at the same time, I recognized that I didn't agree with their morals on this point. I got so that I wasn't needing peer validation. Knowing I was right was enough.

Be able to trust your own moral compass. Listen to that voice in your head that very clearly knows you're in the right, even when the rest of the world says you're crazy.

Dear Reader,

I felt sick knowing that the school was allowing sexual predators to continue teaching. My lawyers contacted Poulet weekly, who always said that his investigation would be ending soon. Eight months after our meeting in Phoenix, Poulet sent an email asking me to take a lie-detector test.

One week after I had sent my initial letter, Mr. Wickham sent me a letter threatening me with revenge. During the investigation, I received emails and phone calls from alums pressuring me to stop attacking esteemed teachers.

My lawyers and I continued to ask the school to do the right thing. In response, The Prep School's administration told us that they were updating their policy regarding teacher conduct and had hired an expert to train faculty on healthy teacher-student relations.

Professor David Lisak ~ Prevention efforts geared toward persuading men not to commit sexual assault are very unlikely to be effective. Lessons can be drawn from many decades of experience in sex-offender treatment, which have demonstrated that it is extremely difficult to change the behavior of a serial predator.[36]

Jacob, age 23 ~ Part of me thinks these schools do what's required from a PR standpoint, so they can say, "Oh, we provided this education. Oh, we did this and this and this. Maybe they really do care about the issues, but a lot of it is that they need to be able to save their own asses in case things go wrong and they get questioned.

We sent Poulet emails, tabulating the number of days

that had passed since the school was informed that they had sexual predators teaching students. 43 days. 123 days. 227 days. 493 days.

A year and a half after I had sent my initial letter, I checked the school website and saw that Mr. Lyon was no longer listed as a faculty member. A few weeks later, in a phone conversation with the Head of the Board of Trustees, I was told that Mr. Lyon had "retired."

When I asked if she was going to notify alums to see if he had sexually abused other students, she said no. I also told her that I was deeply concerned about Mr. Wickham being allowed to continue teaching students. I reminded her that he had sent me a letter threatening revenge.

The Head of the Board of Trustees told me she didn't have sufficient evidence against Mr. Wickham to terminate his employment because Claire wasn't alive to testify.

Wasn't that evidence enough?

She said she'd brought in experts and had updated the school's policies and procedures. She assured me that the school was a better place.

Helen Keller, Optimism ~ *It is a mistake always to contemplate the good and ignore the evil, because by making people neglectful it lets in disaster.*

Two and a half years after I had sent my initial correspondence, I received a form letter from the school announcing Mr. Wickham's upcoming retirement and asking me to submit memories of him for a scrapbook they were making in his honor.

"Profoundly Disturbing" Abuse Documented at Elite [Prep] School

Bella English, *The Boston Globe*, September 1, 2016

After a months-long investigation of sexual abuse...a report released Thursday described the elite...prep school in the 1970s and '80s as a cauldron of sexual exploitation of students.

Sixty-one alumni gave investigators first-hand accounts of the abuse they say they suffered, with 51 saying the abusers were faculty or staff and an additional 10 reporting abuse by classmates. Two staff members abused at least one student every year they worked at [the school].[37]

Zoe, age 22 ~

It was a big moment for me when I said, "Okay, I can't let others dictate my happiness. It has to come from within." I read a quote once that said, "Keep how you feel about yourself and your feelings in two different places, because when you get your feelings hurt, it shouldn't affect how you feel about yourself." I think that's so huge. So many times, when our feelings are hurt, we take it as a reflection of ourselves, but really it's not. It shouldn't change how we feel about ourselves. Yeah, our feelings got hurt, but it doesn't have to change how we view ourselves. The thing I'm working on right now is trying to find happiness from within and to know that I'm the only one who can define myself.

Dear Reader,

Because I had information that could make The Prep School a safer place for its students, I felt I had to say something. I held on to the belief that if a mother across the country knew something that would help keep my child safe, she would tell it, and, if she had to, she would repeat what she knew again and again until it was heard—as if my child were her child.

I want you to know I care about your safety with every cell in my body. You are worth protecting. Even though I may not know you, I care about you. I care about protecting your sense of self worth, your dignity, and your right to a safe and equal education. I care about your well-being, your health, your happiness, and your future.

My request of you is this: Know that you are worthy of respect—even if people you know betray you, even if the institution you attend fails you. You matter, and you are worthy of being treated with respect from the beginning of time to the end of time, all day and every day, morning to night, night to morning, in small ways and big ways, within your family and with strangers. You are worthy of being treated with respect by your friends, your classmates, and your lovers. You matter.

Denise, age 25 ~ If you've got friends in your life who tear you down, cut them loose.

Grace Kaimila-Kanjo,
Girls' Empowerment Educator, Africa ~

Six things that I want girls to know:

Number One: You are as valuable as anybody else. I think that is key.

Number Two: You can be anything that you want to be as long as you put your mind to it. If… if… if… you apply yourself, you persevere, you work at it, you can become whatever you want to be.

Number Three: You should be confident. I want girls to know that the world is your oyster. You should voice whatever your concerns are and not fear anyone. A lot of the time girls are taught and they internalize the belief that they are not supposed to speak out, that they should be silent. I tell you, "You have a right to speak. You have a right to air your opinion. You have a right to participate. So speak out! Get out there. Be part of the flow. Whatever is happening, you can join in and participate on an equal level with anyone." Initiative is very important.

Number Four: Perseverance. You need to persevere because these problems that are affecting girls, they have been entrenched over time in the psyche of the community. And so you should not expect that the community will relent in a very short time. You should push and persevere in order for you to achieve your goals. You should not run away at the first encounter of resistance.

Number Five: You need to be brave. If you've been taught all your life that you're not strong enough and that you can't do something, trying to dispel that myth requires you to be brave. You are going to encounter a lot of opposition, and for you to surmount that opposition you have to be brave and think out of the box and do things that are out of the ordinary.

Number Six: Be knowledgeable. Seek knowledge. Know what opportunities are out there and what activities are going on. If you are going to participate, if you are going to take the initiative, if you are going to reach your goals, you have to be aware of what is going on around you. You have to know critical key events and have tools that will help you get there. Seek knowledge and be knowledgeable about the things you will need that will get you to where you want to be.

Dear Reader,

Yesterday, I took the ferry from Marin to San Francisco. I watched sailboats on the bay as we made our way toward the city. From the ferry building, I walked up Clay Street to an Italian restaurant called Palio d'Asti. A backroom had been reserved for people honoring three young women who had come from Africa to talk about their work. They had been trained by Grace Kaimila-Kanjo and were inspiring radical change in their countries.

The back room was full of people, mostly women. My friend Paola was there, and she was telling me about a workshop she had attended over the weekend with the young women from different countries in Africa. She said one of them had been her partner. Paola looked around the room and saw her workshop partner, Harriet Kamashanyu, leaning against the wall, watching all of us.

"Harriet, join us," Paola called.

We were introduced, and then Harriet started talking. "This past weekend, I attended a workshop in San Francisco with theater people who showed me how to find my voice and connect with my own story."

The room was loud. I leaned in to hear her. Harriet had a lyrical voice, with a hint of an English accent that accompanied the song in how she spoke.

"I live in Uganda. I am 25 years old. I work in the red-light district in Kampala, teaching girls how to be safe, have dreams, think of their own lives—how not to follow their mothers into prostitution. At the workshop, I learned that it is important for me to tell my story and what it means to me. My story is my source of strength." Harriet used her hand to

167

emphasize her point: She made a fist and pressed it against her chest. "I lost a friend, my best friend." Sadness swept over Harriet's face, and then it was gone. Her expression became fierce and determined. "I never, ever want to lose another girl again."

The woman organizing the event was calling us to come into a circle to hear the young women from Africa speak, but I was speechless. I had taken a ferry from Marin to San Francisco. I had walked 10 blocks to an Italian restaurant. I'd had to lean in to hear Harriet's words over the noise in the room. Harriet was a young black woman from Uganda; I am a white woman, twice her age, from Arizona. But we share the same wound. I lost my best friend, and I never, ever want to lose another girl again.

The program began. When Harriet spoke, she talked about her friend whom she had lost. She said her friend had tried to care for her sick mother, who was also a sex worker, and that her friend's mother had died. Harriet said that she speaks to daughters of sex workers and encourages them to look out for their own dreams.

She said, "Society nurtured me to be the next sex worker after my mom. We have to nurture a new generation that has principles and stands for what is right and what they believe in. An educated girl can realize her potential. This is a global problem that needs a global solution." She said she tells the girls, "Follow your own dreams, make a new life, and contribute to your community positively."

After the presentation, I spoke with Harriet. She said many girls she speaks with are looking for a Sugar Daddy who will give them money and buy them fancy clothes. But she said that this creates only a "temporary satisfaction."

Harriet said, "I tell them, in two minutes you can get HIV, which is something that can affect you for the rest of your life. I tell them not to fall into peer pressure. Just because everybody is doing it doesn't mean it is right for you. I ask them to ask themselves, 'What do you believe in? What is your dream?'"

I said I was touched by her work. Then I told her that I had lost a friend too and that was why I was writing a book for girls, to help them be safer and realize their dreams.

"When I talk to girls," Harriet said, "I want them to pick a leaf."

The room was loud again, and I couldn't hear what she said. On my notebook, I wrote out, "Pick a leaf." I pointed to the words. "Is this what you said?"

"Yes," Harriet said.

"I don't know what 'pick a leaf' means," I said.

"The story is a tree, and something that touches you is a leaf. We tell our stories to inspire, so that something offers a lesson or touches you. If it does, you pick it. You can learn, take that lesson with you, and the lesson will empower you. You pick a leaf."

Harriet took her hand, reached up, and picked an imaginary leaf from the air. She handed the imaginary leaf to me.

I smiled, took it, and recalled her words. "My story is a source of strength," I said. "As you do your work, I will keep you in my prayers."

Harriet put her hand on her chest. "As you do your work," she said, "I will keep you in my heart."

Cara, age 23 ~

I volunteered at a camp run by college students for kids who have a parent who has cancer. It's for kids ranging in age from five to 18. It's a place where they can have all the attention on them. I think commonly, when you have a parent who is going through cancer, the focus is shifted away from you. The camp is a time when the kids can be the focus and just be kids, and they don't have to grow up as fast as they did at home.

My mom passed away from cancer when I was six months old. I have an older sister. She had it a lot harder than I did because she navigated all of high school first, and I got to follow in her footsteps and learn from her. We're pretty tight-knit, the three of us—me, my dad, and my sister.

At camp I was a counselor for the youngest group, and I could be that motherly figure that they didn't have or that had been limited by what was going on in their family. I never had a camp like that. It was a not-talked-about experience, and I grew up with that silence being normal.

I think that emotionally it helped me to go to the camp too. This was surprising. I didn't expect that. Being able to provide for the kids what I didn't have—made me more aware of what I had thought was normal growing up. I had missed out on a few things. Being able to provide that for other kids made it really special. It can be healing to provide for someone else what you didn't have, and that, in turn, can be healing for you as well.

Dear Reader,

A few days ago, I attended a prayer retreat run by nuns at my son's school. It had been a long time since I'd been to confession. I chose to meet the priest face to face. The two of us sat in a small room.

I began, "Forgive me, Father, for I have sinned."

The priest was older than I am and had a gentle face. I wanted desperately to release the pain of everything that had happened—not the truth of all the betrayal, but the fact that I couldn't carry its weight any more.

I told the priest that I had sinned against myself because I felt unworthy of love and that, as much as I tried, the feeling wouldn't go away. I shared with him what had happened when I was at The Prep School and about my friend Claire who had died.

The priest listened, and then he spoke. He told me he had attended a prayer retreat at Auschwitz and that he had lived there for two months. He described the horror he felt when he saw the gas showers where Jewish people had been killed. He said he had been overwhelmed by the cruelty of humans.

Then, several weeks into his stay, spring began to arrive, and as he walked the grounds at Auschwitz, he saw flowers growing. He told me that, in the midst of atrocities, wildflowers were blooming all over.

I was silent, and then I shared with the priest the line from Claire's poem that I had found: "Wildflowers bloom all over in unexpected places." The priest's eyes filled with tears, and we sat in silence. And then he gave me a prayer from Mother Teresa to recite to myself daily:

God tenderly loving me.
Jesus in my heart.
Jesus tenderly loving me.
I love you.

I don't know if I've forgiven myself or if I've forgiven the others involved, but I am trying, and the result of my efforts is that I feel closer to the Divine[38] and have more joy and peace in my life. This is why I write to you today about forgiveness and love.

Helen Keller, The Story of My Life *~ Once, when I was puzzled to know why there were so many religions, [the Bishop] said: "There is one universal religion, Helen—the religion of love. Love God with your whole heart and soul, love every child of God as much as you ever can, and remember that the possibilities of good are greater than the possibilities of evil; and you have the key to heaven."*

Dear Reader,

Over time, I began to see that the Divine's love for me was bigger than my shame and that love made its way into my heart. How did this happen?

I made time for quiet prayer, especially when I felt awful. And I studied compassion and began to understand what it means to be kind to myself. This tenderness allowed me to see that there is something incredibly beautiful within a girl, the girl within me, who is connected to the Divine.

Helen Keller, Light in My Darkness *~ I know that life is given us so that we may grow in love. And I believe that God is in me as the sun is in the color and fragrance of the flower, the Light in my darkness, the Voice in my silence.*

If we each knew how divine we are and how sacred that connection is, I believe we would treat ourselves with love and kindness.

No matter what happens, always offer yourself kindness and know that you are worthy of love. The connection is there between you and the Divine. At any time, you can turn to it and receive love. Grace will lead you there. And it will feel like home.

Mary, age 23 ~ The little voice inside that tells you the kind of person you want to be—nothing about college should keep you from listening to that voice. No one who matters is ever going to judge you for listening to that voice.

Dear Reader,

Yesterday, when I was driving home, I was thinking about Claire and wondering what had led her to kill herself. Was she fighting her own civil war within herself? How much did she suffer? How alone did she feel?

If love is the answer, how could others and I have given Claire more love? How could we have better protected her as a young girl? And what if we'd gotten her help immediately? If we had, would she be an inspiring woman and poet today?

Kaufman, (2008) ~ All victims should be screened for suicidal ideation and self-harm behavior.[39]

I want to beg you—don't hate yourself. Pay attention and catch yourself. Notice any thought that is self-disparaging and identify it as part of our cultural sickness; then offer the thought itself kindness instead. Be compassionate with yourself when harsh thoughts arise. This is a cultural disease, and it's everywhere. Listen to your words, your language, and how you talk about yourself, inside your head and to others. Learn how to think, speak, and feel words of encouragement and self-love. Practice soaking in love.

I'd like you to consider taking on one exercise: Every time you look in the mirror, say, "I love you." Say it again, and again, and again. I love you. I love you. I love you. Even if it doesn't feel true. Even if it feels awkward. It takes practice. Daily practice. You're worth the effort.

I wish I could have told this to Claire. I wish I could have told her that her smile lifted my heart, that I loved how playful she was with words, and that I admired how much beauty she was able to see in the world. I wish I could have told her that I loved her.

As I drove home, I told Claire that I was sorry if she'd had a civil war inside of her, and that, whether she did or not, I still loved her. I told her about my letters to you and that I was telling you things no one told us when we were girls, and that I hoped it would make life better for you.

I told Claire that what had happened between her and Mr. Wickham wasn't her fault and that she didn't deserve to be treated that way.

Helen Keller, The World I Live In *~ I sympathized with plants when the flowers were picked, because I thought it hurt them, and that they grieved for their lost blossoms.*

I was still thinking about Claire when I arrived home. I poured myself a glass of water and sat in a wooden chair in my garden. My neighbor knocked on the front gate, and I called her in. She was carrying a mail-order catalogue, and she was telling me about a particular rose.

"It blooms all year long," she said. "I have one growing in my backyard. It's disease-resistant. It never gets mold on its leaves. It's incredibly beautiful and fragrant, and I want to purchase two more just like it."

My neighbor told me she could get a discount if she bought three and asked if I wanted to go in on the purchase.

"I'll go in with you," I said.

My neighbor held up the catalogue for me to see the flower. All roses have names, and many are named after people. I read the name of the rose I had agreed to purchase. Its name was Claire.

Dear Reader,

Claire's rose was on my doorstep. My neighbor had dropped off the bare root rose in a cardboard box. It looked like a handful of sticks. I spent the morning watching patterns of light move across the garden and decided that there was enough sunlight under our Japanese elm for a rose to grow.

Before I planted the rose, I used a plastic bag and picked up some dog poop from the chosen place and put it in the garbage can by the side of the house. I wanted to prepare the ground where I would plant the rose. I decided that the process offered a philosophy on how to live life—shine light on crap, remove it, and replace it with something beautiful.

When the ground was clear, I dug a hole beside the elm. I held the root of Claire's rose and said a prayer. I remembered her stopping to admire the sunset, a tree, a flower. I remembered her reading me poems out loud. I thanked her for being in my life.

I wanted to release the sadness of what had happened and how she had died, and I wanted to honor the joy she had brought to life and how she'd lived. Claire always made time to be in awe and to feel grateful. When I close my eyes, I can still see her smile.

Helen Keller ~ What we once enjoyed and deeply loved we can never lose, for all that we love deeply becomes a part of us.

I put the rose in the empty hole and filled in dirt around the roots. I watered the ground and used my feet to pack down the mud. Then I walked to the hose to wash my feet. When I looked back, I saw a path of muddy footprints on the pavement. It looked as if a mud girl had been following me. That was something Claire would have done, crept up behind me after walking barefoot through a garden.

Sometimes I wonder if the people we love who go to the other side are there, like the muddy footprints, right behind us, when we're missing them or loving them. I wonder whether, if we could see our path as it really is, would we see their footprints following us, checking on us, loving us? Do they whisper wisdom in our ears?

Helen Keller, The Story of My Life *~ I have cherished friends awaiting me in God's beautiful Somewhere. In spite of the lapse of years, they seem so close to me that I should not think it strange if at any moment they should clasp my hand and speak words of endearment as they used to before they went away.*

What would Claire say to me, I wondered.

And then I heard her voice, "Thank you. I love you. Be free. Be free."

I filled the watering can, and as I began to water the bare root rose and the other plants, I noticed that the geraniums were blooming for the first time since they had gone dormant—light pink, hot pink, and red. Maybe winter is only a season, and spring does come bursting with color and new life.

Dear Reader,

This past weekend I attended a meditation retreat. During a break, I took a walk in the woods. Beside the path, there was a display of miniature stone statues for sale. There were many little Buddhas and some goddesses of compassion.

As I passed, a little stone Buddha called out to me. He was about knee-high and was full of sweetness. He looked young and happy. He had a gentle smile on his face and stood with his hands in prayer. I asked him if he wanted to come home with me, and he said yes.

I purchased the little Buddha and buckled him into the passenger seat of my car. As I drove home, I recalled what I had learned at the retreat.

It's all about using our minds to gather the good.

We sat quietly, and Dr. Mendius, a neurologist, led us in a meditation. He asked us to bring to mind a sense of being cared for by someone—finding a port in a storm. He said to imagine that love coming from a person, a pet, or a spiritual being. He asked us to focus on feeling included, feeling seen, feeling appreciated, and feeling loved.

Next we were asked to bring to mind someone for whom we naturally feel compassion, a wish that they not suffer. He asked us to sink into that feeling of compassion in our body. And then he suggested that we turn this compassion toward ourselves and say gently, "May I not suffer. May the pain of the moment pass."

Dr. Mendius explained, "It can be easiest to have compassion for someone else who is suffering. It can be hardest to have compassion for the person in the mirror. It's okay to fail—it's an opportunity to practice compassion and to see your own individual struggles as heroic. This can be hard because of feelings of unworthiness, internalized oppression, and self-criticism. Practicing self-compassion buffers stress and increases resilience."

When I arrived home, I put the little Buddha in my garden at the base of the Japanese elm tree facing Claire's rose. I wanted him to remind me to breathe and to see beauty in the world. I also wanted him to pray for something good to come from something bad.

When a bare root rose is planted, it looks like a few sticks jutting out of the ground. Planting bare root roses requires hope. I suppose planting anything requires hope. Will it grow? Will the miracle of sun and soil and water work?

Together, the little Buddha and I looked at the rose sticks jutting upward, and there we noticed tiny—ever so tiny—green leaves coming out of the branches. And the little Buddha smiled.

Helen Keller, Optimism ~ *I never knew why Green's history thrilled me with the vigor of romance until I read his biography... When he and his wife were too poor to have a fire, he would sit before the unlit hearth and pretend that it was ablaze. "Drill your thoughts," he said; "shut out the gloomy and call in the bright."*

Dear Reader,

I had the most incredible dream last night. Part of what made it incredible was how vivid it was. It feels as if it really happened and that, as I write to you about what I saw, I am not recalling a dream, but a memory of something that was tangible.

I was with my daughter. She and I were walking through the halls at The Prep School. We passed a few students. I walked ahead of my daughter and turned into the office where the English teachers had their desks. I wanted to know if the teachers were still there, to see for myself. To my relief, the desks that had belonged to the three teachers I've told you about were empty. The bare desks were so real that I could have touched them.

There was sunlight in the room. It was coming through an open window. Outside it was spring, and I could see new leaves on the trees. A cool breeze blew through the room and rattled stray pieces of paper. I could hear the wind, and I knew it was a clearing breeze.

I showed my daughter the empty desks. We stood there together, looking at them, and then she put her arm around me. My daughter is taller than I am, and I rested my head on her shoulder. It felt as though I had come to the end of a very long journey.

Grace Kaimila-Kanjo,
Girls' Empowerment Educator, Africa ~

In African, we have a saying—Ubuntu—which goes, "I am only a human being because you are a human being, and together we make the human race. There could not have been a world if there was just me." Do you get what I mean? It is a world because there is me, there is you, there is her, there is him, and we need to interrelate knowing how interconnected we are, knowing that we all need each other. We have to live together in harmony. Respect my rights, and I respect yours. Ubuntu.

Cara, age 23 ~

I studied abroad in Cape Town, South Africa, and I taught life-skills workshops for young men in the local prison. They were ages 18 to 26. I felt that the most important thing for them is to feel that they are important, that they are cared about, and that they can still have a meaningful impact in the world.

Specifically, for youth who are in a juvenile detention center, I think it's important for them to feel they have a voice that can be heard. I taught a rap workshop, and I was paired with a guy who had just graduated from the program. We co-led the class. He focused on how to do the rhythm and make a beat, and I focused on the structure, what a metaphor is and how to make a rhyme.

In the end, I think for all those guys, getting them to stand up in front of a huge group of people and perform was a really big feat. It gave them confidence. I could see it.

A lot of people in my class felt that we had white privilege—we had so much money, we were able to fly there, who were we to help them? We were feeling guilty about our situation. But I learned that guilt isn't helpful to anybody, and that the most helpful thing you can do is leverage your position and your knowledge to help in any way you can—not to feel guilty about your status, but to do whatever you can to help other people.

In hindsight, I took a breath of relief when I left the prison for the last time. My nerves were definitely heightened the entire time when I was there, but the work was incredible.

Dear Reader,

I have wonderful news to report. Claire's rose bush has 17 new buds. They're tiny, the size of my pinky nail. What I didn't realize when I placed the little Buddha beside Claire's rose was that he was also next to a sprinkler head. Every morning the little Buddha gets sprayed in the face, a full dowsing, but, to my amazement, he keeps smiling.

I see the little Buddha when I leave and when I return. He stands with his hands in prayer and a soft, gentle smile on his face, blessing what is good in life to grow. Even when the water is blasting him, he is there with love in his heart.

My news for you today is this: The roses are coming! The roses are coming! The roses are coming! Oh, how important it is to believe in blooming.

There are dreams in you that want to bloom. Give them water, good soil, sunshine, and faithfulness, like the little Buddha who smiles and prays.

Dear Reader,

The other day I attended a meeting at a Jewish temple. Across from the sign in table was the sanctuary. My therapist, Ruth, had told me about a piece of artwork that hung from a skylight there. She said if I ever had the opportunity I should stop in and see it.

I walked into the sanctuary. I had been to several bar mitzvahs and bat mitzvahs. I recalled the cantors who sang at the services, and I could hear remnants of prayers being sung.

Ruth had shared with me the Jewish belief that we all come from one whole and that, when we're born, we're broken apart and sent out into the world. She said that pieces of string hung from a skylight in the sanctuary, with bits of glass attached to each string. When the strings twirled, Ruth said, each piece of glass reflected light. Ruth said we each have our own part of the original light, and we're meant to share it and offer it to the world.

I looked around the room. From a skylight hung strings lined with pieces of broken mirror. There were different shapes—squares, rectangles, and trapezoids. Each one reflected light and color in its own way. Ruth was right—it was beautiful.

No matter what happens to you in life, remember the mirrors hanging from the light. When you hear a small voice in you, a thought, a whisper, a feeling that says, "Maybe I am here for a reason, to offer something unique and beautiful," stop and listen. When you have this feeling or hear this thought, pay attention, listen, and know that you are.

Dear Reader,

Last night, I volunteered at the Safe & Sober grad-night party at my son's school. After the ceremony, I checked in seniors as they arrived. They seemed hopeful, excited, tearful, and relieved to have time with friends.

Every 20 minutes, the volunteers rotated posts. We sat and watched the recent graduates play Ping-Pong, get tattoos, have their fortunes read, and eat nachos. For my first shift, I sat beside an exit door near the basketball court and listened to deep voices echoing throughout the gym.

For my next shift, I rotated to a station at an indoor pool. No one was swimming when I entered the room. "It's an easy shift," the parent ahead of me said. I sat in a white plastic chair in the pool area, alone. A lifeguard came in and took his post on a ladder. Not long after, a group of senior guys entered the pool area. They were the same ones who had been playing basketball.

I felt myself start to sink. Maybe it was the indoor pool late at night, full of senior guys, or maybe it was the girls I had checked in who were beautiful, young, and trusting. My heart started racing. I was traveling back in time.

"What will help me not slide?" I asked myself. My chest was getting tighter, and I was being sucked through hallways where teachers and students snickered. I covered my ears to keep out their loud voices and the sound of the pool. I was desperately searching my mind for a port in a storm—and then I remembered love.

Bring to mind someone you naturally have a feeling of compassion for, a wish that they not suffer.

I thought of my children. I tried to breathe.

Sink into that feeling of compassion in your body.

The seniors' voices were loud.

I was sweating, and my heart was beating fast. I imagined the faces of my children. "See them. Focus on them," I told myself. I pictured each child of mine, and I felt my heart fill with love, a mother's love.

Turn that compassion toward yourself and say gently, "May I not suffer. May the pain of the moment pass." Focus on feeling included, feeling seen, feeling appreciated, and feeling loved.

I closed my eyes and put my hand on my cheek. I tried to breathe and whispered, "May the pain of the moment pass. May the pain of the moment pass. May the pain of the moment pass."

Helen Keller, The Story of My Life *~ Sometimes, it is true, a sense of isolation enfolds me like a cold mist as I sit alone and wait at life's shut gate. Beyond there is light, and music, and sweet companionship; but I may not enter. Fate, silent, pitiless, bars the way... Silence sits immense upon my soul. Then comes hope with a smile and whispers, "There is joy in self-forgetfulness." So I try to make the light in others' eyes my sun, the music in others' ears my symphony, the smile on others' lips my happiness.*

When I opened my eyes, I saw the seniors in the pool. I recognized a few of them. They were friends with my son. I wasn't 16, I was a mother, and this time there was a lifeguard at the pool. I took several deep breaths. I was all right. I was all right.

A mother touched my shoulder. "Time to rotate posts," she said.

For my next station, I sat beside a ring-making booth. A tiny old man made coins into memory rings using a hammer, a file, and a large metal press. His glasses balanced on the end of his crooked nose. I watched him slide metal circles onto girls' fingers to determine their size, and then he used a heavy press to shape the ring. As the old man worked, he was careful and gruff.

When there was a break in the line, the old man turned to me and asked, "What year were you born?" I was surprised when he spoke to me.

The old man sifted through the box, pulled out a ring made from a coin, and tested it on my finger. He removed the ring, pounded it, and pressed it with a large clamp. He worked quickly, and when he was finished, he polished the ring with a cloth and slid it onto my little finger.

"When you get home, use a magnifying glass, and you'll see on the ring the word LIBERTY," he said. He looked at my hand with the ring, nodded, and was pleased.

I could feel the LIBERTY ring on my little finger. I had successfully navigated a memory slide and pulled myself back to the present by focusing on offering love and being loved. Learning how to manage my own mind and happiness is liberating.

Dear Reader,

Today, when I finished my morning walk, I stopped to look at Claire's rosebush. There in the middle of a handful of green leaves was the first rose. A sweet, gentle scent filled the air.

Helen Keller ~ Love is like a beautiful flower which I may not touch, but whose fragrance makes the garden a place of delight just the same.

On one petal I could see a droplet of water, and I wondered if it was a tear. They say that tears, if you study them, are different from each other—that scientists can tell by their chemical makeup if they are tears of sadness, joy, or relief. I wondered what tear the rose had shed. Maybe it was a combination of all three.

There are some things that happen in life that will never, ever be okay. And despite that truth, life itself continues to offer love and beauty.

When you leave home, remember that you are loved, remember who and what you love, and work daily to love yourself.

Helen Keller, The Story of My Life ~

What secret power, I wonder, caused this blossoming miracle? What mysterious force guided the seedling from the dark earth up to the light, through leaf and stem and bud, to glorious fulfillment in the perfect flower? Who could have dreamed that such beauty lurked in the dark earth, was latent in the tiny seed we planted? Beautiful flower, you have taught me to see a little way into the hidden heart of things. Now I understand that the darkness everywhere may hold possibilities better even than my hopes.

Part Two:
Your Story

Denise, age 25 ~

I recommend journaling to someone going into college. It's so much easier to be honest with yourself if you put pen to paper. That's what really helped me—to reflect a lot about who I am today.

Dear Reader,

I end my own story with a request that you practice loving yourself daily. To learn how to do this, we will explore four words—respect, boundaries, discernment, and love—and how we can apply these words to ourselves and others.

Many of the young women I interviewed journal to find and hear their own voice. This has been my experience as well. Throughout this section, I share ideas, quotes, and questions. Please free to respond as you like. You can write out your thoughts and feelings, talk with a friend or parent, or do both.

I recommend selecting a notebook and having a set of colorful pencils and pens that you can use to illustrate your feelings, thoughts, and dreams. Breathing and taking time to check in helps. When I'm journaling, I remind myself that my goal is not to write well but to let myself get lost on the page. Messy is good.

Thank you for joining me on this journey.

Respect

Irene Tsai, Watcher and Alcohol Educator, age 21 ~

Every person, every peer, every friend, even if they're not a friend—whenever you go out, care for the well-being of others.

Kathleen, age 50 ~ And yourself.

RESPECTING ALL OF YOURSELF

Dear Reader,

The first word I'd like to talk about is respect and how we can work on respecting our inner selves.

Last Christmas I was home wrapping presents and listening to a video discussion between two people who are both psychologists and Buddhists—Rick Hanson and Tara Brach. They were talking about how important it is that we practice compassion for ourselves.

Tara shared that she had struggled with weight issues in her late teens and early twenties. She described having a war of negative feelings and thoughts inside herself. But when she learned how to offer loving kindness and compassion to all aspects of herself, the battle stopped and her weight issues resolved. This was a profound shift for her.

I later read Tara's book *Radical Acceptance*, in which she explains that she thinks of loving kindness as a cup of tea. I have always been a tea drinker, and this metaphor was easy for me to imagine. Tara described taking time to notice what voices were talking inside her head and what feelings she had in her body. She said she would pause and ask, "What's happening inside of me right now?" Instead of trying to push hard feelings away or allowing herself to become more self-critical, Tara imagined a table in her mind. She named the voice that was speaking or the feeling that was wanting attention and welcomed each part of herself to the table with love. And then, metaphorically, she offered whoever was there a cup of tea.

Tara's approach seemed both simple and profound. I began to see it as a game—could I make time throughout the day to stop and notice what feeling was wanting attention within me, name it, and offer that part of me love? Could I offer all parts of myself kindness—no matter how awful or ugly or embarrassing the sentiment was?

After I heard the video presentation and read Tara's book, I adjusted how I treated myself. This idea of accepting, even welcoming, all aspects of myself was radical for me. For decades, I had tried to get rid of feeling unworthy and shame, but the feelings persisted. When I started using the cup-of-tea practice, I began to find peace and acceptance for all that I am—including the parts that were uncomfortable and that I didn't respect. For the first time in my life, I made a seat at the table for my shame.

When I befriended my feeling of there being something wrong with me, I felt sad for myself. I saw that having this feeling caused me to suffer, and I offered myself tenderness and said, "I am so sorry that you feel this way, and I love you."

Instead of thinking of myself as a giant self-improvement project—with much to eliminate or improve—I started treating myself with kindness. When I learned to accept that I had parts within myself that I didn't respect and didn't want to accept, I softened and began approaching those aspects with love.

Every day I drew in my journal a giant circular table and tiny cups of tea at each place setting. I drew stick figures of myself at each seat and labeled the different aspects of myself. The "worried me" got a cup of tea. The "unworthy me" got a cup of tea. The "tired-of-feeling-unworthy-and-worried me" got a cup of tea. The "sad me" got a cup of tea. The "it's-all-my-fault me" got a cup of tea. The "relieved me" got a cup of tea. The "jealous me" got a cup of tea. The "having-fun-drawing me" got a cup of tea. And on and on.

Inside each cup of tea, I drew a heart. The point of the exercise, as I saw it, was to be kind, welcoming, and curious. I accepted that I couldn't control the hard feelings that arose within me but that I could choose how I treated them. Offering a cup of tea filled with a heart was a sweet and gentle place to start. When I learned how to do this as a daily practice, I started to change and my internal battles stopped.

Rather than being each of those feelings, I started to become a person who relates to all aspects of myself with respect and kindness. It's a cool trick: No matter what hard feelings arise, I can name them and treat them with kindness, and my ability to do that feels good.

As I applied this tea ceremony to myself daily, I began feeling like a student of emotional and intellectual Jujutsu. Jujutsu is a Japanese martial art in which the student is trained to defeat an armed opponent without using weapons. Jujutsu was originally called the "art of harmony" and the "way of softness."[40] I learned that offering love and compassion to all aspects of myself is the way of softness. For the first time in my life, I began accepting myself, all of myself, and I realized that, in performing this daily tea ceremony, I was learning to practice the art of inner harmony.

I would like to invite you to hold tea ceremonies with yourself—to start noticing what you're feeling, investigating it (how does it feel in your body? where is it?), naming it, and then nurturing it. Sometimes I put a hand on my heart and say, "Sweetheart, I am sorry you are suffering in this way."

The nurturing part is offering loving kindness and compassion to all aspects of yourself.

It is a lovely way to move through each day, pausing every so often to take a breath, check in, and have a cup of tea with whatever aspect of yourself needs love.

Opportunities ~

1) *Thomas, age 19 ~ Take time to think about how your day actually went. If you don't develop this as a skill, you may never know how your day actually went.*

   Sit and notice how you are right now. Check in with yourself. Breathe. Ask yourself, "What's happening inside me right now? What's up in my body? Am I tense anywhere? How's my stomach, my chest, my throat? Does anything feel uncomfortable? What am I most worried about? What am I feeling?"

2) Draw a circular table with a cup of tea at each place setting. Can you name the feelings you have and offer each one kindness? If you are suffering in some way, can you name it and offer that part of yourself a cup of love?

3) I suggest that you begin each journaling session with a tea ceremony. It's an easy way to check in with yourself and practice offering kindness and love to whatever you notice.

RESPECTING YOUR PALETTE
OF EMOTIONS

Dear Reader,

I have found that naming feelings is helpful. Here's a partial list of feelings that might show up to your tea ceremony.[41] I think of it as a potential guest list. I have regulars who show up every day, and there are others who arrive unannounced and want to be included. Remember that the tea ceremony always starts with recognizing who is there, welcoming the feeling or thought to the table, and then offering each part of yourself kindness and love.

Angry

Arrogant

Closed-minded

Competitive

Defensive

Disgusted

Envious

Frustrated

Full of Contempt

Full of Dislike

Grumpy

Impatient

Irritated

Jealous

Judgmental

Pessimistic

Resentful

~

Alienated

Ashamed

Bullied

Defeated

Depressed

Despairing

Disappointed

Discouraged

Embarrassed

Guilty

Heartbroken

Helpless

Homesick

Hurt

Insecure

Insulted

Isolated

Lacking

   Confidence

Lonely

Longing

Powerless

Rejected

Remorseful

Sad

Sensitive

Unhappy

Vulnerable

~

Afraid

Anxious

Clingy

Concerned

Conflicted

Disconnected

Guarded

Hesitant

Nervous

Panicked

Suspicious

Torn

Uneasy

Worried

~

Balanced

Caring

Compassionate

Concerned

Empathetic

Equanimous

Kind

Loving

Non-judgmental

Open-hearted

Open-minded

Trusting

~

Appreciative

Content

Encouraged

Enthusiastic

Excited

Fulfilled

Glad

Grateful

Happy

Hopeful

Joyful

Proud

Relieved

Satisfied

Thankful

Opportunities ~

1) Draw a circular table and go through the list. Who wants to come to the table? Can you name each feeling, welcome it, and offer it kindness and a cup of love? What feelings would you not want to tell anyone about? Can you welcome them to the table too and offer them love?

2) *Sophie, age 22 ~ Before, when I was tired, exhausted, and overwhelmed, I thought I was depressed, when in reality I was angry. For women, we don't often get supported in being really angry or pissed off. People like to talk you through being depressed, sad, or anxious. It's very understandable for others, versus, when you're really pissed off, people don't want to hear it. I was depressed for a year and a half. I was also really angry. Anger can be temporary, but sadness and anxiety can stay. There's nothing worse. Unless you've gone through it, you never know.*

Sometimes recognizing feelings brings up anger, sadness, grief, or other hard feelings. If this is true for you, can you now name the other emotions that showed up? I call these back-row emotions. Often there are emotions in the front row that say, "I'm here! Pick me!" After the front-row emotions get seats at the table, I've noticed that middle-row and back-row emotions arrive. Can you welcome them and offer them tenderness as well?

3) What three feelings on this list would you like to experience more frequently in your life? Name them and make space at the table for them. Can you welcome these feelings, even though you may not feel them yet? Can you offer each of them a cup of love?

RESPECTING YOUR LEARNING PROCESS

Dear Reader,

We allow ourselves to learn and get better in sports, in school, in art, in music—and we can allow ourselves time to reflect, learn, revise, and improve in our social interactions as well. Every day, we can reflect on what happened.

It's helpful to take time to respect all of your feelings. This does not mean that it's best to *act* on all of your feelings. The more deeply I understand that all actions have consequences, the more I make it a priority to practice self-restraint to avoid hurting myself or someone else.

When I look back on a day, I see that all actions have consequences. My goal is to take small steps toward who I want to be in the world and to avoid making choices that take me away from my goals.

Denise, age 25 ~ I try to reflect every night on these questions. I ask myself, "How did I act? How do I feel? How did I treat others?" And I can see, okay, yes, I completed X, Y, and Z off of my to-do list, but was I kind to my dad when he was smacking his food and it was driving me crazy? That's what happened yesterday. It's my biggest pet peeve, and I always have to tell myself not to blow up. When he did it, I said, "That can drive you insane, but you didn't get angry, nice job. But when you went to AA, you saw someone and gossiped about them. That didn't feel right. That's not the person you're trying to become." It's good to reflect on that. It's good every night to ask yourself, "What did I do? Who am I? Who do I want to be?"

Opportunities ~

1) What are three things you did today that you feel good about? What's something you did that you would change? What feeling led to the action that you want to revise? Can you allow yourself the feeling and still resolve not to act on that feeling in the same way the next time it arises?

2) Taking small daily steps toward our goals and dreams helps us answer the question "Who do I want to be?" To live the life I want, it is necessary for me to take positive actions in the direction of my dreams. What's one goal or dream that you have? Write it down. How would you feel if you achieved it?

3) *Lisa, age 18* ~ *Every day I give myself kudos for three brave things I did that day, and I write down what the three actions I took were. This allows me to find value in the actions I am taking even though solutions haven't emerged yet. I can see that even though the problem hasn't been solved, my actions are important and have value.*

What three brave things would you like to do tomorrow? What's one tiny step you can take in the direction of your dream?

RESPECTING YOUR INNER GUIDE

Dear Reader,

I have something sparkly to share with you today. Each person is like a snowflake—complex, original, and beautiful. And this is true of you. I want you to know that you are intricate and unique, and that the world needs what only you can offer.

There is a whispering within you that wants you to listen. This voice is different from the noisy ones that occupy most of our inner thoughts. There is a voice deep within you who is your guide to feeling satisfied and joyful about who you are, why you are here, and what you are living for. Learning to identity your Inner Guide takes time. It's a journey and a process of discovery.

Sometimes we can admire gifts that others have and not see what we have. When I'm focusing on others and comparing myself with them, I miss seeing my own gifts and I can't hear my own inner longings and my own Inner Guide.

The most important journey you can take in your lifetime is learning how to listen to your Inner Guide. This requires making time for yourself and learning how to listen to the longings of your heart. It's important that you make time daily to show up to yourself—as a friend wanting to hear what your Inner Guide has to say. When you want to make a difference in the world, pay attention.

As you learn to listen and take action toward your calling, you will begin to see that you are not alone. Helpful people will appear, and these grace-filled moments will light your way. Learn to notice grace-filled moments and appreciate them. When you start listening to your inner longings and dreams, serendipity will happen, and you will be helped in ways you could never, ever have imagined.

Who you are and what you have to offer are needed. You can make a difference in this world, and you're supposed to; it starts by learning how to tune in and listen to your Inner Guide.

Stephanie Seibel, Counselor, age 25 ~

The most valuable things we can walk away from college with are answers to some of these questions: Who am I? What kind of life do I want to live? What matters to me? What are my gifts and talents? What is my place in the world, and how can I contribute in a way that will make me successful and happy?

A lot of people think answering these questions is simple. I think it is an active process and a life-long process. You can test out your answers. Take classes in areas you're interested in. Join clubs. Volunteer or intern.

It's a two-part process—learning, and reflecting on what you're learning and exploring. I wish I'd kept a journal while I was learning and had taken the time to reflect on my purpose. I wish I'd asked myself more often, "What types of projects am I really enjoying? What types of people am I really enjoying connecting with?"

Opportunities ~

1) Is there a place in your life—at home or in nature—where you can find quiet time each day, walking or

sitting? If not, can you create one? What do you want to name this place?

2) Even if you don't have a quiet place in your external world, you can always pause and find a quiet place in your internal world. Try turning off all electronic devices and paying attention to your breathing as it comes in and goes out. Count to three as you inhale and to three as you exhale. Do this exercise three times. How do you feel afterward?

3) Notice something beautiful that is near you. Now notice something beautiful that is within you—a quality or feeling. What are you noticing?

RESPECTING YOUR INNER GIFTS

Dear Reader,

I want to ask you to respect that you have gifts to share that are important, much needed, and valuable—even if you have no idea what they are right now. These gifts are woven into the fabric of who you already are. When I tell you that you have work to do, I mean it. You have work to do: identifying your gifts and developing skills so that you can share them with others and the world.

It is important that you make it a priority to get to know yourself—not what others are saying about you, but what the inner longings of your heart are saying to you. When you feel a deep sense of joy and peace, pay attention to what you're doing in that moment. When you see your joyful, peaceful actions improving someone else's life, pay attention—your presence is already making a difference in the world.

I keep seeing the image of a message in a bottle. I believe we each have a message that the world needs, like pieces in a puzzle—or shards of glass hanging from a skylight, each reflecting light in its own unique way. Even if you can't read the message yet and don't know what it is, it's still important to search to find that purpose, what is written on your heart.

Opportunities ~

1) Imagine yourself as a wise old woman and ask her to write a letter to you. What three things does she want

you to know? What one thing does she want you to never, ever forget? What's one thing that she'd like you to worry less about? What's one thing she would like to see you doing to make a difference in the world?

2) Now imagine the little girl in you, and ask her to write you a letter. What three things does she want you to know? What one thing does she want you to never, ever forget? What are three joyful things that you used to do that she'd like you to do again? (Hint: Being joyful in and of itself adds a lot to the world.)

RESPECTING YOUR BODY

Dear Reader,

Today I'd like to talk about respecting your body. What I have come to appreciate is that my body is an amazing living organism, and I feel better when I make it a priority to take really good care of my body.

Taking care of my body means that I notice what feels good for me and what doesn't, and I try to make choices throughout the day that feel good later. When I take time to listen, I allow my Inner Guide to evaluate what enters or touches my body and to determine if it is healthy for me. I care about protecting myself because I care about myself.

Food—I work on choosing foods that help my brain work well and my skin be clear. This means I try to choose foods that are natural and basic—fruits, vegetables, whole grains, and proteins. The closer to earth the food is, meaning less processed, the better it is for me. I try to eat proteins and greens throughout the day and to limit my sugars. I've learned that eating too much sugar can make my moods go up and down more than I want.

Skin—I work on wearing clothes that feel good on my skin. I have a favorite robe that I wear in the early morning that feels like I am wrapping myself in heaven. I like wearing certain lotions that feel good. I also try to notice when the sun feels warm and healthy on my skin and when I need to put on sun-block. I love feeling wind on my face and noticing where it is coming from. I love the feel of my dog's fur in my hands when I rub her ears. Touch is an important part of being human. Being touched by someone or touching someone I love can feel calming, comforting, caring, healing, full of sweetness, tender, playful, exciting, delightful, passionate, and exquisite.

Eyes—I try to stop and notice beauty every day, throughout the day: the sunrise, a flower, a friend's smile. It's good to pay attention to what you're seeing and to choose to see things that fill your spirit with inspiration and joy. I try to stop and feel thankful when I notice people being kind to each other—a mother stopping to tie a child's shoe, a man pushing an old woman in a wheel chair, a crossing guard making certain that children pass safely through an intersection.

Nose—I love the scent of good food cooking, my dog after I've given her a bath, and my kids when they come home from school. It's fun to notice what scents you like and what ones you don't. We've had several skunks move into our neighborhood, and we're very careful, whenever we smell a skunk, not to let our dog play outside. Respecting scents is part of being aware of your surroundings.

Taste—I like experiencing different cultures through their spices and food. When I eat the bread my mother used to bake, I am reminded of her love for me. When I taste salt water, I know I am at the beach on vacation. When someone does something awful, I get a stomachache and a bad taste in my mouth. It literally makes me feel sick. Goodness feels good. Bad stuff often makes my stomach hurt. Things that aren't good for me often have a bad taste. Learning to notice these differences is helpful.

Ears—What sounds do you enjoy hearing? I love the sound of people's voices, especially the voices of people I love. Every voice has richness and texture. When I really listen to the variety in a voice I can tell a lot about a person. Genuine warmth and love feel incredibly good. Other times, people say words I want to hear but their tone communicates something else. I learn a lot when I really listen. Sometimes, when people don't say anything, that can say a lot too. I also love music and believe that music helps us tap into the rhythm of life.

Body—My body knows. When I feel sick to my stomach, I listen. When I'm getting a headache, I listen. When my jaw gets tight, I listen. When my heart aches, I listen. My body is constantly communicating information to me. When I tune in, I learn a lot. Sometimes my body is recalling past fears and worries. Other times my body is telling me valuable information about things going on in the present moment, and it's critical that I listen. I try to notice what my body likes—what kinds of touch feel good and what kinds of touch do not. Listening to the wisdom of my body helps me understand my true feelings about people and situations.

Exercise—I know that I am happier when I exercise regularly. This can be as simple as walking my dog every day or as elaborate as driving to the ocean and swimming in the waves. Regular exercise washes away stress and increases my happiness. I cannot express in words how much dancing to music lifts my spirit.

Sleep—Paying attention to how I am sleeping and how much I am sleeping helps me function better during the day. When I stop looking at any glowing screen an hour before I go to bed, I sleep better. When I read something inspiring before I sleep, my sleep is more peaceful. Defending and enhancing my sleep is part of respecting myself. Getting good sleep matters a lot; others may not value it, but getting good sleep is a priority for me. How much sleep one person needs varies, and it's helpful to learn what's optimal for you.

Pay attention to the middle path. Too much sleep can be a sign of depression. Too little sleep can be a sign of anxiety. Eating too little food can be a sign of anorexia. What's a middle path of health for you and your body? If you notice that you have areas of imbalance, seek out help, talk with someone. Respecting the Inner Guide also means noticing when the critical, sad, or fearful voices within you have become overwhelming and are asking for help. We are not meant to suffer alone.

Sophie, age 22 ~

You have to start simple and ask yourself, "Does something ring true to you?" The more you self-assess, the better you get at doing it. You have to get through the phase of "I don't know if I'm right about myself." That describes the majority of my undergraduate experience.

I got really, really sick my freshman year. I had mono and was really tired and had headaches. That catapulted me into very aggressive self-assessment. I had to keep track of everything. I saw a sports psychologist. If you can, see someone. It was informative for me. And I did daily self-assessments. I was trying to figure out a way to get better. I made a list for myself of daily questions: How well are you sleeping? How are your headaches? What times of day do you feel the most exhausted? What foods are you craving? Are the foods healthy for you?

I created a self-assessment list of questions and generated it based on what my biggest problems were: my fatigue level and my quality of sleep. It doesn't have to be on a scale. I made sure I checked in every day. It became normal, but it wasn't normal at the time. I felt like I was a science experiment for myself.

Opportunities ~

1) It's fun to get curious about who you are in this world and to make time to tune in and listen. Write these categories going down the left side of your page: Food, Skin, Eyes, Nose, Taste, Ears, Body, Exercise, and Sleep. Make four columns across the top of your page and write: Things I enjoy, Things that are good for me, Warning signs (when something isn't good for me or when something is dangerous), and Things I'd like to experience more. Fill in each quadrant with your response and notice what you learn. It's helpful to direct our actions toward goodness in our lives.

RESPECTING YOUR EMERGING
SENSUAL, SEXUAL BEING

Dear Reader,

Today I'd like to talk with you about your emerging sensual, sexual being. A flower on a tree can become something delicious and delightful when the conditions are right. A blossom can transform into an apple, or a peach, or a pear. As you grow and develop, you change as well—from a girl into a young woman. If you watch fruit trees, you will know that they bloom at different times—in spring, mid-summer, and early fall. This is also true of how your sensual, sexual being emerges—in its own way and in its own time.

Specific conditions are necessary for trees to blossom: healthy soil, clean air, sunlight, rain, hummingbirds and bees, and protection from harmful insects and people. Temperature matters too. If it's too hot, blossoms wither and there's no fruit; if there's a late freeze, flowers die. Different seasons have different conditions. Many factors must come together in a beautiful, time-sensitive way for a tree to blossom and bear fruit.

During a fruit-bearing season, the tree is blessed with delight—healthy soil feels good, clean air feels good, protection feels good, warm sunlight feels good, hummingbirds and bees feel good, and gentle rain feels good. The blossoming of a flower is beautiful, delicious, and divine.

How we grow into ourselves as sensual, sexual women is a blossoming—and this process too can be delightful, delicious, and divine.

Opportunities ~

1) Notice how people's bodies change at different times. What are changes in your physical body that you notice? What are changes in your thoughts and feelings?

2) What changes are you enjoying? What changes bother you? Can you offer all of your feelings around the changes loving kindness, a cup of tea?

3) You may notice feeling attracted to someone. Some people call this "chemistry." Sometimes this feeling is reciprocal. Sometimes it's not. These feelings and thoughts can be sparkly, distracting, and exciting. When you feel attracted to someone, what do you feel in your body? What thoughts do you think? What feelings do you have?

RESPECTING OTHERS

Dear Reader,

Today I want to write to you about respecting others. This idea is connected to respecting ourselves. When we learn how to treat ourselves with care and respect, we can apply this learning to others.

When we don't treat ourselves well, we get off-balance. Sometimes it means that we try to take care of everyone else's needs and not our own. Other times it means that we treat others poorly—judging them or putting them down to try to make ourselves feel better. Either way, someone is getting hurt and our actions or lack of action are causing harm.

Yesterday at church our minister gave a sermon.[42] He asked us to look at our own lives and see if our actions were predatory or neighborly. Predatory energy means acting in a way that benefits ourselves while ignoring the pain we cause others. A person who is being predatory resists seeing the other person as a person and does not acknowledge someone else's pain or the fact that they caused it.

Ouch. I definitely could think of people who were predators in my life.

Our minister explained that another way of being in the world is being neighborly. This means that we are in touch with our own pain and the pain of others, and this grounds us in compassion. We see ourselves and others as people who have feelings and individual lives, and we acknowledge our own humanity and theirs when we interact.

I smiled as I thought of people who leave me feeling seen and warm after I spend time with them.

This takes me to another word I want to give you. The word is DIGNITY, "the quality of being worthy of esteem or respect."[43] If I could make dignity into a drink, I would. Imbibe dignity. Let dignity sink into your pores, your cells, the way you walk and talk and hold yourself. Let dignity become part of your being so that you know on the deepest level that you are worthy of esteem and respect. Treating yourself with respect and feeling innate worth and dignity will change your life.

When you feel lost, return to respect and dignity. Every human being deserves respect and to have their own inherent dignity acknowledged. Actions matter in how we treat ourselves and others. Being neighborly means that in every human interaction I consciously acknowledge the inherent dignity within myself and the inherent dignity in the other person. I am not better than anyone, and I am not worse than anyone. This is what respect is, and I start with myself.

Opportunities ~

1) Practice walking with your shoulders back, your head up, and a slight smile on your face, while repeating the word "dignity, dignity, dignity." Let yourself feel royal, noble, and connected to the Divine—because you are. That's what your beautiful life force is. Can you see that being alive is itself a miracle worthy of awe and respect? Make a DIGNITY art project. Write out something positive that goes with each letter of the word. Offer it to yourself.

2) When I acknowledge my inherent dignity, I feel _____.

When I acknowledge the inherent dignity in others, I treat them more _____.

Treating myself with respect means I care more about _____.

Treating others with respect means I _____.

One time, when I treated someone with predatory energy, I felt _____.

One time, when I treated someone with neighborly energy, I felt _____.

One time, when someone treated me with predatory energy, I felt _____.

One time, when someone treated me with neighborly energy, I felt _____.

3) Questions to ask yourself before taking any action:

Am I acting in a way that is aligning my gain with another's harm?

Am I forgetting that the person I am interacting with is unique in his or her own needs, dreams, and challenges?

Am I aligning my well-being with the well-being of another?

Am I aware that my well-being and the well-being of the people I'm with are connected?

EXAMINING PREDATORY AND NEIGHBORLY BEHAVIOR

James, age 22 ~

There are different types of approaches to hooking up. There are the guys who are really bold and the ones who are really careful and ask for consent every step of the way. I've never seen a guy who wouldn't take no for an answer, and if I did, hopefully I'd step in and say something.

Some girls are at the party because they want to hook up with a guy, and there are guys like that too, who are there to hook up with a girl. They go to the party, and they want to get laid. They have one goal in mind. They don't care who it is. You see the same guy making out on the dance floor, and, 10 minutes later, he's with someone else. He's going for the shotgun blast, throwing stuff at the wall to see what sticks. He doesn't care who it is. I hate to say it, but there's definitely a culture where some girls want to hook up with an older guy and some guys take advantage of it.

On the opposite end of the spectrum, I had a female friend who came to parties to dance. She brought her own alcohol in a water bottle, and that was all she drank. She always came with friends. She was really pretty. She had the dance moves and wasn't afraid to show it. She had dark, thick-framed glasses and a pretty face. She was a good dancer, not self-conscious at all. She was gorgeous, with long, dark hair. I wanted to hook up with her, but I always struck out, and other guys did too. She was always really fun, and she was always dancing in a group with girls. Other times, another guy or I would join them to show off, and she'd say, "Oh my God, you're such a good dancer. You're so fun." It never worked out the way we wanted it to.

Toward the end of my senior year, we had issues with too many girls getting really drunk and throwing up. We stopped serving hard alcohol. We had beer and mixed drinks. When we served hard alcohol, people got drunk too quickly. Serving mixed drinks and beer slowed them down. Some girls got mad and indignant and yelled at us, "You don't have any shots!" If we ran out of punch, there were always girls who'd say, "You don't have any more punch?" They were super indignant and ugly. This happened every time I worked the bar: No matter how much alcohol we bought, we always ran out, and a girl would always get mad at me and say, "Why don't you have what I want?"

I'd get mad. "This is free for you. If you don't like it, you can leave."

A drunk girl coming on to you is super awkward. You don't want to hurt her feelings. It's a sticky situation. So often it's the other way around, and we coach girls on how to act. But there are girls there who want to hook up with any guy, and they'll hook up with anyone. They're intoxicated. They're younger. They're on the dance floor where it's backlit, with flashing lights and glowing paint on the walls. It's loud. It's dark. People's white shirts are glowing. If it gets awkward, I avoid conflict and usually leave and go upstairs.

When we talk about sexual assault, it's always, "Girls, here's how not to get raped, and, guys, here's how not to rape someone." If you're both drunk, who's responsible? If you're both drunk and neither of you gave consent, you both have grounds to press charges. If neither gave consent, then it's whoever says, "I got raped," first.

Even if a guy feels taken advantage of, there's so much in our culture working against him. Statistically, the males assaulting the females are so much more numerous. With a girl, it's much more part of the education and culture to encourage her to come out and say if she was uncomfortable. If a guy says a girl took advantage of him, people say, "Stop being such a pussy."

It's scary to me, what the legal system says and the school's treatment of the issue. The school has unilateral authority to kick someone out. You can be accused, kicked out of school, but not held legally responsible, and your school life is ruined.

It's also a legitimate issue if a school knows someone has sexually assaulted a woman and doesn't do enough, allowing the attacker to continue going to school and attacking.

It's very complicated. How are we to distinguish between them? Whose responsibility is it to give consent? Is it always the guy who has to ask for consent from a girl? Or is it the person who is trying to go to the next step? I'm sure a sexual-assault educator would say that whoever is trying to go to the next step has to ask and receive verbal consent to progress.

To truly address the problem, there has to be a complete change in terms of how romantic or sexual relationships and interactions are approached. Sneezing into your elbow is one thing, talking during sex is a bigger challenge.

Opportunities ~

1) In this interview, what are some examples of predatory energy? Who was thinking only of his or her own needs regardless of the other person? Who treats another person badly? We can also neglect ourselves and treat

ourselves with predatory energy as well. Who was not respecting him or herself?

2) What are examples in the interview of someone displaying neighborly energy? When does someone consider his or her own needs and the needs of someone else? Who is trying to avoid causing harm? How does someone look out for others?

3) If you were attending this party, what are some danger signs that you might see? What are three things you could do to intervene? To protect a friend? To protect a stranger? To protect yourself? What are some feelings that you might have that might prevent you from intervening? Would it be worth acting to help someone even if you experience discomfort?

Discernment

Stephanie Seibel, Counselor, age 25 ~

My biggest piece of advice is not to worry about getting it all right. Consider this a time of purposeful exploring. Our whole world is waking up to questions like "What really matters to me, and what is my purpose?" We're all on a journey of finding our place. The point is not to have all the answers but to be living into those questions.

What if you're not lost but right where you're supposed to be? So wherever you are—start, go for it, try, fail! And you most likely will fail a bunch. Embrace it. Because a life unlived is a far worse fate than failure.

For me, the hardest thing in grown-up land has been holding onto my youthful optimism, joy, spirit, love, and creativity in a world that seems to tell us it's impractical and frivolous. I am finding, however, that the opposite is true. What fills your heart up is not only what you need but what the world needs and your easiest path to success. Trust me when I say that it's extremely hard to succeed at being anyone other than you.

DISCERNING YOUR GIFTS
AND CHARISMS

Dear Reader,

Several months ago, I attended a spiritual retreat at my son's school run by nuns. After one of the talks, I asked a sister if she would show me a few slides again. I had missed some of the information she had shared during her presentation. The sister looked at my journal filled with notes, smiled, and said, "You have a writing charism" (pronounced "care-ism").

I didn't know the word "charism" and asked what it meant.

The sister explained that the Holy Spirit gives each person spiritual gifts called charisms and that these gifts can be used only for good. She said there are many different types of charisms, and we are meant to use them to make the world better. She said we feel a deep sense of joy and peace when we use our charisms, and that we use them to serve our neighbors, the world, and God. She said charisms aren't inherited, that they're different from talents, and that, when we are using our charisms, we are energized and filled with purpose.

After our conversation, I began studying the subject of charisms. I am still learning, and I feel like a beginning student as I share these ideas with you.

I have always believed that every single person is called in different ways, has special gifts to offer, and possesses the capacity to make a difference in the world. I like having a word for that calling and these gifts: charisms. When we can discern our gifts, our charisms, we can act with the pure intention of making a difference in people's lives, and I believe extraordinary things will occur because we are not acting alone but with help from the Divine.

I find this collaboration with the Divine Mystery exciting and hopeful. It is true for me that when I align my work with good, doors open and synchronicity happens in ways I could never have foreseen. For me, it feels like stepping into the unknown with faith and good intentions and being met with surprisingly helpful, loving, open arms.

What if we truly are each here for a purpose, as agents to do good in the world? And what if the forces of good in the universe want to help us and work through us? Wouldn't we want to know that? Wouldn't we stop comparing ourselves to others and start searching for clues that reveal our gifts and our assignments? I believe that practicing discernment is the conscious act of seeking our authentic and innate goodness and the best way to share it with the world.

Eryn Huntington and Sherry Anne Weddell write in their book on charisms, "We are peering into the mystery: the revelation of who God has created you to be."[44] It is important that you make time to discover what charisms you've been given. They describe your search "like a metal detector on the beach. It will turn up a lot of small change (which may well add up to part of the treasure you're looking for), some bottle caps and, perhaps, a diamond ring. The difference is that seeking charisms isn't a matter of chance; we know the treasure is there. You do have charisms, which God is infinitely more eager for you to receive and use than you are yourself."[45]

The most important jobs you have in your life are learning to appreciate your own unique beauty and life force, working to identify the gifts or charisms you've been given, and figuring out how you can use them to make the world a little bit better.

Opportunities ~

1) What if you believe for a moment that you have been given gifts that are full of goodness and that you are meant to discover them and use them to help others? How does that feel?

2) Read through the list of charisms. Knowing that you have several charisms, what's one you think you might have? (Hint: Sometimes we don't value things that we do easily, but often this very act that we do with ease and joy is a charism.)

Now fill in the blanks in the following sentences: "One time this week, when I was doing _____, I felt joyful and noticed that what I did helped _____. When I _____, I feel peaceful and other people say I helped a lot." What did someone say or notice?

3) Testing and using our spiritual gifts means getting involved in the world. This requires reaching out and trying new things. What's one group that you're part of or that you'd like to join in which you could try using this particular charism? What are three tiny steps you can take in this direction?

A Partial List of Charisms ~

- Administration: providing the planning and coordination needed to accomplish good things.

- Craftsmanship: making creative work that beautifies and/or orders the physical world.

- Encouragement: nurturing others through words of comfort, encouragement, and counsel.

- Faith: trusting in the love, power, and provision of the Divine and having the freedom to act on this trust.

- Giving: giving with exceptional generosity to those in need.

- Healing: curing illness and restoring health when healing is unlikely to occur quickly or to happen at all.

- Helping: enabling others to serve more effectively.

- Hospitality: warmly welcoming and caring for those in need of food, shelter, and friendship.

- Intercessory prayer: praying for others so that love reaches those in need.

- Knowledge: diligently studying to better understand ourselves, the universe, and the Divine.

- Leadership: sharing a compelling vision of a better future with others and directing the overall efforts of a group as they work together to make the vision a reality.

- Mercy: offering practical deeds of compassion that relieve the distress of those who suffer and helping them experience love.

- Music: writing or performing music for the delight of others and the praise of the Divine.

- Service: recognizing unmet needs and personally doing whatever it takes to solve the problem and meet the need.

- Teaching: enabling others to learn information and skills that help them reach their fullest spiritual and personal potential.

- Writing: using words to create works of truth or beauty that reflect the fullness of human experience and bring glory to the Divine.[46]

DISCERNING HOW YOU LIKE
TO PRAY OR MEDITATE

Dear Reader,

Learning how to discern our gifts or charisms requires taking quiet time—asking, reflecting, waiting, and testing. I like to take prayer breaks throughout the day to check in, breathe, and center myself. There are a million ways to pray. Knowing to pray is far more important than knowing how to pray.

On the day that I saw the artwork in the sanctuary at the Jewish temple, I was attending an interfaith breakfast. There were three scheduled speakers: a Muslim woman, an African American minister from a Pentecostal Church, and a woman Rabbi from the temple where we all had gathered. Each spoke about prayer.

The Muslim woman described praying five times a day and learning to accept that she wasn't supposed to fit prayer and faith into her busy life, but rather to allow her faith and prayer a fullness and fit her busy life around the peace and stillness of her devotion.

The Pentecostal minister said he turned to God for comfort, guidance, and substance. He described accepting that we can have our own plans and then God reveals God's plan for us, which can be quite different from what we imagined. He invited us to listen and look for God's plan being revealed in our lives.

The Rabbi was the final speaker. She said that, thousands of years ago, the rabbis said that it was fine to ask God for things when we prayed; it was even important to petition

God—for health, wealth, happiness, guidance, love—but that one day a week, on the Sabbath, the prayers to God should be prayers of thanksgiving, honoring and celebrating God's love and glory.

I liked hearing how each person worked daily to strengthen their relationship with the Divine through prayer—and I came away inspired to do the same.

Opportunities ~

1) There are so many different ways to pray. Some people pray when they dance, or paint, or cook, or run, or walk in nature. Is there a way of thinking about prayer here that is new to you, which you might consider trying? Remembering that you don't have to "get it right," write a prayer that you would like to say. Or maybe you want to dance your prayer or paint it.

2) Write a prayer asking for something you want, and see yourself getting what you want. Draw or dance what that feels like. Then write a prayer offering thanks for something or someone in your life. Draw or dance what that gratitude feels like.

3) Mindfulness is the study of learning how to watch and guide your thoughts in a way that promotes peace, joy, compassion, and love. Practicing the tea ceremony that we reviewed earlier will help you to notice your feelings and thoughts and to offer all aspects of yourself respect and love. Hold a tea ceremony for yourself, and notice which aspects show up to your table. Can you welcome each part, name it, and offer it a cup of love?

DISCERNING ROMANTIC
FACTS OR FICTIONS

Dear Reader,

As we bring more awareness to our inner thoughts, I want to talk about how we think about romantic love.

Last night I went to see our middle-school musical. As I sat in the audience, delighted by the singing and dancing, I watched younger siblings, particularly little girls, looking up at the stage and longing to be in the fairy tale.

Together we saw a parade of princesses coming and going. There was Princess Fiona, the lead princess, who was accompanied by Snow White, Cinderella, Sleeping Beauty, Rapunzel, and the Little Mermaid. The girls playing these roles were dressed beautifully. In each scene, the princess was waiting to be saved by Prince Charming. They longed, they dreamed, and they waited.

In the middle of the play, the music stopped. Fiona, who was trapped in her tower, took out a plastic phone and called a company that supplies Prince Charmings. The school principal appeared on stage. She was dressed as a telephone operator and answered the call.

"I'd like you to send a Prince Charming to rescue me," Fiona said.

The principal replied, "Prince Charmings are in short supply. I suggest you save yourself."

The audience laughed, and then the play continued.

I watched the girls on stage, the younger ones sitting on the floor, and the parents in the chairs. We were all hoping that

Fiona would be saved and that she would find true love. We all know these fairy tales. Some of my earliest memories are of my mom and me listening to musicals on her record player. I grew up with love songs, and I always wanted to be in love.

But here's where we need to stop the fairy tale that may be playing in our minds. When we are feeling in love, it's important to discern if we are loving the idea of being in love or if we are loving a unique person who has specific dreams, needs, and challenges. When we love someone, who that person is matters. That person gets to be a human being. When we are living in the fairy-tale idea of love, we are not in love with a person, but with the idea of being in love, and we are in danger of ignoring or overlooking who that person really is.

Abigail, age 22 ~ There's a lot of pressure to be hooking up. It's important to be realistic. It's never a perfect situation. No one really has it figured out. It's the most non-committal thing. Women, whether or not they want to admit it, want the emotional connection—there's always that hope that this random hook-up will turn into something more. The worst thing is when women are duped by a guy who is so obviously texting when he's drunk on a weekend. A lot of it has to do with how non-committal a text message is. All of a sudden, the contact ends. No time, no money, and no emotion have been invested, and you interpret it as emotional engagement, and it isn't. They were just texts. Nothing else. Take texting with a grain of salt. He has to show some other form of commitment if you think he likes you.

When you are attracted to someone—which is normal and healthy—notice if you are allowing a fairy tale to grow in your mind before you really know the person. If you think someone is perfect, you are wrong; no one is. If you think someone will save you, you have given away responsibility for your own happiness. You are responsible for your own happiness. Even the most kind and loving Prince or Princess Charming can never rescue you. You can work on your own happiness, and learning how to love someone else can be part of that effort—and that person needs to be working on what it means to love you as well.

Professor Gurit Birnbaum, an associate professor of psychology at the Interdisciplinary Center in Israel, studies "responsiveness" to everyday life in relationships. He and his team of researcher have shown that when both people in a romantic relationship practice "responsiveness" to each other, there are many long-term benefits, including a better sex life.

Professor Gurit Birnbaum ~ Responsiveness creates a deep feeling that someone really knows and understands you.[47]

When someone is responsive, understanding, and thoughtful, they do three things:

- They take time to understand what you are really saying.

- They validate what is important to you—such as your values, goals, and desires.

- They care for and express warmth and affection toward you.[48]

When you are "responsive" to someone else, you are practicing these skills. A relationship doesn't begin with all of these skills working perfectly. Both people need to be committed to learning how to listen, share, and improve.

Real love isn't a fairy tale in our minds—it happens between two people, and it's in the details of how two people treat each other every day. Resist the urge to love the fairy tale, and instead focus on what it means to appreciate the intricate details of who you are, who the other person is, and how you treat each other. Attraction is a moment, but love is a conversation that takes time and effort and includes concern, kindness, and curiosity—on both sides.

Opportunities ~

1) What would you like a Prince or Princess Charming to rescue you from? List three things. What items on the list you can you work on yourself?

2) How can you work on being understanding and thoughtful in your relationships with important people in your life? What are three things you can do? Do you know what the important people in your life value? Do you know what their goals are? Can you ask? How can you express warmth to someone important in your life?

3) Do you ever ignore when someone treats you badly? What do you ignore? Would it be okay with you for you to treat that person the same way? Why or why not? If someone was being understanding and thoughtful toward you, what are three things that person might do or say? If someone was asking about your goals and desires, what would you say? If someone was expressing warmth to you, what would feel good?

DISCERNING YOUR OPTIMAL DEVELOPMENT:
HOW DOES CONSENT WORK?

Dear Reader,

For many people, experiencing intimate love is part of how they imagine living and loving fully. Like most things in life, how we love is something we can study, work at, and improve upon. We can get better at how we offer love and how we receive love. Learning to love well takes practice, reflection, honesty, and communication. Sensual, sexual interactions that go well and feel good start with communication and evolve from a tender and caring place.

If you want to experience love, do not start by checking sex acts off a list. If you get good at checking sex acts off a list, you will not be learning how to love someone or how to let someone love you. If you want to get good at loving, you will need to work on what it means to be loving toward yourself and toward someone else.

When you begin to interact with another person, start by getting curious about who they are and try to see their unique beauty and way in the world. Getting to know someone, truly seeing and appreciating them, requires conversation and shared experiences. When you are working on getting better at love, sensual, sexual interactions can become expressions of a mutually agreed-upon affection, connection, tenderness, and warmth.

As a little girl, when I was first introduced to swimming, I played in a shallow kiddie pool that was a foot deep, and toddlers could get in and out with ease. In the kiddie pool, children splashed about, laughing, playing with toys, and enjoying being in the water. If a child ever got in a situation that was uncomfortable or unsafe, someone was always there to pick up the child: "That's too deep, that's not safe." The child was comforted and eventually returned to the steps to play.

As a mother, I have watched many children learn to swim. The process and experience are different for every child. Some went really slowly, testing and re-testing. Who knows what they were taking in? The sounds. The feelings. New sensations. Before a child moved to the next stage, there was discussion about what the child was willing and ready to try next, and then an agreement was made. When a child was exceedingly comfortable in the kiddie pool, that child could decide it was time to move on to the big pool to experience and learn new things.

I've seen a few swim teachers use a philosophy that didn't work well—tossing a child into the deep end and saying, "Swim!" Understandably, the child was terrified. It was too big a step from where that child was comfortable. The deep end was too big, too deep, and too lonely.

I've seen other swim teachers carefully communicate every step of the way—introducing new skills and experiences at the right time. And the child, feeling comfortable and supported in that environment, was usually ready and eager to proceed to the next step. Swimming the length of the big pool was a huge accomplishment. The first time I swam the entire length of the pool by myself, my mother walked backward in front of me in the pool while I swam toward her. "You're safe. I'm here," she said again and again, and I felt safe and supported the entire way.

The pool had two diving boards—a low dive and a high dive. When we were old enough, when we felt ready, and when the swim teacher agreed, we were allowed to jump off the low diving board. It was a big step—jumping off into the deep end, swimming to the side, and using the ladder to climb out. It required a certain level of physical and emotional development and many skills.

There was another big moment: deciding to jump off the high dive. People were allowed to jump off the high dive only when a lifeguard was on duty. The decision of whether or not someone was ready required the right set of conditions, preparation, and conversation. When we were ready, we would climb the tall ladder, walk down the long diving board, and stand on the edge. High in the sky, looking down on everyone, some kids changed their minds. They decided they weren't ready, and they walked back along the long diving board and climbed down the ladder.

Some jumped, belly-flopped, and got the wind knocked out of them, and usually they went back to the big pool for a while. And then there were the ones who jumped off the high dive and said they experienced incredible feelings they'd never known before. Many said it felt like flying. At the right time, with the right skills, the right people, and the lifeguard on duty, the deep end eventually became a place that was fun to explore.

This is how I want you to think of your emerging sensual, sexual being. You are both a beginning swimmer and your own lifeguard. You get to go at a pace that feels safe and delightful to you. At any point in time—no matter what the circumstances—you can always walk back along the diving board and climb down the ladder. You will have your own timing and your own required conditions. It's important that you always feel safe. No one gets to pressure you. You get to decide.

It's healthy and normal and beautiful to grow as a sensual, sexual being. The process is meant to be delightful and respectful, each step of the way. And you can stay and enjoy whatever pool you're in for as long as you want. There are always big kids in the kiddie pool who love splashing around, kicking inflated beach balls, talking, and laughing. Some kids don't feel like swimming at all, and they enjoy sitting in the sun and playing land games.

As both an emerging sensual, sexual being and your own personal lifeguard, you get to take into account a variety of factors as you decide and defend what you're comfortable doing and what you aren't. You get to discern your own sense of the right timing, the right person, and the right conditions. And you can stand by your decision no matter what anyone else says or does, every single time.

I'd like to offer you a caution: If you are being overly generous in a sexual interaction in order to get love, be aware. Stop, notice, and be honest with yourself—using any sexual act to get attention is a recipe for feeling used and being treated badly. If you are hoping to exchange a sexual act for being loved later, it doesn't work. When I was at the pool as a young girl, some swimmers would do crazy, dangerous dives off the high dive—but they only did this when there were onlookers and the lifeguard wasn't watching. They wanted attention for taking risks, and they got it. The trouble with their strategy was they would do more crazy, dangerous dives to keep getting attention, and some eventually got hurt.

It's better to avoid using any sexual interaction to try to get something. Sensual, sexual encounters feel much better when they are mutually agreed-upon expressions of affection.

We all want to be loved and seen. Genuine affection from another person takes time and effort to develop. If you want love, learn how to listen and how to share. See yourself as an architect who carefully builds respectful and caring connections with the people in your life. Love requires work.

Rather than hoping that a sexual interaction will develop into a relationship that is kind and communicative, start by developing two-way communication and two-way respect. When sensual, sexual interactions do begin, the goal is for both people to communicate and listen, to be kind and respectful. Your wanting and asking for two-way sensual, sexual pleasure is healthy and important. Your sensual, sexual being is supposed to experience tender goodness and tingling delight. It is supposed to be playful and fun and feel good. In every interaction, you matter, all of you. Building connection with another person can be a wonderful experience. But it takes time and requires talking.

How does consent work?

from www.loveisrespect.org

Consent is about communicating. Some people are worried that talking about consent will be awkward or that it will ruin the mood, which is far from true. If anything, the mood is much more positive when both partners are happy and can freely communicate what they want. First off, talk about what terms like "hooking up" or "going all the way" mean to each partner.

Consider having these conversations during a time when you're not being physically intimate. If you are in the heat of the moment, here are some suggestions of things to say:

- "Are you comfortable?"
- "Is this okay?"
- "Do you want to slow down?"
- "Do you want to go any further?"

In a healthy relationship, it's important to discuss and respect each other's boundaries consistently. It's not okay to assume that once someone consents to an activity, it means they are consenting to it anytime in the future as well. Whether it's the first time or the hundredth time, a hookup, a committed relationship, or even a marriage, nobody is ever obligated to give consent just because they have done so in the past. A person can decide to stop an activity at any time, even if they agreed to it earlier. Above all, everyone has a right to their own body and to feel comfortable with how they use it— no matter what has happened in the past.[49]

Elisa Pinto de Magalhaes, Studied Bro Culture, age 22 ~

Women aren't asking enough of men. A woman needs to say to a man, "This is what I need from you." Then the men will grow into themselves and become better. It happens when women ask it of them. The parties aren't what's important at the end of the day, and those people who were at the parties are not who I am in touch with now that I've graduated. I'm not wasting my time going to things that aren't important to me. Realizing that has opened up so many doors. I have so much more time because I'm not trying to work around someone else's schedule who doesn't care about mine.

There is a power element to time. Taking back time is taking back power. You need time to be with yourself and create yourself. Whatever it is that makes your clock tick—running or reading—it probably isn't doing keg stands with a bunch of guys in a basement. It's not valued socially, but it takes time to find the voice within.

We are living in a man's world, and we are trying to make ourselves into men. We're losing our power. It's time for a time-out—to find alternatives. What we value is important, but we need to know what that is.

Opportunities ~

1) Imagine yourself as an emotional being, a mental being, a spiritual being, and an emerging sensual, sexual being. Can you see these aspects as part of your whole being? When we see ourselves as a whole being, it can change how we see our sensual, sexual being interacting in the world. What needs do you have as a whole being before you interact with someone in a sensual, sexual way? What do you want to know first? What would you like someone to know about you?

2) The difference between swimming lessons and having sensual, sexual experiences with another person is that you are interacting with another human being. Unfortunately, many people measure sexual interactions as individual actions. This way of seeing a sensual, sexual interaction isn't accurate because it means treating the other person as an object. When two people are involved, two people matter.

Before engaging with someone in a sensual, sexual way, it's helpful to take time and think about what you value. What do you care about? How do you want to be treated? What activities do you enjoy doing?

When you start engaging with someone in a sensual, sexual way, talking about how the interaction is going for both people is the priority. Practicing check-ins with yourself can help you talk with a partner. Internally, ask yourself: "Is this okay with me? Do I feel safe and supported? Am I enjoying myself? Does this interaction feel respectful? What would feel better? How do I want to feel tomorrow about what happens today? What am I willing to do and say now to help me feel good later?"

You can ask your partner these questions: "Is this okay with you? What feels good for you?"

When talking about what you like or don't like, you can say: "That doesn't feel good, I'd rather you _____. I'm not comfortable doing _____, I would rather _____. Someday I might like to try _____, but right now I like _____."

Hannah Gribetz, Sexual Assault Peer Educator, age 22 ~

If you know beforehand that you're not comfortable doing a certain thing with someone until you know and trust them really well, or until you've done other things with them, it's a lot easier to express that to the person in the moment.

Example 1: "Kissing you is really fun, but I'd like to go on a date with you before we go any further. Are you free for coffee this weekend?"

Example 2: "Can I take your bra off?" "No, but I'd love you to kiss my neck."

Write out three phrases you can see yourself saying and practice saying them out loud. You can role-play with a friend as well.

3) Some people use sexual interactions to feel loved. Using sexual interactions to get love doesn't usually work out. If feeling loved is your need—and it's a basic need we all have—a better strategy is to build emotional connections and shared experiences first and then allow sensual, sexual interactions to become an expression of that connection. This creates a foundation for intimacy. Touch feels best when it is wanted, tender, and affectionate, and when it goes both ways.

What are some things you can do to build intimacy with another person that do not involve a sexual activity? What are some sensual things you can do with another person? Can you ask yourself not to use sexual interactions to try to get love? Can you allow yourself baby steps and frequent check-ins with yourself and your partner as you develop as a sensual, sexual being? Can you delay sensual, sexual interactions with another person until they become agreed-upon expressions of affection and you are both capable of supporting each other emotionally?

What conditions would you like to have that would make you feel supported emotionally when you begin exploring a sensual, sexual relationship with someone? Is the person you are with mature enough to handle these emotional responsibilities?

DISCERNING THE NOBLE MALE
AND THE CONQUEST MALE

Dear Reader,

Within nature, animals use a variety of courtship rituals to select a mate. The male bowerbird decorates his nest with blue objects to attract a female, using bottle caps, yarn, flowers, or berries, and the female bowerbird visits his nest to determine if it is tidy and how well he can perform a certain buzz-wing-flip.[50]

Within some species, male-and-female pairs partner for life. Outside my home, the same two geese return every year to build a nest, guard their eggs, and raise their goslings. With seahorses, the male and female dance together, twirling and swirling about. Eventually, the female deposits her eggs in the male's pouch, and he carries the eggs until they are released as tiny seahorses. In some species, males have sex with as many females as possible and the females raise the young on their own.

If we look at humans in biological terms, we know that the roles of males and females in reproduction are quite different. Because the female human is the one who gets pregnant, her investment of time and body is significantly greater than the investment of the male human. This means that it benefits the female to be choosey in selecting a mate, so that she can find someone who will help care for the offspring.

I want to explore two types of male dating behavior. This is important to understand even if you are not interested in dating males, because one type of male is more

2) Look within yourself and notice your own intentions when interacting with someone. Are you using someone to feel better about yourself? Are you seeing the other person as a unique and beautiful being? How are you treating yourself? What does being in balance look like for you?

3) There's an old saying, "Where attention goes, energy flows." Notice who gets attention in our culture, our movies, our schools, our workplaces—the Conquest Male or the Noble Male? What can you do to offer more attention to Noble Males? When you look for them, who do you see? (Hint: They usually aren't overly puffed up.) What do they do? What do they say? What do you admire?

likely to be a sexual predator toward both women and men. If you are romantically interested in males, identifying different types of male dating behavior can help you make informed dating choices.

One strategy for a male human to ensure that his genes survive is to have as many female partners as possible. This reproduction strategy focuses on quantity. Another male human reproduction strategy seeks long-term connection with his partner and participates in assuring the survival of his offspring. This reproduction strategy focuses on quality. The latter type of male seeks fewer offspring and invests more energy in each one. In reproductive terms, a male who has sex and leaves is not as valuable to the female as a male who stays to help with the offspring.

For most species, there is usually one way in which the male behaves—either he helps in caring for the offspring or he doesn't. What's interesting about humans is that we have a variety of mating models for how males treat females. Some males seek quality—I will call them Noble Males. Some males seek quantity—I will call them Conquest Males.

Noble Males seek connection with their potential mates. They invest in their relationships and are interested in long-term commitments. A Noble Male recognizes the otherness in a partner and will postpone sexual gratification in order to preserve the relationship. One research study reported in heterosexual interactions, male college students who were told "no" or "not now" to their sexual advances *and* who respected this refusal were more likely to be interested in a long-term relationship. In the same study, males who ignored a "no" or a "not now" and who continued to pressure the female for sex were not interested in a long-term commitment.[51] The Noble Male will prioritize respect and affection over his own sexual desires.

Conquest Males use sex to increase their feelings of power and dominance. They see sex as a form of scoring and measure themselves by their sexual conquests. They treat females as objects, not as unique individuals. They often puff themselves up and put others down, especially girls and women. In their tactics, they rarely use direct weapons, but instead use flattery, charm, pressure, alcohol, and trickery to accomplish their goals.[52] Sometimes a Conquest Male may pretend to be a Noble Male in order to trick a female into trusting him.

Not all Conquest Males are sexual predators—they may get consent from their partners, but their intention is to use sex as a form of personal gratification or as a bragging right among like-minded peers, not as an expression of affection.[53] Although Conquest Males often seem arrogant, it's possible that many feel inadequate or inferior and are seeking a sense of belonging among other Conquest Males. Either way, they are focusing on meeting their own needs and are using females to accomplish this. For them, sex is a game, one that's about trying to increase one's perceived power in order to reduce feeling inadequate.[54]

What I think is terrifying about our culture right now is that we have elevated the value of impersonal, conquest sex, and many males and females are copying this behavior in how they interact sexually. We now have Conquest Males and Conquest Females, in which sexual acts revolve around individual power and gratification. This leaves many people—both female and male—feeling confused, used, hurt, and lonely.

Stephanie Seibel, Counselor, age 25 ~

I think a lot of women compensate by shutting emotions and by becoming hyper-masculine. We sl nurturing side of ourselves. We turn off our empathy not safe to feel. As women enter the work force, we the driver, and now we want to be the provider. I do the answer is women only becoming stronger. In o genders to be in balance, society as a whole needs more compassionate and in touch with empathy.

Of course we need to protect ourselves to de immediate situation, but if we want to create a fu where we don't have this problem, we're going to n compassion. You can't fight fire with fire.

It's important to respect both sides: the mascul feminine. Both come at a cost if there's too much of I've spent time in both, and I feel it in my body when balance. It doesn't feel good. We need to come in, and stop caring what others think of us, and take care of value when I can be in the middle and hold both the and the feminine because that is where I can be my b eternally searching for balance in my life. We're out Let's bring it back.

Opportunities ~

1) Notice different forms of courtship—at movies, in videos. What do you see? Can noticing when someone is being a Conques a Conquest Female? What words do you he behaviors do you see?

IDENTIFYING SEXUAL PREDATORS' TRAITS, TACTICS, AND TRICKS

Dear Reader,

I want to focus specifically on how to identify Conquest Males who become sexual predators. As I said earlier, not all Conquest Males are sexual predators, but they are more likely to become sexual predators. Noble Males will always respect your boundaries—they care about being honorable in their relationships and are capable of empathy and of seeing you as a person.[55] Conquest Males who have become sexual predators will not respect boundaries—they value dominance in their relationships. You can learn how to pay careful attention to behavior cues to understand if someone's intentions focus on mutual respect or sexual conquest.

Andre Salvage, Self-Defense and Assertiveness Instructor ~ It is not who they are, but what they do that makes someone safe or unsafe.

You can use discernment to identify who are potential predators and what their behavior often looks like leading up to a sexually abusive act. The sooner you identify predatory behavior, the sooner you can take action to protect yourself or help a friend and cut off the possibility of violence.

I am going to share with you many statistics. I want you to understand these percentages to help you identify predatory behavior and risky situations. When I read research studies and statistics on sexual assault, it is deeply disturbing to me, and I always take breaks and walk. I am aware that behind every single number is a person. One sexual assault is too many. As you read through these statistics, I'd like you to understand that there are people behind the numbers.

Who are sexual predators? You can't tell by looking at them. They blend in. They look like people you know because, for the most part, they are. According to the most recent research studies, 11-14% of males on college campuses report committing some form of sexual assault during their college years.[56]

Some sexual predators commit multiple attacks. In one study, the average number of victims for each rapist was seven, and in another study it was 11.[57] College men who have hostile beliefs about women and peers who encouraged sexual conquest were most likely to report committing multiple acts of sexual coercion during college.[58]

Until we find a way to change sexual predators' behavior, the threat they pose to you and your girlfriends is real. Being aware of sexual predators' traits, tactics, tricks, targets, and tests can help you identify who they are and things you can do to protect yourself.

Here are some things we know:

• **Traits**: Many predators speak badly about girls and women, have an exaggerated sense of masculinity, and lack empathy. Many know their target in some capacity and assault girls between the ages of 14 and 24 more than any other age range.[59]

• **Tactics**: Most predators use subtle forms of coercion and manipulation (not direct weapons): pushing alcohol, ignoring verbal and non-verbal refusals, and trying to get their target alone.[60] About four out of 10 sexual assaults take place at the victim's own home, and two in 10 take place in the home of a friend, neighbor, or relative.[61] Many predators use alcohol to increase their ability to assault someone: The vast majority of incapacitated sexual-assault victims (89%) reported drinking alcohol and being drunk (82%) before their victimization.[62]

• **Tricks**: Most predators start an assault with a kiss and may use flattery, gifts, and promises of love to gain someone's trust.[63] Some predators wait until date four or five to attack. Some wait years. In nearly half (47%) of the cases involving an internet-initiated sex crime, the predator offered gifts or money during the relationship-building phase.[64]

• **Targets**: In America, over 500,000 women are subjected to sexual assault per year.[65] **Females age 16-19 are four times more likely than the general population to be victims of rape, attempted rape, or sexual assault.**[66] If you are a girl between the ages of 14 and 24, you are in a sexual predator's most targeted age range.

In a study conducted by the Department of Justice and the Centers for Disease Control and Prevention, researchers interviewed 8,000 women and 8,000 men. Using a definition of rape that included forced vaginal, oral, and anal intercourse, the survey found that **one in six women** had experienced an attempted rape or a completed rape. At the time they were raped, 22% were under the age of 12; 54% were under the age of 18; and 83% were under the age of 25.[67]

Approximately one in five female high school students report being physically and/or sexually abused by a partner.[68] The most common first encounter with predators in internet-initiated sex crimes is in online chat rooms (76%).[69]

- **Tests**: Sexually aggressive men may use domination as a test to identify vulnerable targets, especially early in a relationship. A woman who resists domination may be seen as unavailable, but a subordinate response may indicate that she is a potential target.[70]

We want to reduce the number of sexual assaults that happen, and you can help. Some sexual predators are strangers, but the harsh reality is that most sexual predators are people we know. They can be family members or close friends. If you are in a room with 100 males, there could be 11-13 sexual predators in that room. "90% of campus sexual assaults are committed by perpetrators that the survivor knows. Most victims knew the person who sexually victimized them. For both completed and attempted rapes, about 9 in 10 offenders were known to the victim. Most often, a boyfriend, ex-boyfriend, classmate, friend, acquaintance, or coworker sexually victimized the women."[71]

Since we know that every sexual assault can have significant mental, emotional, and physical impact, it is imperative that you do everything you can to reduce the likelihood of an attack happening to you or someone you know. It's best to learn how to identify predatory behavior both in people you don't know and in people you do know—a boyfriend, an ex-boyfriend, a classmate, a teacher, a cousin, a friend's older brother, an uncle, a step-father, a coach, a relative.

The good news is that many of their traits, tactics, and tricks are known, so you can learn to look for predatory behavior early in an interaction. Because you can't tell what a predator looks like, it's important to be curious about what predators do, so that you can recognize dangerous behavior and exit early. And you can help your friends do the same.

The first step is to memorize **The Three T's:**

1) **Traits**: Puffed up and hyper-masculine; uses language that puts down girls and women, often through jokes; doesn't believe that "No" means no. Lacks empathy. Associates with similar peers.[72]

2) **Tactics**: Uses alcohol; pretends to ignore verbal and non-verbal refusals; tries to get target alone. May use pressure, guilt, joking put-downs and challenges, flattery, and charm.[73] Tests boundaries and ignores any signs of disinterest. Often starts with a kiss and then turns aggressive, overriding any denial or dissent; hears "No" and chooses to ignore it.

3) **Tricks**: Often uses flirting, gifts (dinner, drinks), and promises of love to increase dependency and trust. May pretend to be hurt or in need of help. May use guilt to try to get you to do things sexually that you don't want to do.

Remember that sexual predators are seeking conquest and dominance, not affection and connection, and they can get a sense of power by overriding or ignoring your "No." This is sick, and it shows you how pathetic they really are. You do not want to interact with someone who is seeking to dominate you physically, intellectually, or emotionally. They rely on putting you down to put themselves up. Remember, you are worthy of respect. Always.

Here is a device you can use to remember common predator tactics: A "Take This, Pig!" resistance strategy.

PIG BEHAVIOR:	TAKE THIS, PIG!
Pushing drinks.	Part ways immediately.
Ignoring my no (verbal or non-verbal).	I will fight to get free. Going to use my voice
Getting me alone.	and my body.

An important part of keeping yourself safe is to practice overriding hesitant feelings—such as feeling awkward, unsure, or embarrassed—and fighting for your right to be safe. It is important for girls and women, whether they have already experienced sexual violence or not, to learn how to identify predators' traits, tactics, and tricks, and how to act early. Any unwanted touch is an assault, and you can use your voice—even if you were previously dismissed or ignored—to stop violence. You get to say how you do and don't want to be touched, every single time you interact with another human being.

Red flags that indicate your partner doesn't respect consent:

from www.loveisrespect.org

- They pressure or guilt you into doing things you may not want to do.
- They make you feel like you "owe" them—because you're dating, or they gave you a gift, etc.
- They react negatively (with sadness, anger, or resentment) if you say "no" to something, or don't immediately consent.
- They ignore your wishes and don't pay attention to nonverbal cues that could show you're not consenting (ex: pulling/pushing away).[74]

Opportunities ~

1) Memorize The Three T's and the two types of PIGs. Write them down. Share them with your friends.

2) Review the fact that a kiss is not just a kiss and that most sexual assaults start with a kiss. If you don't want anything to happen, don't allow the kiss. Cut it off. If you only want to kiss, stop anything after a kiss.[75] With a friend, role-play and practice saying "No" and expressing what you do want: e.g., "Just stop. I want you to leave now." Or practice using an excuse to get out of an uncomfortable situation: e.g., "Listen, I just remembered, I need to go check on my friend. I'm really worried about her. I need to go now."

Anne, age 25 ~ *I thought through what I wanted to say because I didn't want to be wishy-washy, and I wanted to be clear. I said what I didn't want, and then I found it helpful when I said, "This is the last time we're meeting." After that, when this person contacted me, I didn't feel as if I had to respond in any way. I set a really clear boundary, and I was done.*

3) Notice when someone says "No" and someone else ignores the no and continues to pressure the person. What words are spoken? What words are ignored? What body language do you notice? Notice when someone sets a boundary and defends it. What do they do with their words and their body? If you are ever in a situation in which you're uncertain whether or not you've said no clearly enough, stop questioning yourself and make an

exit plan—predators will ignore your no; they want you to question yourself.

I read about one survivor who was fighting a date who was trying to force her to have sex, and she said, "This is rape"—and he stopped. Most predators do not think of themselves as rapists, even though they will admit to behavior that is legally defined as rape. Many deny reality and project blame onto someone else.

Definitions of Rape and Sexual Assault

Although the legal definition of rape varies from state to state, rape is generally defined as forced or nonconsensual sexual intercourse... Sexual assault is a broader term than rape. It includes various types of unwanted sexual touching or penetration without consent, such as forced sodomy (anal intercourse), forced oral copulation (oral-genital contact), rape by a foreign object (including a finger), and sexual battery (the unwanted touching of an intimate part of another person).

The term "drug-facilitated sexual assault" is generally used to define situations in which victims are subjected to nonconsensual sexual acts while they are incapacitated or unconscious due to the effects of alcohol and/or other drugs, and are, therefore, prevented from resisting and/or are unable to give consent.[76]

DISCERNING WHEN TO ACT TO
PROTECT YOURSELF OR A FRIEND

Dear Reader,

I want to introduce the idea of discerning when to act. When we respond early, it's more likely that we can prevent something awful from happening. If you see someone in a situation that could become dangerous, don't assume that someone else will help. Keep yourself safe and take action, or call for help.

I've heard it called The Half-Second Pause. When you see something or feel something that isn't quite right, instead of looking away, or ignoring the feeling, take The Half-Second Pause. This pause lets you check your gut—are things okay? If not, what actions can you take that could prevent harm from occurring?

The Half-Second Pause is intended to be a wake-up moment. Sometimes it's acknowledging the sick feeling in your gut and deciding to redirect your actions. Other times it feels like getting a bucket of ice water dumped on your head and you see a situation differently and can take action according to what you now see. The Half-Second Pause can prevent you from doing something you regret later. It lets you check how someone else is treating you or a friend and decide if it is okay. It can help you intervene on a friend's behalf. It can even save your life.

The Half-Second Pause asks you to stop, breathe, listen to yourself, and assess: Given the current set of variables, what is most likely to happen next? Is this what you want?

Is this in alignment with your dreams, values, and goals? Is this something that honors the beautiful being that you are?

I would like to share with you two interviews in which one friend intervenes to help another friend:

Sophie, age 22 ~

It's important to identify when something goes beyond being in your best interest and becomes harmful. People struggle with defining this. I was good at knowing—I'm going to get sick, or I need to go home, or I'm too tired. I'm naturally a very sensitive person. I'm an athlete, and I'm in touch with my body and with whether or not something feels good. It's usually at night, and you're usually intoxicated. I want to say I was lucky, but it's more than that. One of my friends was really in trouble, and I knew we needed to go. I felt it in my gut. I told her, "We need to leave now." And we did. Thankfully, we were okay.

James, age 22 ~

My junior year, I was at a football tailgate during the day. Everyone was having a good time partying. There was a huge group of people. It was a giant mob scene. At one point, this big guy from my dorm pushed me up against a van and was saying, "Kiss me. Kiss me." I was confused and not really totally there. I was pinned between this guy and the van. He was getting in my face, and he was tapping his cheek and telling me to kiss him.

I remember I was turning my face away and saying, "No, no, no, thank you." I'd had a lot to drink and don't remember all of it. I remember being surprised and wondering, "What is this guy trying to do right now?"

"Kiss me, kiss me!" he kept saying. He was getting really close to me, and I was looking from side to side, trying to avoid kissing him. Our faces were too close.

He was gigantic. He was about my height but weighed about a thousand pounds. He was a heavy, heavy guy. I assume he was drunk, but I don't know for sure. I knew him by sight. I didn't know his name. I'd never talked to the guy. It was a situation that definitely was not okay, that girls probably have to deal with all the time. And it's something that would make anyone feel really uncomfortable. It was a bizarre situation. It was definitely an assault-type situation.

This girl, who was my friend and also from my dorm, grabbed my arm and pried me out from between the van and the guy. She knew from being friends with me and from the expression on my face that I was uncomfortable, and she was there at the right time. She said, "Why don't you come over here with me," and I remember feeling grateful to my friend for getting me away from him.

What happened is a testament to having friends who have your back and following a buddy system. Watch out for your friends, and they'll watch out for you. That can help prevent you from getting into trouble through no fault of your own.

One in five women and one in 16 men are sexually assaulted while in college.[77]

Opportunities ~

1) In the first interview, what did the interviewee trust and how did that make a difference? How did she listen to herself? To her body? How did this listening help?

2) In the second interview, what signs did the friend notice that let her know it was important to intervene? What did she do?

3) Practice taking The Half-Second Pause throughout your day to check in with yourself and with what people are doing around you. The Half-Second Pause can help you avoid dangerous situations, recall your own dreams and goals, and make an exit plan. If you were in a situation in which someone was pressuring you, what are three things you would do to get yourself free? How could you help a friend?

USING DISCERNMENT WHEN
SELECTING YOUR FRIENDS

Dear Reader,

Many animals stay together to improve their odds of staying safe from predators: fish, birds, horses, dolphins. An alert group can work together to increase each individual's advantage over a single predator.

Statistically, the first two years away from home are the most vulnerable time for young women, and the first few months of college are the most dangerous. Many of my interviewees said that they were cautious until they found a supportive group. One woman described "friend searching" and said it wasn't until sophomore year in college that she knew she had friends she could trust.

Many people said they formed small groups who went out together, developed hand signs to signal discomfort, set drinking limits with each other, and returned home together.

I'd like to share with you five interviews that concern friendship. Some actively watched out for each other, and some did not.

Alyssa, age 23 ~

On game days, we'd get up early. We were so excited. We'd tailgate and start at a pre-party at someone's house. It was easy to have too much to drink by 2:00 pm and be too far gone at such an early time in the day. When a girlfriend has your back, instead of leaving you to go to the game she says, "Let's not go into the game. Let's walk downtown and get food. Let's get some water."

In a school full of football fanatics, you want that friend, the friend who is willing to miss out in order to take care of you, who will say, "Hey, let's not go." I feel great being in their care, friends like that. You don't want the friend who says, "Oh, she's had too much to drink, let's just leave her at the apartment. We have to get to the game or the party."

I remember, during football season, I was with a girl friend of mine. We'd skipped out on the game. We didn't want to be in the hot stadium, and we'd gone downtown to watch the game in a bar. It was midday. We were walking along and saw a girl who was by herself on the curb. She was clearly out of it. We didn't know who she was or her name. My friend went over to her and said, "Are you okay? Are you with anybody?" It was one of those situations where the girl was alone and out of it. My friend found the girl's phone and called some of her friends and got her help. You want to find friends who will stay with you. And you want to be that kind of friend.

Catherine, age 22 ~

I was in LA with friends from high school who I hadn't seen in years. They said, "We're in LA celebrating a friend's birthday, you should come hang out." We had clearly gone in different paths in college, but I didn't know that. We went to dinner, and everything was normal. They said, "Oh there's a club we want to go to." My friend had a friend from school there who I didn't know beforehand. She was from Ohio, had never been in California before. They said, "Oh, we're going to see if we can get coke." That seemed pretty sketchy to me.

And then, all of a sudden, I noticed that everyone was there except for the girl from Ohio. I said, "Hey, does any one know where she is?" Nobody was concerned at all. I didn't even know this girl, and I was the only one who concerned for her safety. I was like, "What? Seriously. Does anyone know where she is?" I started looking for her. I wouldn't stop asking. Then finally someone said, "She's fine. She met some guys, and they went somewhere." I was like, "What!" I got her phone number from my friend, and I was calling her, and she wasn't picking up, and I was thinking, "Oh my God, we're in the middle of some crazy horror movie where the friends lose the friend and something terrible is happening to her. She's never been to California before."

It turned out she got into a car with two strange men who said they had coke at their home. She didn't know LA. She was drunk and got in the car, and the friends, who were her friends from college, let her get in the car, and I was the only one who was worried about her. She finally answered, and she was like, "Chill out. I'm doing my thing," and I said, "You should come back. This is definitely not safe." She came back, and she was okay. She said, "We did coke at the house, and the guy tried to make a move on me, and I was like, 'Take me back,' and he did." In the end she was okay.

This experience showed me that I was so lucky to have made the friends I did in college, who have the same moral guidelines that I have. We knew what kinds of friends we wanted. We didn't want to just be cool, and we always took care of each other.

I also saw that this was the type of thing that must go on in other places too. Watching the situation unravel seemed like a common thing for the girls I was with in LA. This gave me a glimpse into that party culture, and I understood why bad things could happen so quickly. I was horrified by the idea that nobody cared about that girl's safety and well-being. The party was going to continue, and everybody was going to have fun at the party, regardless of what was happening to this girl.

This wasn't something that happened by accident. More than one person said, "It's fine for you to go in this car." There is some disconnect between what these girls deemed was safe and okay to do for fun and what is actually safe and okay to do for fun. I had never seen anything like this before.

They were supposedly really good friends. I was so concerned, and I had just met her six hours beforehand. I was the only one who was worried about her, and I was the only one who noticed that she was gone. Two people watched her leave, but no one said anything.

When she got back, I asked her, "Why did you do that?" and she said, "They told me they had more coke at their place, and they seemed like nice guys." The only possibilities I could wrap my head around were that maybe she was already an addict and that's what addicts do—they forego their own safety to get the next high—or that she had never been taught not to trust everybody. This is when all the alarm bells should be going off. You're in a strange place. It's late at night. Nobody knows where you are. These are two strangers who nobody you're with knows anything about, and they're promising you free drugs from their home. This is where all of the alarm bells should be going off, and yet zero alarm bells were going off. I aged 15 years that night.

Madison, age 21 ~

A guy came up to me, bought me a drink. I wasn't even drunk, and then all I remember was that one drink. I blacked out, and I couldn't remember the rest of the night.

My friend said to me, "You got roofied last night. That guy totally roofied you."

I said, "I know, I can't remember anything. Thank God I didn't leave with him."

My friend took me home. I'm always with friends. My friends really care about me. They're always with me.

Ali, age 22 ~

My college partying experience was limited to a group of one hundred to two hundred people. Ninety-nine percent of my party experience was in a social network of people where we all knew each other. It was a tight-knit group of people who loved music, art, and poetry. When it's a tight-knit group, you don't run the risk of being taken advantage of because you know everyone there. There were a few incidents where guys were creepy, and they got their asses kicked by guys who are our friends. We always have sober, imposing men making sure nothing bad happens.

Abigail, age 22 ~

It also really helps to have male friends. Male friends are important for safety. I really respect opinions about guys from my male friends. They know what guys are good and what ones aren't. Girlfriends want to endorse the guy you're into. They want to see the romance happen because it's more fun. But my guy friends are honest with me.

Mikayla, age 22 ~

When I was in high school, I was on a soccer team with girls who were two years older, and I really looked up to them. They seemed so much more mature than I was. They were miles ahead of me. During fall break and Christmas break, the older girls would come back from college to see a game and hang out with us. I remember some advice I got from them.

They said that you have to find friends who are on your same wavelength about going out. Find someone who hopefully lives in your dorm, and if you're the kind of person who likes to go out until midnight, find some people who like to leave at midnight too. If you're someone who wants to be the last person at the party, find someone else who wants to go out for that many hours. And the friends who you're planning on going to the party with are the same ones you're planning on leaving with. You have that understanding with them throughout the night. You're a unit. You might do your own thing there, but you're going to stay aware of where the other people go—are they talking to some guy in the corner? Check in. Are they all right? And when you're leaving, you're leaving with the girls you came with.

This can be difficult because, when you go to college, you don't know anybody. It can be hard because immediately, when you get there, you're excited, you want to go out, and it can be tough to find friends where you can have a default plan with, that you're going to keep track of each other.

I think a lot of people are tempted to go to parties especially in the first quarter of school, when they don't know people as well. But because they don't know people, it can be a little awkward, and they tend to drink a little more. And they came with no plan of how they're going to get home, and I think that can sometimes lead to a dangerous situation.

Here are three things that I was told by the older girls on my soccer team and that I tried to stick by immediately:

- *Make your own drinks.*
- *Avoid the communal punch bowl.*
- *Have a plan to go home with the same people you went to the party with.*

I was lucky enough to find a handful of friends, and we could walk all the way across campus, do our own thing at the party, and then check in with each other before we left together.

Opportunities ~

1) It is important to remember that a predator is always responsible for his or her violent behavior, but we can still take actions to reduce our risk. What are some strategies that these young women use to reduce their risk?

2) What are some strategies in these stories you can use in your life now? What strategies can you see yourself using later? Make a list of safety strategies and talk about them with a friend. When you go out with friends, can you use a buddy system? Can you create a hand signal to show when one of you needs help?

3) What are some examples of friends not taking care of friends? Part of discernment is choosing friends who will watch out for you. Do you take care of your friends? Do they take care of you? Do you take action when alarm bells go off? What have you done?

Warning Signs

If someone seems drunk and she hasn't been drinking, or she's acting like the effects of drinking alcohol are stronger than usual, get help right away. This is true for you as well.

Predators will often use drugs to help them sexually assault someone. The most common drug they use is alcohol. Between 50-85% of sexual assaults on campuses include alcohol use by the victim, the predator, or both.

Five percent of sexual assaults include roofies. The most common roofies are Rohypnol, GHB, and Ketamine. These drugs are powerful and can be slipped into someone's drink and cause a variety of symptoms such as a drunk feeling, muscle relaxation, problems talking, inability to remember, passing out, confusion, dizziness, and nausea.[78]

Boundaries

Jessica Chapman-Segal,
Reproductive Health Educator, age 25 ~

There needs to be some sort of workshop for girls to help them feel empowered about who they are and be clear about what they want. If some person, woman or man, approaches you, and you don't want to talk to them—whatever it is—you're not interested in a sex way—women should feel empowered to not be sweet and say "No."

SETTING BOUNDARIES WITHIN
YOUR OWN MIND

Dear Reader,

I have learned that maintaining strong, clear boundaries increases my happiness. This is why I created a Do No Harm policy for my external world and my internal world. It may sound unusual, but I apply this policy to myself as well. The first place where I practice setting boundaries is within my own mind. I have learned that I am capable of building stories in my mind that increase my worry, criticism, and self-doubt. I have come to understand that retelling these harmful stories within my mind is a form of attack on myself. Any attack causes harm.

When I was studying the brain, a teacher explained the nature of thoughts in biological language: A thought is a set of neurons that fire together. The more we add onto a thought, the more the thought builds pathways in our brain. Based on these ideas, I developed a way of understanding how my mind works. The first thought that arises is like a locomotive shooting through my mind. Who knows what triggered it? The answer is often complex or unknowable. I learned that I cannot control the first train-car that arrives on the scene, but I get to choose if I attach second and third train-cars (thoughts) to it. When I notice thoughts that arise from fear or shame, I can choose not to add on to them, and this decision stops an attack on myself.

My sons used to play with tiny wooden train-cars that connected magnetically. They would create long trains by linking train-car to train-car. I now see my thoughts as small train-cars that I string together. My mind can develop elaborate worries quickly. What I've learned to do is stop and notice when I'm adding train-cars onto troubling or harmful thoughts. When I see I am doing this, I pause, breathe, and stop creating more train-cars. I stop the train of negative thinking.

Ruth, my therapist, was the first person who encouraged me to study mindfulness, and I started downloading lectures on how to meditate. Instead of building long trains and adding onto painful stories, I learned how to watch my thoughts. I listened to meditations that invited me to see my thoughts as puffy clouds in the sky that floated across my mind. This image made me laugh, and the person's calm voice usually irritated me, but it did eventually help.

This noticing is a boundary. I learned that I don't have to be my thoughts. When I take a half-second to breathe, I can stop building trains that make me more anxious or self-critical. Years later, I began offering each thought and feeling loving kindness, the cup of tea. I now stop, breathe, and practice treating myself with kindness instead. A half-second can change your life. It is changing mine.

Lisa, age 18 ～

I had to reframe the idea of college in my mind. I struggle with anxiety, and uncertainty is a huge thing for me. I was uncertain about clubs, friends, and classes. And then I reframed it from a world of uncertainty into a world of adventure and possibility. In an adventure, the outcome is uncertain; otherwise it wouldn't be an adventure.

When I thought of college as an adventure, I changed my mindset from "I can't do it" to "This is hard, and I can do it." I changed my mindset from "I'm awkward" to "This is an awkward situation." It helped me not to put blame on myself for being awkward and instead place the blame on the situation. By doing that, I was able to relieve a lot of stress, and it made it not about me, and I was able to get through the situation.

Opportunities ~

1) When I have a lot of thoughts in my head, I write each one on a piece of paper and draw circles around all of them. Something about drawing a circle around a worry helps to contain it. If you have troubling thoughts, write them down and draw circles around them.

2) If something keeps reappearing, I draw a big hand in the center of the page, and then I write down the recurring thought in the middle of the hand. I imagine that the hand belongs to a kind and loving Great Spirit who holds my worry for me. Whenever the troubling thought reappears, I remind myself that it is in Great Spirit's hand. Is there something bothering you deeply? Can you name it, draw a hand, and put it in the palm of that hand?

3) Sometimes I draw train-cars and show myself how I am linking negative thoughts together. I identify the first train-car that arose and show myself where I can stop sooner when a similar thought arises. What's one thought that you have that might be harmful to you? Can you draw the thought and offer it a cup of love?

MAINTAINING BOUNDARIES AND NURTURING GOODNESS AND BEAUTY

Dear Reader,

I live in a neighborhood where deer roam the streets at night. My neighbors are constantly working to keep deer from eating their flowers. One woman built a small fence around her roses. That night the deer hopped over her fence and ate some flowers. The next day my neighbor added sticks to increase the height of her fence, and the deer went under it. A few days later she built a high wall around her flower garden with wire and poles, and now her flowers are flourishing.

Part of the gardener's job is to maintain the garden fence, and another part of the job is to water and nurture what is beautiful inside, to help it grow. I believe that we each have innate goodness and beauty within us that's worth nurturing and protecting. Any time there is an attempt to trample on the beauty: STOP. Up goes the high wire fence.

Learning how to create boundaries is one of the keys to flourishing in life. Creating boundaries and constantly adjusting and maintaining them are how we protect what's beautiful inside. I like the image of a fence from ground to sky around a thriving flower garden. The two go together.

When constructing fences, it's important to work on keeping out threats and allowing in what's good and helpful for life and growth. A beneficial fence must block threats and at the same time allow in sunlight, rain, air, the gardener, and others who will appreciate and nurture beauty.

Part of having internal boundaries is minimizing harmful thoughts and making time to create helpful, healing ones. In addition to maintaining strong, clear boundaries, it's essential for me to make time every day to recall wonderful experiences. This is part of how I rebuilt my mind after I lost it. I worked to do both. I saw and felt hard emotions that had been hidden, and it was also important, even essential, for me to build joyful and loving thoughts and feelings—positive train-tracks in my mind.

I used to watch my sons attach train-track to train-track, filling our playroom floor with new paths for their trains to travel on. What I learned is that my brain and heart are like my playroom floor. I can actively choose which trains I attach together by choosing what thoughts I focus on. The more I make time to see beauty, feel loved, and offer love, the more positive tracks my brain and heart lay down. When I have more positive train-tracks in my brain and heart, my thoughts and feelings travel more easily toward seeing beauty, feeling love, and offering love.

When I lost my mind, I had to learn how to rebuild my thoughts. Bit by bit, I constructed new brain patterns that felt good. I still have hard days, but by intentionally focusing on beautiful places, people, animals, and memories, I continue to build positive trains of thought in my mind and tender connections in my heart. The more I do this, the more easily I am able to generate warm, joyful, loving states of mind and being. I wish someone had taught me how to do this a long time ago—to make time to savor and cherish good things, good moments, and good people in my life.

When I focus on feeling cared about, appreciated, or seen, these trains of thought fill me with warmth and love.

They also reduce my heart rate and improve my creativity. When I recognize my intrinsic worth, I feel peaceful. When I am calm and feel loved, I can access more parts of my brain and I smile more easily.

When I have a self-critical thought or a hard emotion, I now pause and offer the thought or feeling loving kindness, a cup of tea—allowing myself to feel tenderness toward it. I then return to my work of being a gardener—planting seeds of love for beautiful things to grow and noticing the beauty and love that's already here.[79]

Opportunities ~

1) Sometimes I write out things that I love and savor the details in order to create positive train-tracks in my brain. The more I do this, the easier it is for me to recall happiness and joy. I have learned that I can consciously activate good thoughts that then change my brain for the better. This is empowering and quite helpful.

   Recall a memory that brings you happiness and joy. What are the details? The sounds? The smells? How did you feel? Who was there?

2) What person, animal, or spiritual being helps you feel loved and cherished? Write out details of how it feels to spend time with this being. What is one of your favorite places on earth? What does it smell like? Look like? Feel like? What time of year is it? Who is there? Fill in as many details as you can and know that you can return to this place or person in your mind whenever you need to feel joy, love, or peace.

3) Imagine four positive events that could happen to you tomorrow. See each scene completely. Where are you? What are you wearing? What are you doing? How does it feel?

DISCOVERING YOUR INNER PROTECTOR
AND YOUR ANIMAL WARRIOR

Dear Reader,

As we develop our ability to define and defend our boundaries, I want to ask you to tap into your inner energy for surviving and thriving. Within all of us is a life force that is strong and vital.

Animals in the wild are connected to their life force. They rely on it to survive. Notice animals in the wild—they are alive and aware. While they are sunning themselves or taking a drink at a river, part of them is tuned into their surroundings. If a predator arrives on the scene, they are ready to run or fight.

There are always predators in nature, and many use tricks to lure their prey. This is true with humans as well. Think of the fairy tale "Little Red Riding Hood," in which the wolf dresses as a grandmother to lure in Little Red Riding Hood. This story offers lessons in trusting our instincts and noticing when things don't feel right. Your instincts are connected to your animal senses—this is the part of you that is tuned into your surroundings and notices when something is off before you consciously acknowledge a change. It is important for you to trust your instincts.

There is an Inner Protector[80] who lives inside you. She is there. She has always been there. She cares that you survive and thrive. She cares about protecting all of you—your mental well-being, your emotional well-being, your spiritual well-being, and your physical well-being. She is fierce. She is alive. She knows how to survive, and she is always on your side.

Opportunities ~

1) Make time to get to know your Inner Protector. What is her name? What is her favorite color? Who does she remind you of? Does she have a name? Draw a shield in your journal. What spirit, person, or animal would fight to protect you no matter what? Put their initials on your shield.

2) Think of an animal that you admire and picture it fighting. What type of animal is it? Watch online videos of your animal fighting. Write the name of your Animal Warrior beside the name of your Inner Protector, or tape a picture of your Animal Warrior there. List three traits that describe your animal when it is fighting. How do these words connect to you?

3) Have a conversation with your Inner Protector. What does your Inner Protector encourage you to do? What does she ask you to stop doing?

DEVELOPING A SASSY MAMA ATTITUDE:
DEFINING AND DEFENDING WHAT
YOU WANT AND DON'T WANT

Dear Reader,

Earlier I shared interviews with women who consciously work to stop responding to every situation as a "nice girl." One interviewee discovered her Sassy Mama attitude when she was bombarded with uncomfortable male attention while traveling in Europe. She now uses her Sassy Mama attitude to defend herself and her friends from all unwanted attention.

I'd like to invite you to find your Sassy Mama. This is the woman in you who doesn't put up with any crap—toward you or toward your friends. She isn't nice. She isn't polite. She doesn't say, "Please leave us alone" or "Please stop." She's confident, and she knows there are people who do mean things in this world. She trusts her instincts and listens to her gut. She doesn't worry about being embarrassed or hurting someone's feelings to protect you. She knows what behavior is respectful and what isn't. She's willing to speak up when she sees something that's wrong, and she uses a deep strong voice to define and defend your boundaries—again, and again, and again. She's big, bold, and beautiful. And she's got sass.

Here are two interviews with two young women. I hope they inspire you to find your Sassy Mama and practice using her voice.

Irene Tsai, Watcher and Alcohol Educator, age 21 ~

I have friends who say, "I'm afraid to walk away because I don't want to hurt the other person's feelings." This can get to the point where they're stuck in an uncomfortable situation with a guy or girl who wants to keep dancing with them, and they still can't get out. There is an aversion to saying "No," or a fear that they'll be perceived as being standoffish.

If I were to give advice to someone, I'd say I want you to feel comfortable saying "No." If you're scared to say "No" and leave an uncomfortable situation, then that's where more trouble can come from. It's okay to stand by how you want to enjoy the night and not let anyone else ruin that for you.

Personally, I am very comfortable knowing that if I don't want something, I will say something or walk away. Maybe they'll say, "Oh, this girl isn't any fun." I don't care. I still say something, or I walk away. I want you to know that you can say "No," and that it's okay to walk away.

Lily, Assertiveness Training Workshop Attendee, age 11 ~

I learned you can be up front with someone and tell them what you need instead of being afraid of being stuck in an uncomfortable situation. You don't need to be uncomfortable. It's important to say something if someone is making you uncomfortable. You don't need to be polite. No pleases. You don't want to say, "I'd like you to stop, or please stop." It's much better to say, "I need you to stop now." You can also say, "You may not mean to make me uncomfortable, but you are. So stop!"

Opportunities ~

1) Within yourself, find your Sassy Mama. Who does she remind you of? Does she have a name? What color does she wear? What does she want you to know? What words does she want you to learn to say, and how does she want you to say them?

2) Find opportunities to practice saying "No." If you are at a restaurant and the waiter approaches to pour water in your glass, cover your glass with your hand and say, "I don't want any more water." Practice saying "No" with gestures and words. Role-play with a friend and have her ask you if she can borrow your favorite items and practice saying "No."

I like the broken-record technique—you keep repeating what you said, no matter what the other person says. You don't engage in debate. "I am going to check on my friend. I'm really worried about her. I am going to check on my friend. I'm really worried about her." In reality, you may be the friend you're worried about, and you're using your friend as an excuse to leave and get yourself free. Practice using this technique in a role-play with a friend.

Get a group of friends together and make up situations you think you might encounter with boys. Practice what you could say and do to get out of them. Take turns and help each other think of solutions, and then try adding their suggestions to the role-plays.

3) If someone isn't treating you with respect—if the person is putting you down, blaming you, teasing you, pressuring you, or hurting you—call on your Inner Protector, your Sassy Mama, and your Animal Warrior to help you find words and take action. Imagine them helping you fight off two different predators—someone you don't know and someone you do know. Remember, you don't necessarily know what predators look like, but you can look for aggressive behavior and notice when someone does something that makes you uncomfortable. Learn to notice small signs within yourself. When someone does something that makes you uncomfortable, where do you feel it in your body? What red flags do you notice? What can you do?

SETTING YOUR INTENTIONS FIRST

Dear Reader,

When you're interacting with someone you're interested in, it's important to decide what amount of intimacy you want and what circumstances meet those criteria.

A father to his teenage daughters ~ Boys and men only get trust when it's earned.

You get to test them. Are they treating you with kindness, curiosity, and respect? Are they listening to you? Do they honor what you're saying verbally and non-verbally? How do you want to feel tomorrow about what you did today? Do they care? Are both people seeking communication and connection? Is one person seeking conquest?

A healer named Vajra Woolsey explained to me that, when I'm deciding how I want to interact with people, I can imagine myself as a house. Some people I keep outside my garden fence, and that's where I want them. I don't allow them to come any closer. Others I allow to sit on my porch (metaphorically), and we talk there. Good friends I welcome into my family room or kitchen, where we have more meaningful conversations. I allow very few people into my bedroom. The ones who go there are dear to me. They treat me with respect and care about who I am—my dreams, my challenges, and my needs—and I care about them. They have earned my trust.

It's helpful to notice intention, how people approach others: with kindness, respect, and sparkle in their hearts, or as a game that has winners and losers. Pay attention to what you want from an interaction and what someone else wants. These wants can be similar, or they can be very different. If you are pretending that someone is "perfect," you are not seeing the person as a unique, quirky human being who has needs, dreams, and challenges. If you are using a person, at some point that person will feel it. If you are being used, at some point you will feel it. And being used hurts.

Sophie, age 22 ~ When my friends have felt awful and violated, there's something about the way it happened—the intentions weren't the same.

To reduce suffering and increase our capacity to love, it's best to intend kindness, curiosity, and respect when we're interacting with another person. It is also helpful to insist that others treat us the same way. Communicating what we want and don't want is the only way to make sure that our intentions are aligned.

Never letting anyone in can be very lonely. But letting people in before knowing their intentions can create added suffering, if you then discover that they're not who you thought they were. You want to ask questions and study their behavior. Be curious about people—observe who they are and how they treat others, especially you.

Even when we do think we can trust people, they can betray us. Betrayal hurts. It causes deep pain and suffering. Sometimes we don't see hidden insecurities and weaknesses in someone we care about. Sometimes people do hurtful things that we would never, ever have expected. One of my gifts and challenges is that I can see goodness in people.

This means that I am sometimes very wrong about how people choose to act in the world and how they will treat me. I have come to accept that the goodness I see in people is there—I'm not wrong—but there are many factors that contribute to why someone chooses to hurt others, themselves, or both, and I am working on seeing a fuller picture of how people behave.

It's interesting; as I allow myself to see and accept parts of myself that I don't like and offer these parts loving kindness, I am growing in my ability to see parts of others that I don't like, and my compassion for them is growing as well. I don't necessarily keep these people in my life, but I do try to release my anger at them. Because I am seeing the wholeness of being human, I am able to see and accept the challenging parts, offer them love and kindness, and work not to act on the parts of myself that might hurt me or someone else.

Loving is a messy business because we often hurt others and get hurt—but it's still worth working on how we offer love and how we receive love. If someone isn't curious about you—your quirks and interests, your cares and challenges, your limits and boundaries—they belong on the outside of your garden fence.

If someone has hurt you badly, make time to reflect on any early signs you may have ignored. Offer yourself love and kindness in this debriefing period. See where you may have ignored or overridden a feeling of discomfort with something they did or said. We have all done this, and it's important to forgive yourself. I recently heard one mother say to her daughter, "I want you to trust your intuition. Deep down you know. And at the same time, we all make mistakes. I made mistakes, and this is how I learned to trust my intuition the next time."

Ignoring our intuition about someone is not the same as breaking the law. It is a crime to physically hurt another person except in self-defense. When we do ignore our intuition, we can return to ourselves with kindness and honor the voice that spoke and wasn't heard. Offer flowers to yourself, not self-blame.

When you start again, know that there are people who will see you as the beautiful, unique, quirky being that you are. Don't settle. You are always worthy of being treated with respect and kindness. Always.

Here are four interviews about setting intentions, understanding what you want, and practicing communication skills:

Hannah Gribetz, Sexual Assault Peer Educator, age 22 ~

Personally, I like to consider myself an Enlightened Twenty-First-Century Woman, who doesn't let rules about what you can and can't do on a first date get in my way. But I've found that I do like creating rules for myself. In some ways, it makes it a lot less stressful to go into a situation with limits set already. That rule can even be as vague as "listen to your gut," but I always find that for me it feels better to go into a situation, whether it's a party or a date or whatever, with a game plan.

Professor Luci Herman, Resident Fellow and Student Advisor ~

It's important to have consensual discussions before the heat of the moment. Initially, you may think you're not equipped with the language. You may think, "Oh, this is so awkward," or

"This will kill the vibe." But talking can be erotic and useful. It's important to ask, "Does this feel good? Do you like this? Is this okay? Do you want to slow down? Do you want to go further?"

Irene Tsai, Watcher and Alcohol Educator, age 21 ~

What's really special about my school is that we have Consent Ed. This group goes to every organization on campus, and they hold discussions and talk about what consent means to every individual. When they came to talk to my organization, we talked about making sure, before going out with your friends, that everyone knows what every individual is seeking that night. If a person wants to meet someone new and talk with them or see where that goes, you can establish that prior to going out and before that person is potentially intoxicated.

Talking with your friends before you go out lets everyone know what you're looking for and what you want. It means that, if your friends see something different, then they'll step in. Someone might say, "Hey, I just want to dance with you guys tonight and hang out, so let's just make it a girls night." Other times I might say, "I want to meet someone new and make out with them, but that's it." And that's where the line is drawn. It's important to be clear. So if I see one of my friends being dragged into another room, I step in and say, "Hey, are you sure this is what you really want? We talked about this earlier." As friends, we're looking for signs that are different from what each person established earlier.

Monet, age 22 ~

Focus on developing your own personal character and not having that be contingent on what guys think of you or how many dates you have with guys. I don't know if we really think that, but on some level it makes us a little more confident in ourselves when we have that verification from guys. I got caught up in that freshman year. I felt really good about myself when guys were interested. I got a little addicted to that feeling. So, in contrast, when a guy lost interest, I felt bad about myself.

For me, I am such a competitive person that I saw a guy as a competitive game, and when a guy didn't show interest, I felt like I was losing. It took me a while to figure this out about myself, and I found it was a true experience for a lot of my friends as well. I had to learn how to value myself regardless of who liked me or who didn't.

Before going to college, I would recommend making a five-point list of qualities you want to have in a guy—physically, emotionally, and intellectually. Finding common values is the foundation for a great relationship. I recommend dating different kinds of people to find out what those values are.

Before you go to college, write down a list of qualities that you want to portray and embody. College is very much a time to discover who you are—your innate personality traits. And you have the freedom to choose how you want to be a member of society and go about interacting with people.

Opportunities ~

1) What qualities do you value in a potential partner? Make a list of five traits that you value most in each category: physically, emotionally, and intellectually. Can you look for these traits when you are interacting with someone? Can you pay attention to what someone says and does and how that measures with what you value?

2) Write out words that you could say to communicate what you like—even as simple as "That feels good," or "I like that." You could establish a boundary by saying, "I like kissing you a lot, but I'd like to know you better before we do anything else." In your mind, practice using boundary language. Now practice asking questions aimed at understanding what feels good for someone else and what that person is comfortable doing—such as "Does this feel good?" or "Is this okay?" Remember that every person is different and that the only way to know if something feels good is to ask.

3) Imagine yourself as a house with a fence around the yard, a beautiful garden, a front porch, a living room, a hang-out room, a kitchen, and a bedroom. On a sign-post outside, you can write, "My house, my heart, my choice." This means that you get to listen to your own intuition and decide who can enter your house and how far each person is allowed into it. What would you like to know about a person before they are allowed to enter your property? Each room?

You can move people out of a certain room—and even out of the house entirely—if you decide they don't meet your requirements. You can share less personal information with them and talk more casually about the weather, food, pets, or sports—front-porch talk, even over-the-fence conversation. You can also learn how to share your dreams and challenges with the people you do let in. This is how we build connections and love.

DEVELOPING YOUR RANGE OF RESPONSES

Dear Reader,

I'd like to share with you some thoughts I have about how we use our voices to protect ourselves and take care of ourselves. Your voice is your most powerful tool, and using it effectively requires training and practice. Because of a variety of factors, including my upbringing, my personality, my birth order, and my communities, I learned how to use my voice in specific ways in a limited range. Most of the notes I chose to play were "nice girl" notes. My world praised me when I used these "nice girl" notes—be polite, make others happy, and don't hurt anyone's feelings. I often heard, "You're such a good girl!" Unfortunately, this meant that, when I was being nice, sometimes someone did get disappointed or hurt—and that someone was me.

I have learned that in all interactions among humans, there are needs and wants, and people often get disappointed, and that's okay. It's most important that I am true to myself. It has taken me years to learn what this requires—primarily taking breaks throughout each day to pause and listen to my Inner Guide and my Inner Protector. As I learn to identify and honor my own needs, boundaries, and dreams, it is increasingly important for me to access a wider range for how I use my voice.

I like to think of my voice as a piano keyboard. Within all of us, we have a full set of piano keys available to us—octaves of high notes and low notes. You have a full range of notes on a keyboard available to you. Most people use their voices in a narrow range. Imagine for a moment what "nice girl" notes sound like—twinkling, pretty, soft, light, delicate notes.

Now imagine yourself increasing your range. You can still play all the notes you are accustomed to playing—many serve a purpose and are a delightful way of communicating with the world. But try adding more options, so that you can choose which notes you play. What do strong notes sound like? Fierce notes? Angry notes? Boundary notes? You can use low notes on your keyboard when you need to be a Sassy Mama, an Animal Warrior, or your Inner Protector. Practice filling your lower notes with your body and your breath, and you will say "No" with the fire of the earth and the force of the wind.

When I need to say "No" and mean it, I summon what I call my "dog voice." If a dog jumps up on me, I use my low, strong, embodied voice, which is connected to my lungs, belly, and feet, and I say a clear "NO!" and the dog never jumps on me again. If I say in a high-pitched voice, "Please stop," the dog continues to jump on me. Begging or pleading with a dog doesn't work. Unfortunately, the same is true for predators. We need to find our "dog voice," practice using it, and use it whenever we need it.

Most self-defense classes include training on how to use your voice to protect yourself. I'd like you to find a self-defense class and take it. You can check with your local rape crisis center or community college for a referral. It is essential training for every girl and woman. While you wait for your class to begin, go online and search YouTube videos for self-defense lessons for women. In a way that is safe for you, copy the tones of the voices you hear and the moves you see to develop your voice range and your muscle memory. Recently, I watched in awe as a little girl sang an opera aria on a TV show. Later, she said that she had learned to sing by imitating online videos.

Here's the tricky part about self-defense: If you are assaulted and either freeze or fight back and the person still attacks you, you are not to blame. That person is committing the crime, not you. If the predator hadn't been there, the violence would not have occurred. If you are assaulted, it is never your fault. The person who assaults you is morally and legally at fault—regardless of whether you know the person or not. Remember that it doesn't matter who the person is; it's what they do that matters, and it is against the law to physically harm another person unless it's in self-defense.

There are things we can do to reduce our risk. As I have gathered information for this book, I have learned many things I never knew. Going forward, I now understand that as soon as a situation feels uncomfortable or risky, it's best for me to speak up and say something or do something—even if it means disappointing or offending someone. Exiting an uncomfortable situation *early* is one of the best forms of self-defense.

I rehearse over and over the actions and reactions I want to have, to increase the likelihood that I will use my voice and body skillfully when I realize I am in a challenging situation. To do this, I practice saying "No!" and "Stop!" and I picture myself using strong, clear words: "I have to go check on a friend," "Leave now," or "Just stop." Practicing being assertive helps me tap into my strength and escalate my response as needed. I see myself yelling, swearing, breaking a wrist hold, kicking someone in the knee, punching, and scratching. I work to make myself more comfortable with a variety of emotions and responses. This increases my range and my options.

I do all of this because I have studied the research data, and I now know that an assertive response—using my voice and any part of my body to fight back—can stop over 80% of potential attacks.[81] The beautiful change for me is that I feel safer and more at peace knowing I have these tools.

If someone tries to touch you in any way that is unwanted, call on your Sassy Mama, your Inner Protector, or your Animal Warrior—whoever feels most helpful in that particular situation. Call on all three! Many girls and women have learned how to fight using their voices and their bodies, and you can too.

Bella, Assertiveness Training Workshop Attendee, age 13 ~

I learned that it's important to listen to your intuition, the voice inside your head. If your intuition tells you to run, run. If your intuition tells you to fight, fight. If your intuition tells you to say something, say something. If someone comes up to you and says, "I've been watching you or noticing you," get out or fight. And when it comes to fighting, use a free arm, or a free limb, and go for a vital area: the eyes, the throat, the groin, or the knees. If someone is attacking you, you fight to hurt. And you say, "No! No! No!" Saying "No" keeps you breathing. Some people hold their breath when they're being attacked. If you keep shouting "No!" you keep breathing, and you get stronger, and stronger. I learned that I am really strong.

Sexual Assault Resistance Program Reduces Rapes: U of Windsor Initiative Reduced Rape by Almost 50%.

Rosanna Tamburri, *University Affairs*, June 11, 2015[82]

An innovative sexual-assault resistance program designed by University of Windsor professor Charlene Senn has been shown to substantially reduce the incidence of rape and attempted rape among first-year university women, according to a study published June 11 in the *New England Journal of Medicine*.[83]

Dr. Senn, professor of psychology and women's studies, spent 10 years developing and testing the Enhanced Assess, Acknowledge, Act (EAAA) Sexual Assault Resistance program, designed to help women stop aggressive behavior at an early stage and prevent sexual assaults from occurring.

The program consists of four sessions of three hours each that give participants information and skills on how to assess the risk posed by acquaintances and how to use verbal and physical self-defense techniques. The sessions teach how to develop problem-solving strategies to reduce the advantages of the perpetrator, to assess danger in situations, and to overcome emotional barriers to resisting sexual aggression. Participants practice resisting verbal coercion and get self-defense training that focuses on acquaintances rather than strangers.

"It really is about giving [women] knowledge, tools and confidence to use those tools," said Dr. Senn.[84]

Teen Girls Report Less Sexual Victimization after Virtual Reality Assertiveness Training

Margaret Allen, *SMU Guildhall*, January 19, 2015[85]

Teen girls were less likely to report being sexually victimized after learning to assertively resist unwanted sexual overtures and practicing resistance in a realistic virtual environment, finds a new study.

The effects persisted over a three-month period following the training, said Clinical Psychologist Lorelei Simpson Rowe, lead author on the pilot study from Southern Methodist University, Dallas.

The research also found that those girls who had previously experienced dating violence reported lower levels of psychological aggression and psychological distress after completing the program, relative to girls in a comparison group. [...]

The training program, called "My Voice, My Choice," emphasizes that victims do not invite sexual violence and that they have the right to stand up for themselves because violent or coercive behavior is never okay.

"It is very promising that learning resistance skills and practicing them in virtual simulations of coercive interactions could reduce the risk for later sexual victimization," said Simpson Rowe. [...]

Simulations started with less intense scenarios, where the male was mildly pressuring, such as asking repeatedly for the girl's phone number. Scenarios escalated to increasingly more severe situations, such as verbally coercing the girl to kiss him, becoming increasingly aggressive in speech, and being more persistent in the face of resistance.

Following each simulation, other group members and the facilitator provided feedback to each girl on how she could increase the effectiveness of her response. Suggestions included using a firmer tone of voice, and refusing without apologizing.

The researchers reported their findings, "Reducing Sexual Victimization among Adolescent Girls: A Randomized Controlled Pilot Trial of My Voice, My Choice," in the journal *Behavior Therapy.*[86]

Opportunities ~

1) In addition to understanding the word consent, I want you to understand what it means to dissent. Dissent: "To differ in sentiment or opinion, especially from the majority; withhold assent; disagree."[87]

I want you always to trust yourself and to listen to what is right for you. You get to assert what you want and what you don't want, every step of the way. You can dissent. You can disagree. You can object to what others think you should do. You can veto something at any point in time. In a relationship, regardless of any previous interaction, you can deny someone access to your body if it doesn't feel safe and right for you.

Please write out the following words: dissent, veto, disagree, object, protest, and deny. These are boundary words. These are words that say "No." Use them in your everyday language. You get to define, defend, and assert what you do want and what you don't want, every single time you interact with another person. Try using these words in an art project.

2) Write out words you would be willing to say to someone to end an interaction that was becoming uncomfortable. Practice summoning your "dog voice," your Animal Warrior, your Inner Protector, or your Sassy Mama and saying these words.

A self-defense teacher of mine said, "Creating a boundary starts with putting up a fence in front of your house. Defending a boundary is what you do when someone tries to cross it." Practice setting boundaries:

Step One: Practice setting the boundary or limit.

Step Two: Practice defending it. Leave, say something, or fight.

Step Three: Practice escalating your response as needed.

Mantra from Andre Salvage's Assertiveness Class ~ "No one has the right to make me feel uncomfortable. If they do, I will use my voice and body to stop them."

If the person ignores your words, what will you do next? Imagine using your body, your voice, and your creativity to get yourself free. What would you do physically, verbally, and mentally? During a self-defense class, I learned to ask myself, "What's free?" If someone is pinning my arms, what parts of my body that are free can I use in order to escape? Legs. Hips. Voice. Teeth.

3) It's important to think through how you would respond in these four situations:

- If a male I knew tried to kiss me and I did not want to kiss him, I would _____.

- If a male I knew and liked kissed me and tried to do more, and I did not want to do more, I would _____.

- If a stranger tried to force me to have sex with him when I didn't want to, I would _____.

- If a male I knew (i.e., a date) tried to force me to have sex with him when I didn't want to, I would _____.[88] What is a forceful verbal and physical strategy you could use?

Andre Salvage, Self-Defense and Assertiveness Instructor ~ Predators have a really good way of getting you to distrust your intuition. Your intuition is never wrong. It's always right.

BOUNDARIES AND ALCOHOL

Dear Reader,

I've seen videos of baby sea turtles hatching on a beach and making a run to the ocean. Prior to their hatching, predators gathered and waited. Similarly, the most dangerous time for girls is during the first few months away from home, when they don't have an established friend group, they're experimenting with alcohol, and predators are targeting them.[89] The first two years of college are the highest-risk years, and the first few months of the school year are the highest-risk time of the year.[90]

One out of five undergraduate women experiences an attempted or completed sexual assault during their college years, with at least 50% of sexual assaults occurring when women are incapacitated due to their use of substances, primarily alcohol.

Freshmen and sophomores are at greater risk for victimization than juniors and seniors, and the large majority of victims of sexual assault are victimized by men they know and trust, rather than strangers.[91]

Predators know what increases your vulnerability, and I want you to know what they know. Learning to identify potentially dangerous situations and what to do in them is important because it is likely that you will find yourself in situations where you can make early decisions that protect your friends and yourself.

In the early 1800s, surgeons proudly wore the same lab coats every day and boasted about the layers of dried blood on them as badges of honor. People routinely opened hospital windows in an effort to clean the air because they believed that bad air caused infections. Doctors did not wash hands before surgeries and used the same surgical tools for different patients. More than 50% of surgery patients died from infection. Then, in the 1860s, after observing bacteria growth, a British surgeon named Joseph Lister discovered the true causes of infection and created new ways to reduce the risk. Lister introduced new procedures, including washing hands, sterilizing surgical tools, and using a carbonic acid to clean patients' wounds. Because of the precautions he took, Lister's patients' survival odds improved dramatically. He published his findings in a medical journal in 1867, and the high survival rate of his patients encouraged the adoption of these new practices.[92]

Right now, in our culture, we have an idea that's as dangerous as doctors wearing lab coats covered in dried blood during surgery. We have been trained—through movies, advertising, and cultural stories—to believe that getting really drunk and blacked out are desirable and cool, that they're even badges of honor.

By conservative estimates, half of all sexual assaults involve alcohol. Some studies put the number of sexual assaults in which the perpetrator and/or the victim consumes alcohol at 85%. People argue that it isn't right to tell girls to drink less; they say that girls should be able to drink as much as they want and still be safe. I believe that this is wishful thinking that ignores the current reality and encourages harmful behavior by both males and females. Many people are getting hurt when they drink alcohol, and I want both males *and* females to drink less.

Any surgeon who wears a lab coat covered in dried blood dramatically increases the risk of infecting patients. People who drink alcohol increase their risk of being sexually assaulted or of using alcohol as an excuse for sexually assaulting someone else. Alcohol impacts large motor skills (the use of your arms and legs), small motor skills (the use of your voice), and perception skills (the awareness of your surroundings); as a result, it affects your ability to read warning signs and fight off an assault.[93]

Alcohol consumption also can exaggerate personality types. If someone has an aggressive tendency, alcohol can increase their aggressiveness. According to the disinhibition hypothesis, alcohol weakens brain mechanisms that normally restrain impulsive behaviors, including inappropriate aggression.[94] When it comes to sexual assault, this combination creates a perfect storm—decreasing a potential victim's ability to respond and increasing a potential predator's aggression. Predators know this and deliberately use alcohol to their advantage. My goal is to reduce harm, and I want you to know that a party or date where people are consuming large amounts of alcohol is like an operating room from the early 1800s.

Testa and Hoffman, (2012) ~ Occasions of heavy drinking in college are a significant risk factor for sexual victimization for both experienced and inexperienced drinkers. Findings point toward universal prevention, ideally before college entry, as a strategy for reducing heavy episodic drinking and hence, college sexual victimization.[95]

One recent graduate I interviewed shared with me that when he was the president of his fraternity, a freshman girl almost died in his arms from alcohol poisoning. Fortunately, he called 911 and got her help. A few weeks later, he went through a similar experience with a fraternity brother. Those two experiences deeply impacted him. With a few friends, he started a student-run organization called Cayuga's Watchers. This group places trained, sober students at parties who try to blend in and notice early warning signs and intervene. Their goal is to keep the party going in a way that is safe for everyone.

One fraternity created a "No Drunk Sex" policy to protect girls and guys. Someone who is incapacitated (drunk or out of it) because of alcohol or drugs cannot legally give consent. Although definitions vary by state, "No Drunk Sex" is a policy that seeks to keep everyone safe.

If you look carefully at the statistics on sexual assault, you will see that the risk of being sexually assaulted for a college woman decreases as she gets older. College women are learning and taking steps to reduce their risk, and part of their strategy includes understanding how, when, and with whom they use alcohol. I want to share with you what they have learned and what they do. I interviewed many college students and recent graduates, and everyone had something to say about alcohol. Here are some of their advice and strategies:

Hannah Gribetz, Sexual Assault Peer Educator, age 22 ~

If you are going to drink or smoke under-age, or do illegal drugs, be safe about it, and recognize that it is against the law and that you are therefore taking a risk.

Jacob, age 23 ~

I think what is toughest for guys and girls is establishing a limit. I think it's fine to drink, but it can be a problem when you look at what other people are doing and you think that's how you should gauge what you're doing. When people are having mixed drinks, it's hard to calculate. It is to an extent an equation: Your body size and your genetics factor into your tolerance. You need to find your range.

If you're just following what everyone else is doing, it may be appropriate for them, but if you're half their weight and you don't drink as much, it can be very dangerous for you. I wouldn't say, "Oh, be careful." I would say, "Find out what that range is, and know the line before going too far."

Ali, age 22 ~

For my size, I learned what my limits are. This may sound ridiculous, but I recommend that you practice drinking with your friends. You want to know your limits. How much can you drink before you're drunk? It sounds simple, but it's important. A lot of people who have been drinking believe that they only have slightly decreased judgment, but in reality it's a lot more than that.

I was in South Africa, and there was an elevated danger level. They spoke to us often about being aware of our surroundings and not getting drugged or kidnapped. At parties, I rubber-banded my drink to my wrist to make certain that no one put anything in it. I still do this sometimes when I'm at parties. If I were trying to rape someone, I would not go to someone who had rubber-banded her drink to her wrist and was guarding it.

Laura, age 22 ~

It's hard when you don't have that close friendship. Until you have that, don't get significantly intoxicated. When going to a party, I would go with a girl or guy you trust and look out for each other—and DON'T leave without them.

Lela, age 22 ~

Don't get blacked out so that you don't know what's happening. If you do, you may never figure out what happened—and that would be really scary. Don't drink until you're blacked out.

Find really good friends. In reality you probably will at some point come into a dangerous situation, even though I still believe you owe it to yourself to protect yourself. You may find yourself in a potentially dangerous situation, and that's when having really good, trustworthy friends around is so incredibly important, because, more often than not, one of them will realize that something is not right and will do something. The sad reality is that alcohol plays a big part in all of this.

Jessica Chapman-Segal,
Reproductive Health Educator, age 25 ~

When you are severely under the influence of something, you do not have all your senses about you, and you are not able to make consensual decisions. I want to point out that I am not blaming the person, but you put yourself in a more vulnerable position when you don't have all your faculties. It could lead to a really fun night, or to you accidentally getting pregnant, or getting an STI, or getting sexually assaulted, or getting raped.

Mark, age 21 ~

At my fraternity, we've developed what we call The Social Zone. The goal is that if you want to be drinking, you never go too far. In life you have dreams and ambitions, and you have The Social Zone when you're drinking. The two can overlap. The goal is to stay in The Social Zone while always remembering your dreams and ambitions.

When you're in The Social Zone, you're able to talk well. People are too awkward to talk to each other, and they use alcohol as a social lubricant. But you don't want to drink too much where you start slurring your words or doing embarrassing things or losing your memory or crashing into walls. Alcohol doesn't affect all people in the same way. Some can't talk, and they're still okay physically. Some aren't okay physically, but they can still talk. Monitor yourself and stay in The Social Zone. You don't want to be the person who drinks too much, gets naked, runs around your dorm, and everyone makes fun of you. If you're drinking, stay in The Social Zone.

Gabby, age 22 ~

When I drink a lot, I get tired, and it's not fun for me or the people I'm with. I don't like being drunk. I still don't drink much. I saw my friends who drank too much not feeling good often and missing out on a lot of stuff that we were all enjoying. They felt sick or needed to sleep it off, and the rest of us were hanging out and talking until the middle of the night.

What my friends and I have realized as we've gotten older is that we know our limits. We can have a few drinks when we're out, and we can be tipsy when we're dancing, and we know,

"Okay, I'll need an hour or an hour and a half to be sober so I'm not drunk on the train"—which is a miserable experience. We are aware of our limits alcohol-wise and of the amount of time the group can be out—we do the math. Each one of us has a different limit, and we know how long it will take us to get sober so we can enjoy being out, going to clubs, and keep enjoying each other's company. We're all trying to be as responsible as we can.

Lindsey, age 24 ~

The best way to try to prevent a really bad problem is to avoid the situations where it happens the most frequently. With sexual assault, you could take every precaution and still be victimized.

Assertiveness training and self-defense are useful to a point, but you're having to use those skills when you're already in the bad situation. I'm not trying to say that you can prevent sexual assault. Sexual assault can happen when everyone is sober and home. It doesn't have to be at a party, but I think the best bet is combining those skills (assertiveness training and self-defense) with avoiding certain situations.

Irene Tsai, Watcher and Alcohol Educator, age 21 ~

I want to stress that within our training we do have a section that's on the impact of alcohol on the brain and the body. We teach about the different BAC (blood alcohol content) zones:

- There's a BAC zone under .05, and that's called the buzz zone.

- Between .06 and .11—that's the drunk zone.

- *Between .12 and .15—that's the elevated-risk zone. This is where they're making poor decisions, and their balance and movement are impaired. This is where someone might appear to be slumped over because they don't have complete control of all their actions and body movement.*

- *After that, we have a high-risk zone—that's a BAC of .15 to .25, and this is where blackouts occur and there's a risk of choking on your own vomit.*

- *Even after that, there's a medical-emergency zone—that's a BAC of .25 or above, and that's when we're definitely calling for medical emergency services.*

Within our training we make sure we start with how alcohol impacts the brain and what behaviors are associated with a higher BAC. It's really useful information for people coming into college—maybe they've never had much to drink before, and maybe they don't know the symptoms.

We talk about different factors that can influence how someone is impacted by alcohol—this could be gender, whether or not they've eaten throughout the day, dehydration, whether or not they're on medication, or if they're in a different mood—particularly stress. The workload is insane here, and there are so many tests. Sometimes people party as a stress relief, and they say, "Oh, I've been so stressed the entire week, and now I just want to drink my worries away." We'll use this as an example to help people be more aware with alcohol, because students know how that feels.

Within all these conversations, we have recommendations, which include the ABCDs. This is an acronym that we try to get everyone to remember. It's Alert, Breathing, Color, and Doubt. Within each of the categories, we're looking for specific signs.

For A, alert, we're looking to see if the person can answer simple questions and if they can stay awake for more than two to three minutes. We want to know if they're conscious and able to control their actions. If they're not alert, we call 911.

For B, breathing, we're looking for flow or irregular breathing. If someone's continuously vomiting, then they're not going to be getting enough oxygen, or if they're complaining of any difficulty breathing or chest pain, we call 911.

For C, color, we're observing the person's condition and seeing if they're pale or have a bluish or green skin tone. That can indicate excessive amounts of alcohol intake, and we call 911.

For D, doubt, we want to know if there are any other medications, drugs, or injuries involved. If there's any doubt that the situation might escalate into something harmful, we recommend that you stay on the safe side and call 911.

Opportunities ~

1) How each person processes alcohol varies enormously—even from day to day. However, knowing your limits approximately is still possible. On the blood alcohol percentage chart, find your weight and see how many drinks in one hour it might take to put you in the buzz zone (.05). How many drinks might it take to put you in the blackout or high-risk zone (.15–.25)?

2) Notice how many shots of hard alcohol equal a can of soda. If you have the equivalent of one can of soda of hard alcohol—8 shots, what will your BAC be? For my size, it means I could be dead.

3) Some recent graduates I spoke with said that they had switched to drinking only light beer because it made them full before they were drunk. Others said that they always pour their own drinks to reduce the risk of being over-served.

One recent graduate said that for every drink of alcohol she has, she stops and drinks a full glass of water. Others said that they pretend to drink and then empty their glasses into planters. Every woman I interviewed had developed strategies for how to drink less, or not at all. What strategies and limits can you set for yourself?

Women
Approximate Blood Alcohol Percentage

Gender, time of month, genetics, diet and hydration can impact how one processes alcohol. Most females get drunk faster than males because of how the female body processes alcohol. Most bodies can get rid of one drink per hour but this varies.

DRINKS	BODY WEIGHT IN POUNDS								
	90	100	120	140	160	180	200	220	240
0	.00	.00	.00	.00	.00	.00	.00	.00	.00
1	.05	.05	.04	.03	.03	.03	.02	.02	.02
2	.10	.09	.08	.07	.06	.05	.05	.04	.04
3	.15	.14	.11	.10	.09	.08	.07	.06	.06
4	.20	.18	.15	.13	.11	.10	.09	.08	.08
5	.25	.23	.19	.17	.15	.13	.11	.10	.09
6	.30	.27	.23	.19	.17	.15	.14	.12	.11
7	.35	.32	.27	.23	.20	.18	.16	.14	.13
8	.40	.36	.30	.26	.23	.20	.18	.17	.15
9	.45	.41	.34	.29	.26	.23	.20	.19	.17
10	.51								

(One drink is about 1.5 oz of 80 proof liquor, 12 oz of beer, or 5 oz wine.)

- Buzz zone under .05
- Drunk zone .06 and .11
- If you are 21 years old or older, it is illegal to drive if your BAC is .08 and above.
- Elevated risk zone .12 and .15
- High-risk zone .15 and .25
- Medical emergency zone .25 and above

Unfortunately, although the "standard" drink amounts are helpful for following health guidelines, they may not reflect customary serving sizes. A large cup of beer, an over-poured glass of wine, or a single mixed drink could contain much more alcohol than a standard drink.[96]

Comparing Drink Types
Understanding Quantity

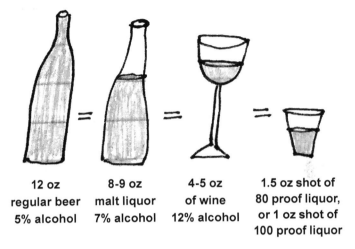

| 12 oz regular beer 5% alcohol | 8-9 oz malt liquor 7% alcohol | 4-5 oz of wine 12% alcohol | 1.5 oz shot of 80 proof liquor, or 1 oz shot of 100 proof liquor |

12 oz of 80 proof liquor, 40% alcohol (whiskey, rum, vodka, tequila—please check individual bottles to learn alcohol content)

=

8 1.5 oz shots of 80 proof liquor, 40% alcohol

Love

Sophie, age 22 ~

I had a professor explain static aesthetics to me. When you're looking at a picture of Monet's haystacks, you miss the beauty of it when you start analyzing it. I'm interested in that moment when something ceases to be a means to an end. It transcends utility. My professor explained that that's what art is and that's what love is. When you talk about love, that's when someone isn't a means to an end. They exist totally in their own otherness, and it's not about explaining or naming or labeling them, and it's not about using them.

LOVING YOURSELF

Dear Reader,

A friend of mine from college named Carianne James created a workshop for girls called Spirit Warriors. Carianne is also an artist and a teacher. In her classes, she seeks to empower girls "to be themselves and help awaken the creative spark within." During one session, Carianne asks each girl to imagine her own cloak of unconditional love. What is it made of? Does it have a hood? Is it heavy? Light?

After each girl has called to mind what her cloak of unconditional love looks like, Carianne asks her to imagine how it feels to wear it. The girls close their eyes, picture themselves wearing the cloaks, and imagine feeling deeply appreciated, accepted, and cherished. Later they purchase fabric and make cloaks in order to remember to wrap themselves in unconditional love—often.

Life can be challenging and hard. We all make mistakes, and awful things happen to good people, to us. Life can be messy, and at the same time we can learn to nurture ourselves, share our gifts with others, and grow—especially in our capacity to offer kindness to ourselves and others. No matter what we do, no matter what happens to us, deep down, at all times, it's essential to remember that we are all worthy of love. Having your own imagined cloak of unconditional love helps.

Opportunities ~

1) What does your cloak of unconditional love look like? What is it made of? Does it have a hood? Draw a picture of it. What colors do you choose?

2) Whose love—people, animals, and spiritual beings— can you sew into your cloak? Write their initials on your cloak to remind you of their love. Is there a place where you feel unconditional love? Add a color or symbol to your cloak that reminds you of this place.

3) When you've had a hard day or you want to do something challenging or brave, picture yourself wearing your cloak of unconditional love. What does it feel like to be wrapped in it?

DISCOVERING YOUR INNER NURTURER

Dear Reader,

Earlier, I asked you to get to know your Inner Protector. Today, I'd like to ask you to meet your Inner Nurturer. Your Inner Nurturer is someone who cares about your well-being. She wants to make certain that you eat, sleep, and have safe shelter, clean water, and nurturing people around you. She cares about how you are treated, and she cares when you are mistreated. She sees your deepest wounds and day-to-day challenges. She wants to make certain that you have down time—for rest, reflection, tenderness, good food, fun, laughter, exercise, and friends. She also honors your dreams and your reason for being here, and she wants to make certain that you make time to identify your gifts and build skills to share them.

Your Inner Nurturer wants to see you engage in life. She believes you can and that what you have to offer is unique and deeply needed in the world. At your core, she knows that you are full of goodness and worthy of respect, kindness, and love.

Opportunities ~

1) What is your Inner Nurturer's name? What does she look like? What colors does she wear? What music does she like?

2) Draw or cut out pictures that remind you of her. Make a collage and use words and images.

3) Write out helpful phrases that your Inner Nurturer can say to you often. Here are some I love:

"Ouch, that hurt."

"Sweetheart, I am sorry you are suffering."

"Breathing is a good thing. Try taking one deep breath, exhaling, and then taking another."

"You don't deserve to be treated badly. Ever."

"I'm enough, as I am."

"Crying usually helps."

"Laughing usually helps."

"Talking with someone kind usually helps."

"Remember not to suffer alone. Who can I call today?"

"Remember to draw what you feel with colorful pens and pencils."

"Dancing always helps."

"I want you to be with people you love and to do work you love."

"When you cut out pictures and words from magazines, you see your dreams more clearly."

"It's okay to be afraid and to still go for your dreams."

"What is one tiny baby step that you can take today toward your dream?"

"I can do it. You can do it."

"You can do hard things. I can do hard things."

"Make it a priority to stay focused on your values and goals."

"When something doesn't go as planned, I can learn from it."

"Your ability to feel compassion for yourself and others makes you rich."

"I have a kind and beautiful heart."

"I can see your goodness shining through the pain."

"You can make a difference in other people's lives when you reach out and engage with others."

"I can do three brave things today."

"I understand that I can't always do what I hoped to do. Tomorrow, I can resolve again to do three brave things."

"You have unique and important gifts to offer, and I believe in you."

"I can work to understand my gifts, develop my skills, and find opportunities to share them."

"People need what only you can offer."

"You matter. I matter."

"I love you."

APPROACHING ROMANTIC LOVE
AND FEELING AWKWARD

Dear Reader,

Today I'd like us to look at romantic love—crushes, flirting, attraction, and sparkle. Wanting to offer love and receive love is one of the most basic human needs. Babies in intensive-care units do better when they are given attention and affection. We all benefit from love—healthy, tender, respectful love. Love is food for our soul.

We've been focused on listening to your intuition and paying attention to when you're feeling uncomfortable. Feeling uncomfortable is an invitation for us to stop and notice a voice within. Sometimes it's a message that says, "Leave now." Other times it's a feeling that's saying, "I'm excited about a crush. I'm afraid this person won't like me. I'm afraid this person might like me. I'm afraid of not knowing what will happen."

It can be hard to tell the difference between a fear that is telling us we need to take immediate action to keep ourselves or a friend safe and a fear that is trying to protect us from possibly experiencing rejection. Both are valid and usually require action. We always want to stop and acknowledge when we feel uncomfortable, and then decide what to do next. If someone else is doing something that makes us uncomfortable, it's best to take note—create distance, remove ourselves or others, or say something and define our boundaries.

When I am feeling uncomfortable about talking to someone, I now know that this feeling is normal. Accepting this insecure feeling and approaching someone anyways is part of learning how to connect. In order to experience love, it's important to learn how to experience awkwardness and still reach out. A sailing coach named Jay Kehoe tells beginning sailors, "To learn to sail a boat, you have to get comfortable being uncomfortable." At first, being on a boat that is tipping can make someone feel uneasy, but becoming accustomed to that feeling is part of learning how to sail.

Starting a conversation with another person is awkward at first. Being vulnerable is uncomfortable. But, without the feeling of awkwardness, there's no possibility of connection. You have to risk talking with someone before you can receive the reward of getting to know someone. Learning to take initiative, even if we are feeling uncomfortable or awkward, is how we grow.

It's tricky because I'm asking you to practice two seemingly contradictory things—notice when you're feeling uncomfortable and leave, and notice when you're feeling uncomfortable and reach out and connect. When I break it down, I want you to pay attention to when you're feeling uncomfortable with someone's actions. Those actions are giving you clues about how that person treats others. If what someone is doing is making you uncomfortable, listen, act, and leave.

If, however, you're feeling uncomfortable inside because you yourself are feeling awkward or self-conscious or inadequate in some way, then offer those feelings a giant cup of love and approach your dreams anyway. Moving toward your dreams will always involve feeling uncomfortable internally (you might feel doubt or fear) and taking steps forward anyway. This is true of connecting with people as well.

If you are too afraid to talk with someone new, then

you limit the possibilities of whom you will know in your life. Smile. Make eye contact. Ask questions. Can you get curious about them as a person? Learn how to listen.

Also, notice the other person's behavior. Are they respecting you in their actions? Are they curious about you as a person? Do they treat you with kindness? Do they respect your boundaries?

In one study, many men reported that they would stop pressuring their girlfriends to have sex if the women said, "I really care about you, but I want to wait until the relationship is stronger."[97] In fact, not only would they stop pressuring their girlfriends to have sex, but this approach had a positive effect on the relationship.[98]

About a year ago, I was sitting next to an older man at a dinner. George was telling me about his life—his divorces, his regrets, and his accomplishments. Then he told me that he had figured out the secret to dating.

"Really?" I said.

"Yes," he said. "I tell everyone, if you're interested in someone, then ask them out for coffee. That way you can talk and get to know each other. It's a good way to begin."

A year later, I met George's grandson, who had just gotten married. I was talking with the newlyweds. "How did you two meet?" I asked.

"I asked her out for coffee," the groom said.

Opportunities ~

1) How do you approach talking with a crush? Do you? What's something you could say? Can you practice initiating a conversation? Will you?

2) Love is in the details—of a person, a day, a moment. What details do you appreciate about someone you admire? What other details would you like to know?

3) Is there someone you'd like to ask out for coffee or on a casual date? Review Professor Kerry Cronin's guidelines on pages 110-111 for how to ask someone on a date. Afterward, reflect, learn, and congratulate yourself on doing something brave—even if it didn't go how you hoped. What did it feel like to ask someone out? Can you do it again?

CREATING LOVE

Dear Reader,

Humans are unique creatures—we are intricate, complex, and beautiful in our quirks, our wounds, and our passions. If you look carefully, each one of us comes postmarked with words that say, "Handle with care." When we practice talking, sharing, listening, honoring, laughing, and playing, we have the opportunity to get to know and love another person. This is where true love lies, and experiencing it is exquisite.

I want to share something quite personal with you. The greatest joy I have known in my life is experiencing how liberating it feels to be loved completely by another person. I can share my dreams, challenges, and needs fully, and who I am is treated with tenderness, love, and respect.

I tell anyone who asks that no one could have prepared me for how much I love my children. The same is true for how I feel for my husband.

I would like to share with you two interviews that talk about how two people treat each other. I'd like you to pay attention to what causes harm and what creates connection.

Sophie, age 22 ~

I had one encounter where I was living in a house with a guy friend, and we'd been friends for a long time, and we were both drinking one night and got together. Something about the way it happened felt really, really bad. I trusted him, and I knew his family. He knew my family. Once it crossed over, we had zero communication. There was a disconnect about how we were viewing it. I wanted to be acknowledged. What got lost was that he didn't treat me like a person he knew. As soon as we slept together, he treated me differently. It felt really bad. He was so immature. That was the only time I ever slept with a male friend, and I haven't slept with any of my male friends since. It's fine for me to have these people as friends, but nothing more.

I came out of it thinking, "Wow, that was really shitty for my self-esteem." It was hard for me to break off from him emotionally. When people talk about casual sex, on an interior level, can you make it casual? Sometimes, you catch yourself talking about things casually that don't feel casual. When I slept with my friend, I spoke casually about it. I said it was okay and that I was fine, but inside it had a huge effect. People numb themselves out. You normalize self-doubt and feelings of anxiety.

This normalization is really toxic. I wasn't raised with any religious dogma. I didn't have someone telling me not to have sex before marriage. And I still think what's really dangerous is the normalization of an experience. That's what's most dangerous about the hook-up culture. Even the name itself normalizes it. The discourse around the hook-up culture and how people talk about it is making it a normal part of being 18.

Think about what they're unifying. Maybe it's a person's first sexual experience. Maybe it meant more to one person than to the other. People may think, "I did something that is 'normal,' but I feel horrible." If a girl feels bad, she can say she's not okay and that she's not going to affirm that experience as something she's okay with.

Cara, age 23 ~

Over time, my boyfriend and I learned that communication is so important. That is true for all relationships, whether they're romantic or not. If something is bothering you or something makes your uncomfortable, it's important to say it outright instead of letting it fester and brew and grow. That is something we did a lot in the beginning.

My boyfriend has an identical twin brother. They are the best of friends. They bicker constantly, but then they apologize immediately after. He's really good at apologizing, whereas, with my older sister, I always wanted to be right. I'm getting better, but I'm pretty bad at apologizing. It's hard for me to say, "You're right."

In the beginning, because I wouldn't naturally apologize, he would always say, "You're right, I'm sorry," even if he felt that I was in the wrong. I think it's important to stand up for how you feel and what you believe in. I also think it's important to be open to changing your perspective, but still being strong as an individual.

Another thing that might seem really small but I think is really important: We spent a lot of time doing our homework together, and that feels like you're spending time together, but it shouldn't count as time because it's not quality time, because you're not focused on each other. I think you can get stuck thinking, "Oh, we're spending so much time together, but our relationship isn't growing, we're not having fun, and all we're doing is working all the time." It took us two years to figure that out.

We were having a really serious talk about our relationship. We both weren't particularly happy. My boyfriend was saying he wanted to spend more time with his friends and that he wanted to make sure he had a healthy balance. I was saying that I didn't need to spend more time with him; that wasn't the feeling that I had. Then I asked myself, "Why do I still have the feeling that I'm not getting everything that I need or want?" Then I thought, "It's probably about the actual quality of the time we're spending together." You spend the day apart, and at 11 pm, when you're done with your homework, you get together, and you spend the night together, but again that's not quality time if you're sleeping. Whatever it is, if you're tied up in another task, it's important to have time together where your sole focus is just each other. We started making an effort to spend quality time with each other, and we both got a lot happier.

Opportunities ~

1) In your relationships, what is your first response to conflict? Do you avoid conflict? Do you tend to apologize for things that weren't your fault? Do you tend to want to be always right? Can you notice your tendencies and allow yourself new approaches—perhaps not apologizing when something isn't your fault, or working to listen to a different perspective?

2) What are some things you can learn from these interviews and apply in your own life to reduce harm and increase connection?

3) What does working on receiving love mean to you? What does working on offering love mean to you? What will you do?

BEING A LOVING FRIEND

Hannah Gribetz, Sexual Assault Peer Educator, age 22 ~

More types of people you should cultivate friendships with: People who care too much about everything, people who don't care about anything, people who like trying new things, people who already know exactly what they like, people who love to debate with you, people who just want to make you laugh, people who love learning from qualifiable experiences, people who love learning from quantifiable data, people who dress like you, people who wear things you wouldn't in a million years, people from your grade, people in grades above and below you, people who like sitcoms, dramas, cartoons, reality shows (most important, people who can recommend good TV to you), people who can take care of you, people who need someone to take care of them, people who come from cities, from suburbs, and from rural areas, from the Northeast, the West, the South, and the Midwest, from other countries entirely, people who come from money, from poverty, from the middle class, people who have the same sexual orientation as you, people who don't, people who aren't sure, people from every race and every gender, people who take medication, and people who go to therapy, and people who use canes, and people who have never been to a doctor for anything other than a check-up. The absolute best part of college was the people, and I found so many more kinds of people there than I could have ever imagined.

Dear Reader,

Being a caring friend to someone in need can truly change someone's life. Here's some advice that another one of my interviewees offered:

Irene Tsai, Watcher and Alcohol Educator, age 21 ~ Look out for your friends. Even if you might know exactly what you want for the night, it's not always clear that your friends will. This involves not only your direct and immediate close friends but all students, wherever you are going. This includes if you're an undergraduate or if you're in high school. It includes people you may not be friends with and even people you may have had fights with and don't necessarily get along with, who aren't part of your friend group. It doesn't really matter, because what it comes down to is that all of us are human beings who have different stories, different pasts, and we should be looking out for each other.

It is very likely that you will someday be a First Friend Responder when someone is really hurting. If something challenging is happening or has happened in a friend's life, you may be the first to know, and how you respond matters.

I want to go through some situations you may encounter. At any time, please reach out to others for additional help—a trained counselor, a teacher, a parent, or a hotline. There are many resources available for tough situations, and it is not your responsibility to go through difficulties alone. The situations we will cover include:

- How to respond to a friend who has been sexually assaulted.

- How to support a friend who is filing a police report or having a sexual-assault exam.

- What to say to a friend whom you think might have an eating disorder.

- How to identify anxiety, depression, or suicidal thinking and get help.

These are hard topics, and I know that teenagers and young adults encounter these situations personally and with their friends. Talking about how to identify these challenging situations and what to do can help you make a positive difference in your own life and your friends' lives.

Thank you for taking time to read through these interviews. It's important information.

Hannah Gribetz, Sexual Assault Peer Educator, age 22 ~ Creating a caring community is idealist, but the only way to make it realistic is to start living it.

RESPONDING TO A FRIEND WHO HAS BEEN SEXUALLY ASSAULTED

Dear Reader,

Because one purpose of this book is to bring to light suffering caused by sexual assault, I want to share with you what two different survivors said about how a friend responded and the effect one person's response can have.

Zoe, age 22 ~ The next day, I went on a hike with the girls we'd been camping with because all the guys left. We were staying for another night, and I told them what had happened. One of my friends said, "Oh my gosh, yeah, that's really scary, that's awful." And then another one of my friends said, "Well, you were sitting on his lap by the campfire." She ways saying, "I could see how that could have happened." After that, I just shut down.

Sofie Karasek, Co-founder End Rape on Campus, age 22 ~

What was really important to me was how my friend responded when I told her. It's important for everyone to know how to respond when someone says they've been sexually assaulted.

What my friend did was tell me specifically that it was not my fault, and that it was up to me what I wanted to do next. If I wanted to report, she would support me in that decision. If I didn't, she would support me in that decision as well. This places the agency back on the survivor. Having someone give control back to you can make a big difference in how someone heals.

I was really lucky that that's how someone responded to me.

Typically, someone responding will try to minimize the problem and make it seem as if it's not as bad as it was. With sexual assault, you need the opposite. You need someone to validate that what happened was wrong and that it's not your fault.

If a survivor comes to you, you should not impose yourself at all. They are coming to you. And you can say, "You can share or not share. I'm here to listen to whatever you want to share. I'm here for you." That puts the control back with the survivor.

Also, if possible (it depends on where you are), you can offer to go with them to make an appointment at the student health center with a counselor, or offer to go with them to have a sexual-assault exam. You are giving the survivor the ability to make that choice. This should apply when someone wants to report or not. You can offer to go with them, or if they don't want to report, that's okay.

It's important to prioritize the survivor's healing. Some people question why it's okay not to report. But I believe it's okay not to report because often reporting doesn't work out well. It can lead to an even more traumatic experience if you report and are not believed. If someone does not want to put themselves through that, that is completely valid.

Opportunities ~

1) Make a list of what friends said or did that seemed helpful and kind.

2) Hannah Gribetz, Sexual Assault Peer Educator, age 22 ~
Sexual violence doesn't always involve alcohol. It definitely does sometimes, maybe even a lot of the time, but a person does not have to be drunk not to consent to sexual activity. I'm very glad that the national conversation is shifting

toward a broader recognition of the effect of intoxication on the ability to give consent. I just always want to make sure that we include in the conversation ideas about how sober people can be forced, coerced, or manipulated into sexual activity. It's easy to imagine how a drunk person might be "taken advantage of," but that doesn't mean that the same thing can't happen to someone who is "in control of their faculties," even if physical force is not involved.

There are many different ways to pressure someone to do something they may not want to do. What are some strategies you've seen people use?

3) Some helpful words you could say to a friend who has been sexually assaulted:

- "I believe you."

- "This isn't your fault."

- "I'm sorry this happened to you. You didn't deserve this."

- "I appreciate your strength in sharing this."

- "You are not alone."

- "Help is available, and it can make a big difference."

HOW TO SUPPORT A FRIEND WHO IS FILING A POLICE REPORT OR HAVING A SEXUAL-ASSAULT EXAM

Dear Reader,

Another aspect of being a friend to someone who has been sexually assaulted is knowing how to support them if they decide to file a police report or have a sexual-assault exam conducted at a hospital. One of my interviewees volunteered at a hospital helping survivors after a sexual assault.

Grace Miller, Sexual Health Educator and
Hospital Advocate for Sexual Assault Survivors, age 22 ～

What's important is for the survivor to have control over what happens, to begin to restore their sense of autonomy. It's important to know that you absolutely do not have to report. Some choose not to because they don't want to deal with what happens when they report, and that's totally valid.

If you do choose to report, it allows for the possibility that the assailant will be removed from campus—which some people need in order to feel safe again in that space.

At my school, if someone is raped or sexually assaulted, there's a hotline they can call. There are also national hotlines. If you're in immediate danger, you should call 911.

If you call the hotline and decide you want a police presence, then they take your account. And then if you want, the police can take you to the hospital to get a rape kit done. It's important to know that you do not need a police escort to get a rape kit done.

A rape kit is an exam where a specially trained nurse takes samples of DNA off of your body—swabbing your mouth, or even doing a gynecological exam and swabbing the vaginal canal. How this exam is administered will depend on what happened during the assault. You have the right to say "No" to any aspect of the exam.

The purpose of the exam is to have physical evidence in the event that the case goes to court. That evidence will not be used unless you want it to be used.[99] You have to get a rape kit done within a certain time-period after the assault. The best time is immediately after.

I would recommend that you get a rape kit done whether or not you decide to report later because it's a powerful piece of evidence. However, getting a rape kit done can be traumatic.

When I was working at a rape crisis center, I was a hospital advocate, and I was there when people came into the Emergency Room. I was with the survivors the entire time they were in the ER. I explained what a rape kit was and the exam process, and I provided emotional support. I also helped with safety planning and made sure they had somewhere to go afterward.

I know firsthand what that experience is like. It can be further traumatizing. You have to explain what happened to you in detail in order for the rape kit to be administered, and you have to be touched again in those same places. That's really hard. When I say I would recommend that you get a rape kit done—if you choose not to, that's beyond understandable.

If you do choose to go to the hospital or go to the cops, you can have someone with you, a friend or a family member. You do not have to go alone. That emotional support is important, and you have that right.

From here on, it differs from school to school what to do next.

Calling a hotline doesn't necessarily mean you're reporting it. If you decide to report, you have a choice how to report. Generally, the best place is with a Title IX officer at your school. Title IX is a piece of national legislation that recognizes your right to feel safe on campus.[100] If you talk with a Title IX officer, you can learn what your rights are in the context of your school.[101] You can also go to a dean. If you want to read more about your rights, go to www.knowyourix.org. It has resources that students created.

If you choose to pursue judicial action within your school, there might be a hearing—this will depend on the school. At my school, a panel of staff members, professors, and peers listened to each case. Both parties have help, or you can hire your own lawyer, and the evidence is presented. The panel deliberates and makes a decision.

It is hotly debated what your burden of proof is, which means, to what extent you need to prove that you're right. In a school system, the burden of proof is not as high as it would be in a court of law. In a school system, the decision being made is how the accused person should be treated within the context of the school. The stakes aren't as high because the accused person isn't going to jail.

In the best-case scenario, the panel would rule in your favor, finding it more likely than not that you were sexually assaulted. At my school, if 51% agree, then the accused person is found guilty and is required to leave school. The harshest punishment possible is being expelled, and that is not common. The person could be removed from classes you're in or might not be allowed to participate on sports teams. The punishments can vary. It is the subject of a lot of activism, making these censures harsher.

If you were to go through government recourse, there is the possibility that the person could be punished more severely, but that is unlikely because the burden of proof is much higher. In a criminal court, the burden of proof has to be beyond a reasonable doubt: A judge and jury have to decide that your case is so strong that it can't be doubted by a reasonable person. The problem is that the court's definition of what a reasonable person is is not universal. It is generally skewed to doubt the survivor.

Survivors, when they go through any of these processes, have to deal with a lot of victim-blaming—meaning that they're blamed for being at the party, for wearing the wrong sort of clothes, or for being a tease, saying yes to one thing and not to another, which, again, survivors have the right to do. This makes these trials very, very difficult and very emotionally taxing for the survivor.

The strictest punishment that an assailant might receive in a court of law is jail time, and that's very unlikely and probably would cost you a lot of money in legal fees just trying to get it to court. The court would assign you a lawyer, but if you wanted a fighting chance of winning, you'd have to hire a lawyer. And it's going to be a long, drawn-out process. It may never even go to court. It's frustrating, and most people don't ever go to court for that reason. Only three out of every hundred rapists will ever spend even a single day in prison.[102]

I do want to say that there are many reasons why people choose not to report. If you are in this situation, you are the one who decides what is best for you. Whatever decision you make should be respected.

Something I hear a lot is that female survivors won't speak up or pursue action in a court of any kind because they don't want to ruin the assailant's life. This sentiment can come from very different places. A woman is significantly more likely to be assaulted by someone she knows. The myth is that people are assaulted by strangers, but it's likely that you cared, to some extent, about this person. Often people won't speak up because they believe that, if they do, they'll ruin the person's life. They can also blame themselves on some level, an internalized form of victim-blaming: "Oh, I shouldn't have been at that party or worn that dress." Women, in particular, for many different reasons, are made to believe that it's their fault, and that's simply not true. I want to dispel that.

I want to validate a survivor's choice and make it clear that your body was violated. You have the right to ensure that it doesn't happen again to you or to anyone else. Moreover, if you choose to pursue recourse in a university setting, it is highly unlikely that the assailant's life will be ruined. Even if they are expelled from school, they will find another school, and they will find people who don't know what happened or don't care.

It's messed up that someone can rape someone else and there's very little recourse for the survivor. I believe there should be harsher punishments for rapists. But the point is that it's unlikely that you will permanently alter their life for the worse. I urge survivors not to let that be the reason they don't report. Even if there wasn't penetration, if you felt at all violated, you can seek this kind of recourse.

Opportunities ~

1) In your area, where can someone go if she needs to have a sexual-assault exam?

2) Where can someone go if she needs to report an assault?

3) If someone is sexually assaulted or has unprotected sex, do you know where to purchase Plan B? Where can she have an STI test done?

WHAT TO SAY TO A FRIEND
WHO MAY HAVE AN EATING DISORDER

Dear Reader,

Last November I interviewed Lynn Grefe for this book. Although we never met in person, I could hear in her voice a woman committed to making the world a better place for girls. For over 10 years, Lynn worked as the president of the National Eating Disorder Association. Five months after we spoke, Lynn died of cancer. After I heard the news, I returned to my notes from our conversation. I knew Lynn had entrusted me with wisdom that she wanted me to share with you.

"I want girls to feel good about who they are," she said. "It's a tough time to grow up. There's more vanity and more focus on how we look. Now we have size zero. Zero is nothing. Who wants to be nothing? I always say that I wish we could measure the size of our hearts and not the size of our hips."

Lynn told me that there's a strong link between being sexually assaulted and developing an eating disorder. "Seventy-five percent of people who have eating disorders have been sexually abused," she said. "Think about bulimia—on some level it makes sense: You're trying to purge the unhappiness."

She went on to tell me how important it is for someone with an eating disorder to get help. "Apathy is one of the worst things we have on college campuses," Lynn said. "The number one best thing to do is to get diagnosed early and to get help."

"It's time to talk about it," Lynn said. "If we say something and someone gets help early, they don't need to be sick so long." She added, "If you notice that someone is dieting, binging, purging, hiding, skipping meals, or compulsively focusing on weight loss, it's important to say something. Roommates know. Dorm-mates know."

"Instead of saying, 'Hey, you look good,' say, 'I care about you, and I think you're struggling, and I'd love to find some resources to help you.'" Lynn said that these words could come from anyone who knows and cares—family, roommates, friends, teammates, coaches, RAs.

She gave me some statistics: Over one half of teenage girls and nearly one third of teenage boys use unhealthy weight-control behaviors, such as skipping meals, fasting, smoking cigarettes, vomiting, and taking laxatives.[103] Even among clearly non-overweight girls, over one third report dieting.[104]

Lynn told me that eating disorders have the highest death rate of any psychiatric illness—higher than depression or schizophrenia. "People don't understand that people die. It's brutal. People think bulimia doesn't do harm, but it does—you can go into a coma. With anorexia, you can wither away. It's like taking poison every day."

Lynn explained, "We have a culture that perpetuates a focus on size and not health. Unrealistic images come to us through the media, models, magazines, TV, movies, and advertising. As a society, we need to circle the wagons and ask ourselves how can we focus on health instead of how skinny you are. How can we allow for a diversity of bodies? How can we change the dialogue?"

Lynn gave me several statistics that concerned her

deeply: 81% of 10-year-olds are afraid of being fat,[105] and 42% of 1st- to 3rd-grade girls want to be thinner.[106]

"You can help someone with early intervention and a therapist who specializes in eating-disorder treatment," Lynn said, and she added, "Someone with an eating disorder has a distorted relationship with their body and with food. They can also feel tired of being isolated, of hiding, and of the shame, and they can get help. When a patient gets help, they can start to see what's causing them to show anxiety through their behavior with food. Anxiety and Obsessive Compulsive Disorder drive eating disorders in a big way. With help, recovery is possible."

Lynn then offered young women five pieces of advice:

1) Put your shoulders back and be proud of what you're bringing to your school.

2) Learn what resources are available and use them. Don't be afraid to get counseling.

3) Set your own goals and measure your own success for yourself. Don't let someone else's standards define you. This includes your parents. Find your own way.

4) Self-care. Take care of yourself—your body and your head. Practice forgiving yourself and saying, "I'm enough."

5) Let things go. Don't hold onto things that don't serve you. Look ahead.

Lynn finished our conversation by telling me about a young woman who recently stopped by her office. When the woman was 18, she had a severe eating disorder and refused treatment. Because she was an adult, her mother could not force her to get care. Nevertheless, Lynn told me, the mother arranged for Lynn to meet with both of them. After the meeting, the daughter agreed to get help.

"What did you say?" I asked Lynn.

"I looked at the daughter, and I could tell that she really loved her mother. I said to her, 'If your mother had cancer, a potentially terminal disease—as serious as a heart disease or having a malignant tumor—and a doctor said she needed treatment, how would you deal with it?'"

The daughter started to cry and said, "I'd tell my mom that she had to see a doctor and get care."

"This is what your mother is saying to you," Lynn replied.

"The daughter stopped by my office a few weeks ago," Lynn told me in our interview. "She was healthy and vibrant." I could hear relief and joy in Lynn's voice. "She thanked me and told me that I had saved her life."

Opportunities ~

1) Practice role-playing with a friend and saying that you're concerned about them and want to help them get help. Then switch roles and have your friend practice on you.

2) Write down something that Lynn Grefe said about bodies that you want to remember.

3) Lynn Grefe dedicated her life to helping empower girls. This is one of the last interviews she gave. What messages can you take with you?

HOW TO IDENTIFY ANXIETY, DEPRESSION, OR SUICIDAL THINKING, AND GET HELP

Dear Reader,

I considered interviewing an expert to help me write this letter on depression and suicide. Then I decided that it would be more honest for me to tell you about my experience. When I was uncovering the truth about my past, in addition to experiencing anxiety, I fell into a severe depression.

There was one day that I remember. I went to see my chiropractor. He is a dear person. I told him I was thinking of ending my life. He asked me why, and I told him I didn't want to live in a world where teachers sexually abuse their students. He was quiet, and then he told me that he understood. I could tell that he could see the weight and horror I felt as I came to terms with this truth. His response was a moment of grace for me. He was kind and honored my feelings of despair. His presence and his offering of compassion and understanding touched me, and I felt heard. He also knew that I was seeing a therapist and asked me to talk with her.

When I thought I couldn't continue and my pain was truly unbearable, I learned to reach out for help—to a friend, a counselor, a family member, a spiritual being, or my dog. There were many distinct moments when someone was kind to me, and that kindness made all the difference.

Anxiety and depression are like many illnesses: They have a variety of symptoms, and there are many known ways to recover. The problem with anxiety and depression is that when you're in the pit, you can feel and believe that it will never end. I felt this way, and it was agonizing. Still, as much as it seemed as if the darkness and pain would last forever, I found people who knew how to help me. If you're ever feeling depressed, it's really important to reach out and get help. If one person isn't able to help, try someone else.

As my therapist, Ruth, told me, "Suicide is a permanent solution to a temporary problem." In honoring my policy to Do No Harm, I knew I didn't want to hurt people I loved, and so I worked hard to get help and get better. It took effort, time, grace-filled moments, loving people, pets, and long walks in nature.

Part of my getting better was deciding to accept that I didn't like living in a world where people are sexually abused, and resolving to work to change that. I also love love and believe that it is the best part of being alive—loving other people, the earth, flowers, pets, sunshine, rain, life itself. I decided to become an agent of change and to do my best to make a difference—even if it is a small difference—to reduce harm and increase love.

A high school senior read an early draft of this book before she went to college. Recently, she sent me an email that filled me with hope. During her freshman year, she told me, she struggled with depression. But, because she had read this book, she got help and got better. In college, she started a blog on depression, and other students wrote to her about their experiences. She shared her story and made a difference—people connected to each other and offered each other kindness and concern.

We are meant to cast loving rocks in a pond, sending ripples out until they touch the edge. Eventually the ripples come back and wash over us.

Catherine, age 22 ~ When we moved in with my grandparents, I went through a seriously depressed couple of years. I would spend most of my time in the basement—summer time, school time. I didn't want to have friends. I didn't care to have friends. I would wake up, go to school, come back, and go downstairs and read or watch TV, and then do it again. On the weekends, I'd spend most of my time isolated. And I didn't care, that was the crazy thing. But then I started to get past it, and I started to try, but I was lost. The most immediate thing to try with in high school was the social scene, but I was really uncomfortable with it, and I was really uncomfortable with people. I decided I would talk to three new people a day. I had a very mechanical approach about learning to integrate back into young society. The biggest thing I did was creating this strategy of talking to three new people a day—longer conversations than just "Hi." You see in the movies where kids have lunch in the bathroom. I really wanted to do that, but it was something I also assigned myself: "You can't spend lunch in the library or the bathroom." I kept track of my progress, and I worked through it.

Opportunities ~

1) It is powerful to become an agent of change in the world, to decide that you can make a difference, even if it is a small difference. I invite you to embrace your own agency—know that you can be an actor for good, for yourself, for others, and for the world; know that you can make a difference. Can you make a pledge out loud that you will say something if you see a friend in need of help?

2) Imagine yourself noticing if someone isn't doing well: They're pushing friends away, changing their behavior, isolating themselves. Can you see yourself taking a risk and saying something to that person or to a helpful adult?

3) Can you make a pledge out loud that if you are suffering, you will seek help? Imagine yourself reaching out for help. It's important to remember that we're not alone in the world and that we are not meant to suffer alone. If you or someone you know is suffering from anxiety or depression, please get help.

If someone you know is suffering from anxiety or depression, some signs to pay attention to include:

from www.suicidepreventionlifeline.org

Expressing hopelessness about the future, displaying severe overwhelming pain or distress, withdrawing from friends, being angry or hostile, sleeping all the time or not sleeping, consuming a lot of alcohol or drugs, talking about, or writing about, or making plans for suicide, experiencing stressful situations, including those that involve loss, humiliation, or getting in trouble. If you notice any of these warning signs, you can help by expressing your concern about what you're observing in their behavior.

- It can be helpful to say, "I'm seeing what you're doing, and I'm really worried."
- It's okay to ask directly about suicide—whether someone is thinking about it.
- If someone you care about is suffering, encourage them to call the National Suicide Prevention Lifeline. 1-800-273-TALK (8255) There are people who are trained to help. It's also important to involve an adult they trust.
- If you are concerned about their immediate safety, call 911.[107]

Additional words you could say to a friend who is suffering or to yourself, if you are suffering:

- "I'm sorry this is happening to you."
- "You don't deserve this. It's not your fault."
- "I'm worried about your health and your safety."
- "You're not alone."
- "Help is available. Please reach out to a family member, a counselor, a teacher, a coach, or an emergency hotline."

LOVING THE BOYS AND MEN IN YOUR LIFE

Dear Reader,

Today I'd like to talk about loving and respecting the boys and men in our lives. As a mother of two sons and as a wife with a husband whose kindness changed my life, it breaks my heart to hear how much anger is being directed at men. The same way in which I was treated badly, for being female, I see boys and men being treated badly for being male. Gender prejudices are real, and they go both ways.

Being angry and upset about the abuse and treatment of girls and women is more than understandable. Blaming all men, however, isn't fair or helpful. We can end up pushing away and hurting important allies and potential friends.

When people elevate their own gender by putting another gender down, they are relying on a power dynamic to feel good about themselves. Some men put women down to put up themselves; and some women put men down to put up themselves. This model is broken because it hurts people.

I always enjoy the Winter Olympics, especially the figure-skating pairs. I admire the grace and skill of the male and female skaters. My favorite part is when the male skater lifts the female skater. He is strong and confident. She is strong and confident. Together they reach a height and beauty that neither could have attained alone.

I want us to embrace a different model of how humans relate to each other. I want us to care more about mutual love and respect than power and dominance. We only can truly lift each other up when we have shared with each other whatever it is that gets us down. Sharing, caring, and respecting one another are the way forward.

As we develop an awareness and acceptance of our full palette of emotions, I believe it is essential to offer this range to boys and men as well. Behind anger there may be wounds and insecurities. Behind a quest for power there may be a fear of inadequacy, a feeling of not being enough, or a feeling of being inferior. Keeping girls in a "nice girl" place and boys in a "don't be a sissy" place cuts off our experience of life. When we allow boys and girls to feel the full range of being human—sad, scared, angry, happy—we open up possibilities for how we can experience compassion and love.

With some gentle conversation about predatory cues—traits, tactics, and tricks—Noble Boys and Men can learn how to identify when guys are behaving badly. We can ask them to notice guys being creeps and to say something. We want to encourage Noble Males to become heroes. We need their help. And their help matters. The goal is to make predatory behavior socially unacceptable and Noble Males—who protect and honor girl and women—social heroes.

We want to encourage and recognize positive words and actions that celebrate girls and women. Noble Boys and Men can lift up girls and women by talking lovingly about qualities they admire, appreciate, and respect in the girls and women in their own lives. They can also support other Noble Males who do the same.

I'm thinking of humpback whales. Every year, male humpback whales sing a new song, and they sing it together.

It changes from year to year, and somehow the whales learn the new tune, and the song is heard around the world.

And what can we do as girls and women? We can honor Noble Boys and Men by offering them our gratitude and respect.[108]

Opportunities ~

1) Take time to notice the Noble Males in your life. Whom do you admire? What do they do?

2) Find a way to say thank you—to show that you appreciate their respectful behavior toward girls and women.

3) Ask a boy or man in your life to share with you some things he admires or respects about some of the girls and women in his life.

How we can build bridges with the boys and men in our lives:

- Encourage, honor, and recognize the boys and men in our lives who are supporting girls and women. Offer them praise and gratitude regularly.
- Make time to listen to their insights and perspectives. They notice and know a lot. What do they see? Hear? What makes them uncomfortable? (Practice listening without thinking of what you want to say next.)
- Discourage bragging about conquests, pushing drinks, ignoring "No."
- Ask them to speak up and stop friends who are being creepy. "That's not cool. Stop. Losers do that."

- Notice our own self-sabotaging behavior when we allow ourselves to continue to interact with boys and men who treat us badly. End these relationships. We can't change them.
- Seek and honor boys and men who respect girls and women—true heroes.
- Value love and kindness more than power and dominance. Sexual conquest is about power, not love.
- Start with communication and respect before beginning sensual and sexual interactions. Remember every person is unique, with challenges, dreams, and needs.
- Communicate even when it feels uncomfortable.
- Resolve to speak up about your own sensual and sexual wants, limits, and needs. Be honest about what's working and what isn't.
- Remember that any interaction between two people is defined by how both people treat each other. Respect matters.

LOVING YOUR FAMILY

Dear Reader,

One aspect of love that can be easy to overlook is the love our families give to us. I know families can be messy and that people aren't perfect. This means it can be easy to find fault. The faults are often real. And so is the love.

I want to share with you a suggestion that I heard from one of my interviewees on families and gratitude.

Alyssa, age 23 ~ Before I left for college, I wrote notes to my mom and dad and put them under their pillows. They moved me into my dorm freshman year and got me all settled in. We said our goodbyes, and they drove home. Later they found the notes and read them. I handwrote them each a note saying something along the lines of "I'm going to be okay. Thanks for this opportunity and for giving me a good foundation. I'll remember to call you. Thank you so much for everything. I love you." My mom told me that my dad cried when he read his letter. And, literally, they still bring it up. Thank goodness I did that. It really meant a lot to them and to me.

You don't have to wait until you leave home to write gratitude letters to people in your life. The letters that my children have written to me are saved in a wooden box beside my desk. If something were to happen to my house and I had minutes to leave, I would take that box with me.

Opportunities ~

1) Write a letter of gratitude to a parent or caregiver who has shown you love. Tell them the specifics of what they did and how what they did touched you.

2) Give them the letter.

3) Write in your journal how their response felt to you. Sharing love and gratitude is like a pair of mirrors that bounce light back and forth.

LOVING THE DISCOVERY PROCESS

Sophie, age 22 ~

I hesitate to use my experience to offer advice to another person, because you are your own person. The only thing I can say for certain is that just because you haven't defined who you are, it doesn't mean that yourself isn't still inside of you—you're in the process of finding that out.

I see college—even though it was difficult—as a really good experience because I was committed to developing and to the process. Looking back, I wish I hadn't been so hard on myself for being in process. Internally, you might have no idea what feels good and what doesn't, who you like, and who you don't. It may seem like you have no idea, but, in reality, you do.

Be more accepting of that state.

Opportunities ~

1) Have a tea ceremony for yourself. Check in, say hello. What's there?

2) Offer yourself loving kindness.

3) Accept the offer.

IT'S ALL ABOUT RECOVERY

Dear Reader,

Before I end, I'd like to share with you one more story. I know a family who drove across the country one summer. Before their journey began, they created a motto: "It's all about recovery." Each day, they acknowledged that each person would occasionally lose it about something—they would get hungry for good food, angry about traffic, tired of someone else's music, desperate for alone time, exhausted from a poor night's sleep. Whatever the cause, life on the road has its beauty and its challenges. And when something didn't go as planned and someone lost it, everyone agreed to say, "It's all about recovery," and try to respond to the person who was suffering with kindness—including the person who lost it. Together they remembered that recovery matters most, returning to joy and to the adventure forward.

As humans, we have the freedom to choose love. We are meant to offer love and to receive love. It is our most precious way of being—experiencing tenderness, warmth, connection, and kindness. Love is not about exerting power over someone. It's about learning how to share the journey of our suffering and successes with another person, and to be there with them on their journey. How we treat one another is what matters most.

We can start with ourselves. When you leave home, take with you your loving-kindness tea ceremony, your Cloak of Unconditional Love, your Half-Second Pause, your Inner Protector, your Animal Warrior, your Sassy Mama, your Inner Nurturer, your Lifeguard, and your First Friend Responder. Remember to make quiet time every day to listen to your Inner Guide and recall your Charisms. Your goal is to actively create a home within yourself that is filled with respect, kindness, and love. This is a practice, and it takes work.

When things don't go as planned or as you hoped, return to your inner sparkle and goodness. It's always there, and it will feel like home.

I believe that an alternate reality exists—it is separate from time and space, and it is a world constructed out of love. When we work to build love, with kindness, respect, and compassion, something that lasts beyond us is created and remains. Learning how to love—to offer love and receive love—is worthy of your attention and effort. And you can start with yourself.

Thank you for taking this journey with me. I wish you love, joy, peace, and hope along your path.

Kathleen

Acknowledgments

In sickness and in health...

I am thankful for all the people who helped put me back together, especially the young people I interviewed who told me their own stories. I am thankful for my girl friends, who listened, shared, and opened their hearts to me. I am thankful for my writer friends, who walked beside me and encouraged me to keep going. I am thankful for my father, who taught me to sing and was kind when I was struggling. I am thankful for my mother, who taught me how to love and see beauty, so that when I was lost I knew a way back. I am thankful for my children, who give me joy and love every-day. With all of my heart, I am thankful for my husband, Dan—you walked through the dark place with me. No one, except God, knows how much your love and kindness have meant to me. It seems fitting to let one of my interviewees say it for me: "You essentially saved my life."

Experts and Advisors

I offer gratitude to all of these people for what they have given to this book and to me. Many are quoted; all informed the wisdom that is shared in these pages. Most of the authors have written multiple books—I include the one that influenced me the most.

Kayleen Asbo, Ph.D., Acclaimed Cultural Historian, Musician, Writer and Teacher. Dedicated to sharing the transformative stories of powerful and creative women in mythology and history. www.kayleenasbo.com.

Marybeth Bond, Advises women on how to travel alone. World Traveler and Writer, *National Geographic*. Author of *Gutsy Women: Advice, Inspiration, Stories* (Travelers' Tales, 2012). www.gutsytraveler.com.

Tara Brach, Ph.D., Clinical Psychologist. International Teacher of Buddhist Meditation. Author of *Radical Acceptance: Embracing Your Life with the Heart of a Buddha* (Bantam, 2003). www.tarabrach.com.

Jennifer Calvert, Ph.D., Associate Dean, Stanford University. Advises on residential life issues.

Don Carney, Director of Restorative Service, YMCA Marin County Youth Court. Restorative Justice Advocate for more than 40 years. www.marinyouthcourt.org.

Jessica Chapman-Segal, M.A., Reproductive Health Education Program Supervisor, San Ysidro Health Center, San Diego.

Annie E. Clark, Co-founder and Executive Director, End Rape on Campus, a nonprofit organization that focuses on empowering students to stop sexual violence. Co-author of *We Believe You: Survivors of Campus Sexual Assault Speak Out* (Holt, 2016.) www.endrapeoncampus.org.

Casey Corcoran, M.A.T., Program Director, Futures Without Violence, a nonprofit organization that develops innovative ways to end violence against women, children, and families. www.futureswithoutviolence.org.

Catherine Criswell Spear, J.D., Title IX Coordinator, Stanford University (2014-2015). Attorney, Office for Civil Rights, U.S. Department of Education (19 years).

Stephanie Cyr, J.D., Self-Defense Instructor, San Francisco State University. Taekwondo Martial Artist. Founder and Owner, Martial Arts Movement.

Denise Raquel Dunning, M.P.A., Ph.D., Founder and Executive Director, Rise Up, an international nonprofit organization focused on advancing health, education, and equity for girls, youth, and women. www.riseuptogether.org.

Angela Exson, M.Ed., Assistant Dean and Director, Office of Sexual Assault & Relationship Abuse, Education, & Response, Stanford University (2011-2015).

Paola Gianturco, Photojournalist and Author of *Women Who Light the Dark* (Powerhouse, 2007), focusing on women around the world who have overcome difficult issues. www.paolagianturco.com.

Lynn Grefe, President and Chief Executive Officer, National Eating Disorders Association (2003-2015). www.nationaleatingdisorders.org.

Hannah Gribetz, Sexual Assault Peer Educator, BWell Health Promotion, Brown University.

Rick Hanson, Ph.D., Neuropsychologist. Senior Fellow, Greater Good Science Center, University of California, Berkeley. Author of *Hardwiring Happiness: The New Brain Science of Contentment, Calm, and Confidence* (Harmony, 2013). Creator of the internet program "The Foundations of Well-Being." www.thefoundationsofwellbeing.com.

Luciana Herman, Ph.D., All-freshmen Dorm Resident Fellow, Student Advisor, Lecturer, Writing and Rhetoric Program and Stanford Law School, Stanford University.

Stephen Hinshaw, Ph.D., Professor and Department Chair, Department of Psychology, University of California, Berkeley. Author of *The Triple Bind: Saving Our Teenage Girls from Today's Pressures* (Ballantine, 2009).

Carianne James, Artist, Teacher and Founder of Spirit Warriors, a workshop to uplift and encourage girls to reach their highest potential. www.cariannejames.com.

Grace Kaimila-Kanjo, M.A., Girls' Empowerment Educator and Africa Regional Senior Advisor for Rise Up, an international nonprofit organization focused on advancing health, education, and equity for girls, youth, and women. www.riseuptogether.org.

Harriet Kamashanyu, Founder and Executive Director, Rhythm Of Life, a nonprofit organization working to empower female sex workers and their daughters in the red light districts of Uganda. www.rhthymoflifeuganda.org.

Sofie Karasek, Co-founder and Director of Education, End Rape on Campus, a nonprofit organization focused on empowering students to stop sexual violence. www.endrapeoncampus.org.

Renee McDonald, Ph.D., Associate Dean for Research, Dedman College of Humanities and Sciences, and Associate Professor, Department of Psychology, Southern Methodist University. Co-creator of a virtual reality training program for girls.

Catharine A. MacKinnon, J.D., Ph.D., Elizabeth A. Long Professor of Law, University of Michigan; James Barr Ames Visiting Professor of Law, Harvard Law School. Author specializing in sex equality issues.

Richard Mendius, M.D., Neurologist. Meditation Teacher. Co-founder, The Wellspring Institute for Neuroscience and Contemplative Wisdom. Co-author of *Meditations to Change Your Brain* (Audio book, 2009). www.wisebrain.org

Grace Miller, Co-Founder and Operations Director of Uplift—Online Communities Against Sexual Violence. Hospital Advocate for Sexual Assault Survivors, Dallas Area Rape Crisis Center. Educator, Center for Sexual Pleasure and Health, Brown University. www.uplifttogether.org.

Marshall Miller, Co-author of *I Love Female Orgasm* (Da Capo, 2007) Nationally known Sex Educator, Sex Discussed Here! Degree in Sexuality & Society, Brown University. www.sexualityeducation.com

Barbara Minneti, O-Sensei, eighth degree black belt, Stanford Kenpo Karate.

Audrey Monke, M.A., Parenting Blogger. Camp Owner and Director, Gold Arrow Camp. Has worked with children, college-age counselors, and parents for more than 30 years. www.sunshine-parenting.com.

Elisa Pinto de Magalhaes, M.A., Advocacy Coordinator, International Planned Parenthood Federation. Undergraduate thesis: *BroBibles: Hegemonic Masculinity on College Campuses*, Tufts University.

Andre Salvage, Master in Kung Fu San Soo. Nationally recognized Inspirational Speaker and Assertiveness Teacher. www.andresalvage.com.

Anne Scott, M.B.A., Ph.D., Survivors' Rights Activist. In 2015, Anne broke a 25 year silence and went public with her account of sexual abuse at a New England prep school.

Stephanie Seibel, Counselor and Mentor. Focuses on young adults and expressive arts therapy.

Charlene Senn, Ph.D., Professor in Applied Social Psychology, Department of Psychology and Women's and Gender Studies, University of Windsor, Canada. Creator of the Sexual Assault Resistance Education Program (EAAA) for first-year university women. Founder of SARE, the Sexual Assault Resistance Education Centre, offering training in the administration and delivery of the EAAA sexual assault resistance program. www.sarecentre.org.

Eric Silverberg, Co-founder, Cayuga's Watchers, a student-run organization at Cornell University that trains students to work undercover at parties to prevent alcohol abuse and sexual misconduct. www.cayugaswatchers.org.

Natasha Singh, Youth Advocate and Educational Consultant, focusing on sex education, navigating the porn culture and gender-based violence prevention. Co-Founder and Executive Director of Asha Rising, a nonprofit organization helping women who have aged out of India's sex industry. www.asharising.org.

Donnovan Somera Yisrael, M.A., Manager of Social and Emotional Health Programs, Stanford University. National Speaker on Sexual and Emotional Health. www.youtube.com/watch?v=p54LL1p5CPc.

Irene Tsai, Alcohol Educator and Watcher, Cayuga's Watchers, a student-run organization at Cornell University that trains students to work undercover at parties to prevent alcohol abuse and sexual misconduct. www.cayugaswatchers.org.

Amy Cerier Tyre, Yoga Instructor. Speaker. Spiritual Guide, helping people find their way home to their own luminosity.

Kenneth Van Vleck, Sensei and Head Instructor, sixth degree black belt, Stanford Kenpo Karate.

Kate Weinberg, Nationally known Sex-Educator, Sex Discussed Here! Hotline Volunteer, Rape, Abuse, Incest National Network (RAINN). Author and Yoga Instructor. www.sexualityeducation.com

David Wolowitz, J.D., Director and Co-chair, McLane Middleton's Education Group, a leading legal authority and consultant on student and campus safety, risk management, and crisis response for independent and boarding schools.

Vajra Woolsey, Healer, Artist, and Spiritual Coach, Pomona, CA. Focuses on helping people live happy, healthy, and integrated lives.

Endnotes

1. I am grateful to Doctor Bessel van der Kolk, a pioneer researcher and expert on traumatic stress, who compared Helen Keller's transition from darkness to understanding with trauma survivors in his book *The Body Keeps the Score* (Viking, 2014).

2. Leonard and Bane, (1992); McKenry, Julian, and Gavazzi, (1995); Rosenbaum and O'Leary, (1981); Van Hassel, Morrison, and Bellack, (1985).

3. Hammock and Richardson, (1997); Jacquelyn W. White, (2007), "Violence in Intimate Relationships." *Children and Youth Services Review.*

4. Swartout, Kevin M. and Jacquelyn W. White, (2010), "The Relationship Between Drug Use and Sexual Aggression in Men Across Time." *Journal of Interpersonal Violence. Vol.25, Issue 9;* Krebs, C.P., Lindquist, C.H., Warner, T.D., Fisher, B.S., and Martin, S.L. (2007), *The Campus Sexual Assault (CSA) Study.* Washington, DC: U.S. National Institute of Justice.

5. Brendgen, Vitaro, and Tremblay, (2002); Hall and Hirschman, (1991).

6. Abbey et al., (2001); White and Koss, (1993).

7. Snyder, Howard N., (2000): *"Sexual Assault of Young Children as Reported to Law Enforcement."* Bureau of Justice Statistics, U.S. Department of Justice.

8. From Professor MacKinnon's speech, October 16, 2016 at Stanford University's conference "Anita: Speaking Truth to Power."

9. When I was working on this book, I heard three young women from Africa talk, and I was inspired by their confidence, vision, and activism. Each was taking on issues like child marriage laws, prostitution, and girls' education, and they were making major changes. I later learned that all three had attended a girls' empowerment workshop through an organization called Rise Up. It took me several months to find the woman who had trained these young women, Grace Kaimila-Kanjo. When Grace and I spoke, she was in South Africa and I was in California. It was late afternoon for her and early morning for me, but we realized that we shared the same dream of seeing girls reach their full potential.

10. From an interview with Lena Dunham. www.lennyletter.com/life/interviews/a271/the-lenny-interview-gavin-de-becker/.

11. en.wikipedia.org/wiki/Statutory_rape. "Statutory Rape Known to Law Enforcement," pdf. U.S. Department of Justice, Office of Juvenile Justice and Delinquency Prevention. Retrieved 2008-03-24.

12. www.urbandictionary.com/define.php?term=Grooming.

13. www.urbandictionary.com/define.php?term=pedophile.

14. Hersh, Keith; Gray-Little, Bernadette, (1998). "Psychopathic Traits and Attitudes Associated with Self-Reported Sexual Aggression in College Men." *Sage Journals, Vol.13, Issue 4.*

15. From a helpful website called www.loveisrespect.org/is-this-abuse/.

16. Ackard, D.M., and D. Neumark-Sztainer, (2002). "Dating Violence and Date Rape Among Adolescents." *Child Abuse & Neglect*, 26 455-473.

17. www.suicide.org/rape-victims-prone-to-suicide.html.

18. Girelli SA, Resick PA, Marhoefer-Dvorak S, Hutter CK. (1986). "Subjective distress and violence during rape: their effects on long-term fear." *Violence Vict.* 1(1):35-46.

19. Cayuga's Watchers is a student-led 501 (c) (3) independent organization designed to mitigate the harms associated with high-risk drinking while promoting student safety at Cornell University.

20. From *The Facilitator's Guide: The Enhanced Assess, Acknowledge, Act Sexual Resistance Program, Program Overview Guide,* Written and adapted by Professor Charlene Y. Senn, (2008). (Accessed through Prof. Senn's NEJM's article *Efficacy of a Sexual Assault Resistance Program,* (2015), under Supplementary Material.)

21. National Institute of Justice, Oct. 1, 2008, www.ncjrs.gov/pdffiles1/nij/182369.pdf.

22. Lisak, David, "Predators: Uncomfortable Truths about Campus Rapists." *New England Board of Higher Education, Summer 2004.*

23. Based on the STEP UP! Be a Leader, Make a Difference Program. More information is available at stepupprogram.org/about/.

24. There are differences in how states define sexual assault. California enacted a law, SB967, requiring all colleges receiving state funding for student financial aid to use an affirmative-consent standard when investigating sexual assault and throughout the hearings. This means that consent can't be given if someone is asleep or incapacitated by drugs or alcohol. "Lack of protest or resistance does not mean consent," the law states, "nor does silence mean consent. Affirmative consent must be ongoing throughout a sexual activity and can be revoked at any time." (www.npr.org/sections/thetwo-way/2014/09/29/352482932/california-enacts-yes-means-yes-law-defining-sexual-consent)

25. Garcia, J. R., Reiber, C., Merriwether, A. M., Heywood, L. L., and Fisher, H. E. (2010). "Touch me in the morning: Intimately affiliative gestures in uncommitted and romantic relationships." Paper presented at the Annual Conference of the North Eastern Evolutionary Psychology Society. New Paltz, NY.

26. "Kerry Cronin's Assignment Rules," *Boston Globe,* 16 May 2014. Cicchese, Heather. "College Class Tries to Revive the Lost Art of Dating." *Boston Globe,* 15 May 2014. Print.

27. The decision to use medication is an individual decision. It's important to consult professionals and yourself as you make the decisions determining what's best for you. I found that combining counseling with mindfulness training, yoga, and acupuncture was enormously helpful.

28. From a phone interview with Prof. McDonald discussing their research work: Simpson Rowe, L; Jouriles, E. N.; McDonald, R. (2015). "Reducing sexual victimization among adolescent girls: A randomized controlled pilot trial of My Voice, My Choice." *Behavior Therapy, 46,* 315-327.

29. In a recent study, 10.8% of college men reported perpetrating at least one rape from fourteen years of age through the end of college. (Swartout, Kevin M. Mary P. Koss, Jacquelyn W. White, Martie P. Thompson, Antonia Abbey, and Alexandra L. Bellis (2015). "Trajectory Analysis of the Campus Serial Rapist Assumption." *JAMA Pediatrics* 169.12: 1148.)

30. Lisak, David and Paul M. Miller, (2002). "Repeat Rape and Multiple Offending Among Undetected Rapists." *Violence and Victims*, Vol. 17, No.1.
31. Lisak and Miller, (2002).
32. Lisak and Miller, (2002).
33. Lisak and Miller, (2002).
34. Craig, M. (1990). "Coercive sexuality in dating relationships: A situational model." *Clinical Psychology Review* 10, 395-423.
35. Lisak, David, "Predators: Uncomfortable Truths about Campus Rapists." *New England Board of Higher Education, Summer 2004.*
36. Lisak, Hopper, and Song, (1996); White and Smith, (2004).
37. This report documented extensive sexual abuse at a prestigious prep school. This is not the school I attended; however, *The Boston Globe*, received hundred of accounts of abuse from former students who attended private and public high schools. Many students who attended the school I did contacted *The Boston Globe* and shared details of sexual and emotional abuse.
38. Sometimes I use the name God; other times I use the Divine. I respect your tradition and your questions, and I encourage you to substitute whatever word you're comfortable using.
39. Kaufman, Miriam (2008). "Care of the Adolescent Sexual Assault Victim," *Pediatrics. Vol. 122, Issue 2.*
40. en.wikipedia.org/wiki/Jujutsu.
41. I found this list of emotions on a free phone app called "Stop, Breathe & Think." The app helps you identify emotions and offers short meditations. I think it's fun to use. www.stopbreathethink.org/.
42. Pastor Rob McClellan gave this sermon, and the theologian Walter Brueggemann informed his ideas.
43. Memidex, online.
44. Eryn Huntington and Sherry Anne Weddell (2000), *Discerning Charisms: A workbook for navigating the discernment process,* 14.
45. Huntington and Weddell, 14.
46. Modified from the list offered at stfrancisnewman.org/discerning-your-charisms.
47. Bernstein, Elizabeth: "How to Rekindle Sexual Desire in a Long-Term Relationship." WSJ 10/18/16.
48. Bernstein, Elizabeth: "How to Rekindle Sexual Desire in a Long-Term Relationship." WSJ 10/18/16.
49. www.loveisrespect.org/healthy-relationships/what-consent/.
50. www.odditycentral.com/animals/romantic-bowerbird-builds-intricate-structures-to-seduce-females.html.
51. Nurius, Norris, Dimeff, and Graham, (1996).
52. Hersh and Gray-Little, 1998; Craig, (1990).
53. White, McMullin, Swartout, et al., (2008).
54. White and Koss, (1993). Further References:
    Craig, M. (1990). "Coercive sexuality in dating relationships: A situational model." *Clinical Psychology Review* 10, 395–423.
    Hersh, K. and Gray-Little, B. (1998). "Psychopathic traits and attitudes associated with self-reported sexual aggression in college men." *Journal of Interpersonal Violence* 13(4), 456–471.

Muehlenhard, C.L., Andrews, S.L., and Beal, G.K. (1996). "Beyond 'just saying no': Dealing with men's unwanted sexual advances in heterosexual dating contexts." *Journal of Psychology and Human Sexuality* 8(1/2), 141-167.

Nurius, P.S., Norris, J., Dimeff, L.A., and Graham, T.L. (1996). "Expectations regarding acquaintance sexual aggression among sorority and fraternity members." *Sex Roles* 35(7/8), 427-444.

Senn C.Y., Eliasziw M., Barata P.C., et al. (2015). "Enhanced AAA Intervention Facilitator Manual." Supplement to: Senn C.Y., Eliasziw M., Barata P.C., et al. "Efficacy of a sexual assault resistance program for university women." *New England Journal of Medicine*; 372:2326-35. DOI: 10.1056/NEJMsa1411131.

White, Jacquelyn W., Darcy McMullin, Kevin Swartout, Stacy Sechrist, and Ashlyn Gollehon (2008). "Violence in Intimate Relationships: A Conceptual and Empirical Examination of Sexual and Physical Aggression." *Children and Youth Services Review* 30.3: 338-51. Web.

White, J.W. and Koss, M.P. (1993). "Adolescent sexual aggression within heterosexual relationships: Prevalence, characteristics, and causes." In H.E. Barbaree, W.L. Marshall, and S.M. Hudson, eds., *The Juvenile Sex Offender*. New York, NY: Guilford Press, 182–202.

55. Wheeler, George, and Dahl, (2002).

56. Abbey and McAuslan, (2004); Monson and Langhinrichsen-Rohling, (2002); Thompson, Koss, Kingree, Goree, and Rice, (2011); White and Smith, (2004).

57. Abel et al., (1988); Weinrott and Saylor, (1991).

58. Thompson, Swartout, and Koss, (2013).

59. Abbey and McAuslan, (2004).

60. Lisak and Miller, (2002).

61. Sex Offenses and Offenders. Bureau of Justice Statistics, U.S. Department of Justice, February (1997).

62. A 2007 study for the National Institute of Justice on drug-facilitated, incapacitated, and forcible rape.

63. Koss, (1988).

64. Wolak, Finkelhor, and Mitchell, (2004).

65. Alvidrez et al., 2011; Truman and Langton, (2014).

66. Department of Justice, Office of Justice Programs, Bureau of Justice Statistics, Sex Offenses and Offenders, (1997).

67. Prevalence, Incidence, and Consequences of Violence Against Women, U.S. Department of Justice, (1998).

68. Silverman, Raj, Mucci, and Hathaway, (2001).

69. Wolak, Finkelhor, and Mitchell, (2004).

70. Malamuth and Thornhill, (1994).

71. Fisher, Cullen, and Turner, (2000).

72. Swartout et al., (2015).

73. Craig, (1990).

74. www.loveisrespect.org/healthy-relationships/what-consent/.

75. Insights on stopping an unwanted kiss came from Prof. Renee McDonald's virtual-reality work with college women. When she introduced this idea,

the women in her study noticed danger signs earlier and resisted earlier.

76. www.911rape.org/facts-quotes/definitions. Further References:

Abel, G.G., Becker, J.V., Cunningham-Rathner, J., Mittelmann, M.S., and Rouleau, J.L. (1988). "Multiple paraphilic diagnoses among sex offenders." *Bulletin of the American Academy of Psychiatry and the Law* 16, 153-168.

Abbey, A. and McAuslan, P. (2004). "A longitudinal examination of male college students' perpetration of sexual assault." *Journal of Consulting and Clinical Psychology* 72, 747–756. doi:10.1037/0022-006X.72.5.747.

Alvidrez, J., Shumway, M., Morazes, J., and Boccellari, A. (2011). "Ethnic disparities in mental health treatment engagement among female sexual assault victims." *Journal of Aggression, Maltreatment and Trauma* 20(4), 415-425.

Craig, M. (1990). "Coercive sexuality in dating relationships: A situational model." *Clinical Psychology Review* 10, 395–423.

Fisher, Bonnie S., Francis T. Cullen, and Michael G. Turner (December 2000). "The Sexual Victimization of College Women." U.S. Department of Justice. Web.

Koss, M.P. (1988). "Hidden rape: Sexual aggression and victimization in a national sample of students in higher education." In Burgess, A.W., ed. *Rape and Sexual Assault*, vol. 2. New York: Garland, 3-25.

Lisak, D. and Miller, P.M. (2002). "Repeat rape and multiple offending among undetected rapists." *Violence and Victims* 17, 73-84.

Malamuth, N.M. and Thornhill, N.W. (1994). Hostile masculinity, sexual aggression, and gender biased domineeringness in conversations. Aggressive Behavior, 20(3), 185–193.

Monson, C. M. and Langhinrichsen-Rohling, J. (2002). "Sexual and nonsexual dating violence perpetration: Testing an integrated perpetrator typology." *Violence and Victims* 17, 403– 428. doi: 10.1891/vivi.17.4.403.33684.

Silverman, J. G., A. Raj, L. A. Mucci, and J. E. Hathaway (2001). "Dating Violence Against Adolescent Girls and Associated Substance Use, Unhealthy Weight Control, Sexual Risk Behavior, Pregnancy, and Suicidality." *Journal of the American Medical Association*, vol. 286 (No. 5).

Swartout, Kevin M., Mary P. Koss, Jacquelyn W. White, Martie P. Thompson, Antonia Abbey, and Alexandra L. Bellis (2015). "Trajectory Analysis of the Campus Serial Rapist Assumption." *JAMA Pediatrics* 169.12: 1148. Web.

Thompson, Martie P., Kevin M. Swartout, and Mary P. Koss (2013). "Trajectories and Predictors of Sexually Aggressive Behaviors during Emerging Adulthood." *Psychology of Violence* 3.3: 247-59. Web.

Thompson, M. P., Koss, M. P., Kingree, J. B., Goree, J., and Rice, J. (2011). "A prospective mediational model of sexual aggression among college men." *Journal of Interpersonal Violence* 26, 2716 –2734. doi:10.1177/0886260510388285.

Truman, J. L. and Langton, L. (2014). "Criminal victimization." Retrieved May 2, 2015, from www.bjs.gov/index.cfm?ty=pbdetail&iid=5111.

Wheeler, Jennifer G., William H. George, and Barbara J. Dahl (2002).

"Sexually Aggressive College Males: Empathy as a Moderator in the 'Confluence Model' of Sexual Aggression." *Personality and Individual Differences* 33.5: 759-75. Web.

White, J. W. and Smith, P. H. (2004). "Sexual assault perpetration and re-perpetration: From adolescence to young adulthood." *Criminal Justice and Behavior* 31, 182–202. doi:10.1177/ 0093854803261342.

Weinrott, M.R. and Saylor, M. (1991). "Self-report of crimes committed by sex offenders." *Journal of Interpersonal Violence*, 6, 286-300.

Wolak, Janis, David Finkelhor, and Kimberly J. Mitchell (2004). "Internet-Initiated Sex Crimes Against Minors: Implications for Prevention Based on Findings from a National Study." *Journal of Adolescent Health*, vol. 35 (No. 5), 11–20. (http://www.unh.edu/ccrc/pdf/CV71. pdf). November 11, 2010.

77. Krebs, C. P., Lindquist, C., Warner, T., Fisher, B., and Martin, S. (2007). *The Campus Sexual Assault (CSA) Study: Final Report.* Retrieved from the National Criminal Justice Reference Service: www.ncjrs.gov/pdffiles1/nij/ grants/221153.pdf.

78. "Estimate of the Incidence of Drug-Facilitated Sexual Assault in the U.S.", (2005). Report prepared by: Negrusz, A., Juhascik, M., Gaensslen, R.E., College of Pharmacy, University of Illinois at Chicago.

79. Many of the ideas in this letter I learned from an online class on Positive Neuroplasticity, taught by Rick Hanson, called "The Foundations of Well-Being." He is also the author of *Hardwiring Happiness* (Harmony, 2013).

80. The idea of having an Inner Protector was first introduced to me by Rick Hanson.

81. "Certain Self-Defense Actions Can Decrease Risk." *www.nij.gov/topics/ crime/rape-sexual-violence/campus/pages/decrease-risk.aspx.* (1 Oct. 2008). (Web. 5 Dec 2016.)

82. www.universityaffairs.ca/news/news-article/sexual-assault-resistance-program-reduces-rapes/.

83. Senn, Charlene Y., and Misha Eliasziw, Paula C. Barata, Wilfreda E. Thurston, Ian R. Newby-Clark, H. Lorraine Radtke, and Karen L. Hobden, (2015). "Efficacy of a Sexual Assault Resistance Program for University Women." *New England Journal of Medicine* 372: 2326-2335 June 11, 2015. DOI: 10.1056/NEJMsa1411131.

84. Founder of SARE, the Sexual Assault Resistance Education Centre, offering training in the administration and delivery of the EAAA sexual assault resistance program. www.sacrecentre.org.

85. Allen, Margaret (2015). "Teen Girls Report Less Sexual Victimization after Virtual Reality Training." *SMU Guildhall.*

86. This article is published online at www.sciencedirect.com/science/article/ pii/S0005789414001385.

87. www.dictionary.com.

88. Resistance measures: Testa et al., (2006); see also the qualitative items listed by Senn.

89. Gross, Roberts, Winslett and Gohm, (2006). "An examination of sexual victimization against college women." *Violence Against Women.*

90. www.nij.gov/topics/crime/rape-sexual-violence/campus/Pages/increased-risk.aspx.

91. Abbey, (2002); Fisher et al., (2000); Testa and Parks, (1996). See also the CSA, Campus Sexual Assault Survey, www.ncjrs.gov/pdffiles1/nij/grants/221153.pdf.

92. www.wikipedia.org/wiki/Joseph Lister, 1st Baron_Lister. See also Metcalfe, Peter and Roger Metcalfe (2006). Engineering Studies: Year 11. Glebe, N.S.W.: Pascal Press, 151. Retrieved 2014-07-07.

93. Abbey, Antonia. "Alcohol and Sexual Assault." *Encyclopedia of Human Relationships.* Web.

94. National Institute on Alcohol Abuse and Alcoholism. No. 38, October 1997.

95. Testa and Hoffman, (2012). "Naturally occurring changes in women's drinking from high school to college and implications for sexual victimization." *JStud Alcohol Drugs.*

96. pubs.niaaa.nih.gov/publications/CollegeFactSheet/CollegeFactSheet.pdf.

97. Muehlenhard, C.L., Andrews, S.L., and Beal, G.K. (1996). "Beyond 'Just Saying No': Dealing with men's unwanted sexual advances in heterosexual dating contexts." *Journal of Psychology and Human Sexuality* 8, 141-167.

98. Senn, Appendix. See also Muehlenhard, Andrews, and Beal, (1996).

99. This can depend on your state's laws.

100. Title IX is a public law, No 92-318, 86 Stat. 235. It states, "No person in the United States shall, on the basis of sex, be excluded from participation in, be denied the benefits of, or be subjected to discrimination under any education program or activity receiving federal financial assistance."

101. A Title IX officer is an administrator at a college or university who handles Title IX complaints. A Title IX complaint can be filed with the U.S. Department of Education's Office of Civil Rights when a student has been discriminated against.

102. Department of Justice, Office of Justice Programs, Bureau of Justice Statistics, National Crime Victimization Survey, 2010-2014 (2015); ii. Federal Bureau of Investigation, National Incident-Based Reporting System, 2012-2014 (2015); iii. Federal Bureau of Investigation, National Incident-Based Reporting System, 2012-2014 (2015); iv. Department of Justice, Office of Justice Programs, Bureau of Justice Statistics, Felony Defendants in Large Urban Counties, 2009 (2013).

103. Neumark-Sztainer, (2005).

104. Wertheim et al., (2009).

105. Mellin et al., (1991).

106. Collins, (1991).

107. www.sptsusa.org/wp-content/uploads/2015/05/FACTS-Green.pdf

108. To see some inspiring videos, check out www.MenForWomen.us and www.MamaHope.org, which offer videos of men talking about women they love and sharing their vision for women and girls.

Select Bibliography

Becker, Gavin de. *The Gift of Fear: Survival Signals That Protect Us from Violence.* Boston, MA: Little, Brown 1997.

Bond, Marybeth. *Gutsy Women: Advise, Inspiration, Stories.* Palo Alto, CA: Travelers' Tales, 2012.

Brach, Tara. *Radical Acceptance: Embracing Your Life with the Heart of a Buddha.* New York, NY: Bantam, 2003.

Bryant-Davis, Thema. *Surviving Sexual Violence: A Guide to Recovery and Empowerment.* Lanham, MD: Rowman & Littlefield, 2011.

Cameron, Julia. *The Artist's Way: A Spiritual Path to Higher Creativity.* Los Angeles, CA: Jeremy P. Tarcher/Perigee, 1992.

Clark, Annie E., and Andrea L. Pino. *We Believe You: Survivors of Campus Sexual Assault Speak out.* New York, NY: Henry Holt, 2016.

Dweck, Carol S. *Mindset: The New Psychology of Success.* New York, NY: Random House, 2006.

Friedman, Jaclyn. *What You Really Really Want: The Smart Girl's Shame-free Guide to Sex and Safety.* Berkeley, CA: Seal, 2011.

Hanh, Thich Nhat. *Teachings on Love.* Berkeley, CA: Parallax, 1997.

Hanson, Rick. *Hardwiring Happiness: The New Brain Science of Contentment, Calm, and Confidence.* New York, NY: Harmony, 2013.

Huntington, Eryn, and Sherry Anne Weddell. *Discerning Charisms: A Workbook for Navigating the Discernment Process.* Colorado Springs, CO: Siena Institute, 2000.

Keller, Helen. *Light in My Darkness (My Religion).* New York, NY: Doubleday Page, 1927.

Keller, Helen. *Optimism, An Essay.* New York, NY: Crowell and Company, 1903.

Keller, Helen. *The Story of My Life: Helen Keller.* Radford, VA: Wilder Publications, 1902.

Keller, Helen. *The World I Live In.* New York, NY: Century, 1908.

Lama, Dalai HH, and Howard C. Cutler. *The Art of Happiness.* London, England: Hodder and Stoughton, 1998.

Luskin, Fred. *Forgive for Good: A Proven Prescription for Health and Happiness.* New York, NY: Harper, an imprint of Harper Collins Publishers, 2002.

Raub, John Jacob. *Who Told You That You Were Naked? Freedom from Judgment, Guilt and Fear of Punishment.* New York, NY: Crossroad, 1992.

Solot, Dorian, and Marshall Miller. *I Love Female Orgasm: An Extraordinary Orgasm Guide.* Cambridge, MA: Da Capo, Life Long, 2007.

Stern, Robin. *The Gaslight Effect: How to Spot and Survive the Hidden Manipulations Other People Use to Control Your Life.* New York, NY: Morgan Road, 2007.

van der Kolk, Bessel, M.D.. *The Body Keeps the Score: Brain, Mind, and Body in the Healing of Trauma.* New York, NY: Viking, 2014.

Williamson, Marianne. *A Return to Love: Reflections on the Principles of a Course in Miracles.* New York, NY: Harper Collins, 1992.

Zimbardo, Philip. *The Lucifer Effect: Understanding How Good People Turn Evil.* New York, NY: Random House, 2007.

Index

A

V

W

Y & Z

About the Author

Photo: Chiara Headrick

Kathleen Buckstaff lives in Marin, California, with Dan, her husband, and their lab, Lily. She is the mother of three young adults who fill her life with love and joy. Kathleen received her BA in Creative Writing from Stanford and her MA in Journalism from Stanford. She began her writing career as a humor and inspirational columnist for the *Los Angeles Times* and *The Arizona Republic*.

Kathleen's first book, *The Tiffany Box, a memoir*, was created from emails, letters, and columns that she wrote during the last two years of her mother's life. *The Tiffany Box* was originally a one-woman play that Kathleen performed to sold-out theaters in Phoenix, San Francisco, and New York.

Her second book, *Mother Advice To Take With You To College: Humor, Inspiration and Wisdom To Go*, was created from drawings she made for her college-bound son; it inspired the creation of this book for girls.

In Kathleen's free time, she loves to hike, take photographs, and laugh with friends.

P.S. For the past three weeks, we've been pummeled by rain and wind. Yesterday there was finally sunshine. Dan and I took our dog, Lily, and we drove to Yosemite. I wanted to see the snow and the waterfalls.

As we walked on a trail toward Yosemite Falls, Dan held my hand on the icy parts. The valley was covered in fresh snow and flowing streams. As we approached the waterfall, we could hear its powerful thundering. When we arrived, people were standing on a bridge looking up. They were speaking different languages, and all said a variation on the word "Wow!"

One group held glasses filled with champagne. Two of their friends had just gotten engaged. A woman asked me to take their picture. They stood together with Yosemite Falls behind them and toasted to love. The same woman offered to take a picture of Dan, Lily, and me.

Afterward, I noticed that a pile of fallen trees separated the raging river from us. The tree on top still held hues of bright orange and yellow, and I could smell the scent of fresh pine. Then it occurred to me—in the most recent storm, that tree had gone over the falls and been cast onto the shore. It was a new arrival.

I touched the tree and said, "If you could talk, what a story you would tell." I took a piece of bark from the tree and held it in my hand. "That's life," I said to Dan, "to go over the falls, make it to shore, and live to tell about it."

As we walked back along the path, Dan, who grew up in snow, taught me, the Arizona girl, how to shuffle my feet and glide—we were laughing and sliding in the snow. A gust of wind blew through a grove of oak trees. Snow that had piled on the branches was set loose, and rays of sun streamed through the falling snow crystals, sending cascades of rainbow light throughout the grove. It was truly beautiful.

I thought of the fallen tree and imagined that over time it would decompose into nutrient-rich soil. And maybe someday flowers would grow there.

Claire, age 17 ~

Wildflowers bloom all over in unexpected places.

Yosemite Falls January 14, 2017

Please check out www.walksavvy.com.
You can sign up to receive Kathleen's newsletter at
www.kathleenbuckstaff.com
and follow @walksavvygirls on Twitter and Instagram.

69316870R10240

Made in the USA
Columbia, SC
14 August 2019